Praise
My Spiritual Walk
A Grunt in . --------.

MW00615053

"I haven't read anything so moving about Vietnam since *The Things They Carried*. After a year in-country, almost all of it in a hostile jungle cursed with death, Sgt. Maes returns to California with a hard-earned CIB and a well-deserved Purple Heart. This is a story rich with honesty, powerful in its telling, and heart-wrenching it its aftermath. The reader is duty-bound to feel what Sgt. Maes and his fellow grunts endured to survive the hell of battle."

    -- John Britto, MSCM, USN, Retired, USS Jennings County (LST 846), one of four modified support ships (Ha Tien, Song Ong Duc) for PBR's and Helicopter Gunships, 9/1969-8/1970; author of *The Ship That Vanished* (forthcoming).

"What Joe went through is almost the same thing I went through in Vietnam myself. We were boys barely out of high school when we were called to combat duty in a land far, far away. It did not take long for us boys to transform into a mean fighting machine, not that we had a choice — you either fight or get killed in the process. I myself can relate to all my Grunt brothers who sacrificed so much in the Vietnam War, and the scars of all our sacrifices will forever be ingrained in our memory."

    -- Rudy Molina, USMC, 1967-1970, 1st AmTrac Bn, 3rd Marine Division, Vietnam 1967-68; US Army 1971-1974, 101st Airborne Division, 2nd tour 1971-72; author of *The 13 Unsung Heroes* (as told to Adrian Miguel Nuñez).

"Maes writes a heartfelt and gripping memoir with honest emotions still raw from war. His amazing memory for detail brings us into his world, a world that we experience through his senses: the terror, the longings, and the small joys. A terrific storyteller."

    -- Lucy Sanna, author of *The Cherry Harvest*, a novel of WW2

"My Spiritual Walk as a Wolfhound: A Grunt in Vietnam is a powerful story by a young Native American man, telling his story his way. He honestly speaks about his fears and struggles. Returning home without parades and thank you's but to an ungrateful nation that to this day is still affecting our Vietnam veterans. Welcome Home brother and thank you for your service."

    -- Richard Campos, Iraq Veteran, 2003 invasion forces,
      Sgt., USMC, Retired, producer of documentary, *The Longest Road*

"My father served in Vietnam as a corpsman with the 3rd Marine Division, and over the years he struggled to open up about his experiences. Joe's book gave me a window into a world that many of us will never know."
> -- Jeffrey Hole, Associate Professor of English, University of the Pacific

"I loved this book. We really need to hear more voices from Native American veterans like this. Joseph Maes, an indigenous warrior grunt in Vietnam, has documented in vivid chilling terms the life of a warrior in Vietnam. Maes shares with us his experience growing up learning the ways of a warrior from his father and other elders and then heading off to war. This is an outstanding book from the perspective of a warrior."
> -- Richard Soto, Surgical Nurse attached to the Marines, 1966-68, Co-Founder & Director of the Chicano Research Center, Stockton, California

"War as a 'soul killer.' Young soldiers fresh from home as 'replacements for the dead.' Told in a raw, authentic voice with a vividness capable of haunting our dreams, this book kept me enthralled from the moment Joe landed in Vietnam until he was on the bus headed for home. It has forever changed the way I think about war and soldiers in battle."
> -- Faye Snowden, Navy Veteran, and writer of "One Bullet. One Vote," (*The Best Mystery and Suspense Short Stories of 2021*) and several novels, including *The Killing* series.

"*A Grunt in Vietnam* moved me. Having inherited a form of epilepsy, I was not drafted and sent to Vietnam. During those years, I taught Homer's *Iliad*, the classic war epic set in an unending Trojan war. I encouraged the many returning veterans in my classes to consider the epic through the lens of their own experiences; I took the pay, but they made the class worth attending. They brought up the heart of the reasoning that contextualizes valor, disgrace, hate, love, despair, triumph and tragedy. That's what Joseph Maes does in this book, too. He reminds us in immense detail that life on earth may not only be hellish, but Hell itself, and he means exactly that. Like my students' contributions in class, the innumerable specific details force you to conceive the thing 'war,' as well as its setting in Vietnam, as the kinds of forces and places most of us can never imagine. *A Grunt in Vietnam* is an archive of one soldier's memories in such detail that he fills in what we who did not serve cannot have known."
> -- Patrick W. Conner, Eberly College Centennial Professor in Humanities Emeritus, West Virginia University

"As I read Joe's book, it terrified me to remember what a generation paid for a war that was doomed from the beginning. Joe fought to survive the terror, and his book rips at the soul of a soldier. His story tells the truth of taking away innocence – it's a gripping story of a boy shoved into a godless war. Joe touches nerves that will drive you to a reality of the darkness of war."
    -- Stanley Rapada, Senior Chief, USN, Retired

"I felt an emotional connection to Joe and what he was going through as a 19-year-old boy. While I cannot completely comprehend the horror he endured, I can now empathize more with him and all the other Vietnam veterans. I am truly grateful for this opportunity to look inside Vietnam because many of the people who served will not or cannot tell their stories."
    -- Destiny Goddu, USMC, 2007-2012

MY SPIRITUAL WALK AS A WOLFHOUND:
A GRUNT IN VIETNAM

Published by Tuleburg Press
Stockton, California

www.tuleburgpress.com
tuleburgpress@gmail.com

Library Control Number 2021941177
ISBN 978-1-7321347-6-8

Cover Photograph Courtesy, Joseph Maes
Back Cover Wolf Illustration, Daniel Villa

This publication was funded in part by the California Arts Council,
CB Merchant Services Charitable Fund, and the John F. Hardiman Charitable Fund

Printed at Tokay Press, Stockton, CA
www.tokaypress.com

MY SPIRITUAL WALK AS A WOLFHOUND: A GRUNT IN VIETNAM

Joseph F. Maes

I Dedicate This Book To:

My wife Susan Jessica, my daughter Zatanee, and my son Joseph Jr. I hope they understand the way I am. I love them all, and I'm sorry I couldn't show them my emotions when they were growing up. I hope they understand me better after reading this book. I love all of you very much.

Contents

Joe's Story

To read this book, imagine Joe talking to you.

With my first try at editing his manuscript, I blew it. I cut repetitions, broke up paragraphs, tightened phrasing, corrected grammar, and made all the verb tenses consistent. Then I gave it to back to Joe. He read it and showed it to a friend, along with the original. "This new version sounds nice," said his friend, a fellow combat veteran. "But it doesn't sound like you."

I started again. A big part of any story is how you tell it – in your own voice. What you've got in front of you now has run-on sentences, sentence fragments, and some very long paragraphs. Sometimes the action is in present tense and sometimes, past tense. Joe's not a novelist – he's a guy telling his truth about Vietnam. As for those verb tenses switching back and forth, the fact is: time stopped working the same way for Joe anyway, after getting drafted and sent to war.

Here's another thing – Joe likes to capitalize words that are important to the way he sees the world. That includes Mom and Dad, Sun, Moon, East, West, and some other words that might seem a bit strange in capital letters. Go with it, and you'll be a better listener for his story.

I've only changed errors that got in the way of meaning and only cut repetitions that were unintentional, all with Joe's okay. Maybe you'll notice how often he repeats "this hellhole" and "like it or not" and "damned if you do damned if you don't." Also, there's lots of "Boy is it hot" and "I was scared to beat all hell" and "I don't need this shit anymore!" And "I don't know if I can keep it together!" And "this could be your last step on Mother Earth!" And especially, "I wish I was home with Mom and Dad."

He was 19 and he felt and thought and lived all of those things, again and again.

How does he remember such specific detail about things that happened over 50 years ago? Joe's mother kept every letter he wrote her and every photograph he sent. There were more photos that he didn't send, too, ones he never wanted her to see. Also, Joe is Native American, of Southern Ute heritage. Memory and oral tradition are central to his culture.

Joe's story is a painful one – but he wants it to be heard and remembered. Not everyone who went to Vietnam lived to tell their own story.

Amy Elizabeth Smith, editor
University of the Pacific, Department of English
Faculty Advisor, Student Veterans Organization

SELECTIVE SERVICE SYSTEM

ORDER TO REPORT FOR INDUCTION

Approval Not Required.

The President of the United States,

To

Local Board No. 33
Rm. 205 Federal Bldg.
San Joaquin & Lindsay **Sts.**
Stockton, Calif. 95202
(LOCAL BOARD STAMP)

JOSEPH FRANK MAES
3327 Waterloo Rd. 652 So. Golden Gate ave
Stockton, Ca. 95205

OCT 1 9 1967
(Date of mailing)

SELECTIVE SERVICE NO.			
4	33	47	736

GREETING:

You are hereby ordered for induction into the Armed Forces of the United States, and to report

at GREYHOUND BUS DEPOT, SUTTER & WASHINGTON STS., STOCKTON, CALIF.
(Place of reporting).

on NOV 1 5 1967 at 6:45 A.M.
(Date)   (Hour)

for forwarding to an Armed Forces Induction Station.

Gail Zuso
(Member or clerk of Local Board)

IMPORTANT NOTICE
(Read Each Paragraph Carefully)

IF YOU HAVE HAD PREVIOUS MILITARY SERVICE, OR ARE NOW A MEMBER OF THE NATIONAL GUARD OR A RESERVE COMPONENT OF THE ARMED FORCES, BRING EVIDENCE WITH YOU. IF YOU WEAR GLASSES, BRING THEM. IF MARRIED, BRING PROOF OF YOUR MARRIAGE. IF YOU HAVE ANY PHYSICAL OR MENTAL CONDITION WHICH, IN YOUR OPINION, MAY DISQUALIFY YOU FOR SERVICE IN THE ARMED FORCES, BRING A PHYSICIAN'S CERTIFICATE DESCRIBING THAT CONDITION, IF NOT ALREADY FURNISHED TO YOUR LOCAL BOARD.

Valid documents are required to substantiate dependency claims in order to receive basic allowance for quarters. Be sure to take the following with you when reporting to the induction station. The documents will be returned to you. (a) FOR LAWFUL WIFE OR LEGITIMATE CHILD UNDER 21 YEARS OF AGE—original, certified copy or photostat of a certified copy of marriage certificate, child's birth certificate, or a public or church record of marriage issued over the signature and seal of the custodian of the church or public records; (b) FOR LEGALLY ADOPTED CHILD—certified court order of adoption; (c) FOR CHILD OF DIVORCED SERVICE MEMBER (Child in custody of person other than claimant)—(1) Certified or photostatic copies of receipts from custodian of child evidencing servicemans contributions for support, and (2) Divorce decree, court support order or separation order; (d) FOR DEPENDENT PARENT—affidavits establishing that dependency.

Bring your Social Security Account Number Card. If you do not have one, apply at nearest Social Security Administration Office. If you have life insurance, bring a record of the insurance company's address and your policy number. Bring enough clean clothes for 3 days. Bring enough money to last 1 month for personal purchases.

This Local Board will furnish transportation, and meals and lodging when necessary, from the place of reporting to the induction station where you will be examined. If found qualified, you will be inducted into the Armed Forces. If found not qualified, return transportation and meals and lodging when necessary, will be furnished to the place of reporting.

You may be found not qualified for induction. Keep this in mind in arranging your affairs, to prevent any undue hardship if you are not inducted. If employed, inform your employer of this possibility. Your employer can then be prepared to continue your employment if you are not inducted. To protect your right to return to your job if you are not inducted, you must report for work as soon as possible after the completion of your induction examination. You may jeopardize your reemployment rights if you do not report for work at the beginning of your next regularly scheduled working period after you have returned to your place of employment.

Willful failure to report at the place and hour of the day named in this Order subjects the violator to fine and imprisonment. Bring this Order with you when you report.

If you are so far from your own local board that reporting in compliance with this Order will be a serious hardship, go immediately to any local board and make written request for transfer of your delivery for induction, taking this Order with you.

SSS Form 252 (Revised 4-28-65)   (Previous printings may be used until exhausted.)   U.S. GOVERNMENT PRINTING OFFICE : 1965 O—765-193

This draft notice put me on a path to a place and a year of scary decision making. At the right is me in the bunker making life or death decisions for me and the other men.

DRAFTED

October 1967-April 1968

WHEN I GOT MY DRAFT NOTICE
October 1967

This story is about me, Joseph F. Maes, born in Stockton, California and going off to war in Vietnam. I'm going to tell the story just the way it happened, and tell what I felt. I'm not a writer, so maybe it's a little rough.

I'm Native American of Southern Ute heritage. Our lands are in the Southwestern corner of Colorado, by the four corners where the four states meet. The Southern Ute Reservation straddles Colorado and New Mexico. My Dad told me a lot about our Southern Ute Native heritage and how to be strong in my Native ways. If it wasn't for my Mother and Father and the way they raised me I would not have made it back from the War in Vietnam. I knew a lot had to do with my parents for me to make it home from the war.

I didn't really want to go to Vietnam. I had no idea about Vietnam and what kind of a war it was. In the end I got drafted into the Army and went to Vietnam. Also this story is about the 1st Battalion, 27th Infantry, 25th Infantry Division ("Tropic Lightning"), Wolfhound Unit, Alpha Company, in Cu Chi base camp. It's about my walk into the battlefields of Vietnam, and my journey into the LIFE OF A GRUNT and a true Warrior in my Native culture.

I can remember the day I got my notice in the mail in October 1967 right after my 19th birthday. My Mom and Dad read it to me when I got home in the living room. It read, "Greeting: You are hereby ordered for induction into the Armed Forces of the United States." I had to report to the Oakland Induction Center November 15, 1967! That was the last thing I wanted to hear. I couldn't believe it! Of all the people in the world, they wanted me a poor Native American kid to be in the service. I wondered to myself what branch of service I would be in. All it said, I was inducted into the Armed Forces! I didn't know at the time, when you got drafted you didn't have a choice in what branch of service or what kind of MOS (Military Occupational Specialty – type of jobs) you would be in. All I could do is hope for the best.

I was just out of high school. I'd never been away from my parents and I was scared as all hell to go. I really didn't want to go it wasn't my war and I didn't hate those people. I had just gotten a good job. I'd been working a lot of odd jobs to pay for the things to put on my '55 Chevy hard top. I'd just finished fixing up my nice '55 Chevy and put in a 327cu. engine from a '64 Chevy Corvette. I'd just put on a new paint job and new tuck and roll interior, and it looked *real* nice. Me and my Dad had worked hard on the Chevy, together, for almost two to three years. He taught me a lot about cars and engines, and we had a lot of fun working together on it.

My Dad was a very smart man . . . not at all like people think of us Native Americans. Like he said to me, here it's a lot easier to buy parts for a car than it is on the Reservation. Because they didn't have an auto store on the Reservation. They were lucky to have a store to buy food at. He really had a hard life but that didn't stop him from being a strong and smart man. He could handle whatever life threw at him. He didn't let things bring him down. Like he told me, take the negative and always try to make it positive and don't take life for granted. Life is not fair for anybody on Mother Earth.

My Mom had the same outlook on life like my Dad. My Mom showed me how to have a big heart and try to be kind to everybody. She also showed me how to cook – that way I didn't have to depend on a girl to cook for me. She showed me how to make flour tortillas and Indian fry bread, and how to prepare meals. And a lot of other things that women had to do. She could make a meal with hardly anything and clothes too. I loved being with my Mom. She was so kind and nice – she used to make flour tortillas and fry bread for the kids in our neighborhood when they'd come over with me and my brother to our one-bedroom house. There were six of the same type one-bedroom homes on the same block. My Dad called them cabins. Boy! That fry bread and those tortillas smelled *so* good! The kids in the neighborhood really liked eating them.

Even though we didn't have much, Mom seemed to have enough food to feed all of us kids. I found out that sometimes she didn't eat just so she could feed us. That's the way my Mom was a very nice and considerate woman. She was a very beautiful woman in her ways and her looks. She looked like a Princess when she cleaned herself up after working hard. At the time I didn't know I was poor. I guess because I never really went hungry and I guess that's what made me feel rich inside. Me and my brother were very close to our parents, we loved them so much. Me and my brother were very close to each other too. We always covered each other's back when we were picked on. That's the way our Dad taught us to be. A lot of times we were the only Native kids around. That was the hard part of growing up back then because of who we were. When we played with other kids we were always the bad guys. We were never the hero. A lot of the time they thought we were Mexican. It was funny when they said Mexican jokes and bad things about them. We would laugh with them, they thought we were cool about it. But when they found out we were Native and said bad things about us the fight was on. Those were the days of survival. Kids back then could be real mean when the odds were against you, we had no choice but to stand our ground.

My Dad and Mom took me and my brother camping and hunting and fishing a lot – and my friends too. We were always gone on the weekends. We didn't stay in town much. It wasn't our way of life, we were too close to Mother Nature. We were outdoors a lot going camping and fishing. My Dad and Mom showed me a lot about survival in the wilderness.

My Mom really liked fishing, and wasn't too much into hunting . . . but she did like to go with us when we went hunting. My Dad used to show us how to hunt and to clean our weapons and game and to cure the meat. My Mom showed us how to hunt for food that Mother Earth provided us out in the wilderness. We were always under my Mom and Dad's wings. We were a tight family. My Mom and Dad tried to keep us away from the city life. They didn't like city life. That was another way my Mom and Dad kept us from harassment. It was always a challenge when they found out you were Native and that you weren't Mexican.

When I was in Vietnam, my Mom wrote me every day. About my Dad and brother and how things were going on at home. Both of my parents had to work to make ends meet. She didn't miss sending one single letter to me daily for the two years I served. She must have known how important it was to me and how important it was for me to *get* those letters. She did the same for my brother when he was in Vietnam too. When I received those letters, I could feel my whole body change . . . and for that moment all the stress and pressure of being in the bush "jungle" just melted off me. I knew she really loved her sons. If it weren't for those letters, I would have gone nuts, and I don't know if I would have been able to get through the trauma of battle, the pain, the suffering, the guilt, and all the other emotions of war! At the end my Mom was the only one writing to me. All my friends stopped writing, I guess they were too busy doing their thing back in the USA and didn't have time for me.

I really didn't want to leave my parents, anyway. I was too close to them. I even had a nice girlfriend, we had been together for two years, and my parents were real good to her, too. Why should I leave? I didn't want to go anywhere, especially not over There! I had everything going for me here at home. Why would anybody want to leave a good thing! I didn't know any of those people over There! It wasn't my war. They weren't shooting at us at home. I didn't understand it. All I knew was that I had to go like it or not, it was the law.

When I was getting ready to leave, my dad told me to *always* do my best in anything I did in life. Keep faith in your Native ways and always use common sense when you have to do something. Then my Mom told me always pray to the Creator to help me make it through life. I had to report to the Induction Center in Oakland, California, on November 15, 1967. I wasn't ready to go in.

The day before I left, I said my goodbyes to my friends. It was kind of funny about me and my friends, we were all kids. None of us realized how bad it was to go off to war.

I guess we thought it was a game back then or like the movies, nobody gets killed for real in the movies. What do kids know? For me, I tried to make myself think it would be like going to a new job. Maybe I could work on engines or be an electrician. I already had a job as an electrician, and I knew electrical work and how to work on engines. Why would they put me in the Infantry? I could do other jobs they had there. They didn't need to train me to be an electrician, I already knew how to be an electrician.

So I was hoping for the best. My older brother Selzo was drafted one year before me. When he got drafted, I didn't think anything about it. I didn't realize how serious war was and how hard it was to be in those circumstances – and how hard it was for him, as well! I guess when you're young, you don't think of those things . . . until it happens to you. When it does! It's a hell of a wakeup call. I also realized and felt that being a draftee in the service, they have a different outlook on draftees. The RA (Regular Army) didn't care for us, they thought it was a waste of time training us for two years.

THE DAY I LEFT FOR THE SERVICE
November 15, 1967

The day I left to go in the service, it was cold. I was nervous that day. Things seemed so different seeing my Mom and Dad so sad. Now, I realize they were scared to see me off. They'd been watching the news, and they knew what was going on over There. I didn't have a clue. I was too busy being a kid and having fun. I guess I just didn't want to believe it was bad over there. I was still thinking to myself that they'd give me a job as an electrician. At least I had some kind of hope.

My Mom and Dad woke me up to take me to the Greyhound bus station in Stockton, here in California. It was 5:00 a.m. I ate breakfast. We had to be there before 7:00 a.m. We waited for the Greyhound bus to come. We had a half hour. There were seven other families with their kids waiting for the bus to come. Then the bus pulled into the station. It was full of young kids going to the same place. They loaded us on the Greyhound bus (When my son Joseph Jr. went into the Army 35 years later, I was sad and scared for him. Now! I know how my Mom and Dad felt when my brother left – they were sad and scared for him, too, the same way they were sad and scared for me as I was leaving). It was before 7:00 a.m., now.

At our bus station, there were seven other kids leaving that morning from Stockton, and I didn't know any of them. We all said our goodbyes to our parents and family members. It was kind of funny that none of us had any luggage, or suitcases, just hand bags. I guess we all got the same orders. After we got on the bus the Greyhound bus driver closed the doors. You heard the air brakes release and we started to move out of the station.

We were downtown, and the streets were empty. Hardly anyone was out. It was quiet everywhere. It was quiet on the bus. I started thinking about the bus ride . . . it reminded me of going to a track meet at another school, except I didn't know any of these kids. We all looked lost in our own deep thoughts. You could hear a pin drop. We each felt alone and isolated from one another. We didn't know each other, and we were all from different towns, but we were all going to the same place.

On the way to the Induction Center, we stopped in Tracy where five more kids got on. They were on their way to the Induction Center, too. We could see them saying their goodbyes to their parents and families the same way we did, as we pulled up to the bus station. The bus driver opened the door and the kids came up the steps into the doorway and down the aisles to empty seats and sat down and they all had sad looks on their faces. Then you heard the door close and that sound again of the air brakes releasing and the bus started moving out of the bus station and headed out of town. Back then, Highway 50 went right through the middle of Tracy, which was a small railroad town and farming community.

Driving west along the old Altamont Pass Road, we could see the construction for the new freeway being built through the pass. I used to drive my car over it, a lot, to see my girlfriend. She lived in the town of Fremont, California, in the Bay Area. She went to live there with her father. On that bus ride through the pass, I wondered if I would ever see those things again. It was a lonely ride. Everybody was in deep thought and no one made a sound.

When we got to Oakland and arrived at the Induction Center it was a cold morning on that day November 15, 1967. You heard those air brakes again then the door opened and the bus driver told us to get off the bus. We were standing around in a giant cluster fuck trying to stay warm, when an Army recruiter came out to ask us which of us were enlisted and which of us were draftees. He took all the enlisted in first, I didn't know it at the time, but draftees didn't have the choice of choosing what service branch you could enter.

Anyway, after standing around in a cluster for about an hour, and after the recruiter asked us which of us were enlisted and draftees, he told us draftees to line up, walk up the stairs, and take our physicals. There were at least a hundred guys lined up with me now. The enlisted were in one line and the draftees in another line.

I just couldn't believe how many guys there were. Most of us were draftees. We walked up an old wooden stairway to the second floor – and since most of us were lost in our own thoughts, all you heard was the sound of hundreds of feet stepping up creaky wooden stairs. We entered a giant room that looked like a converted auditorium or banquet hall.

There were hundreds of kids in different stages of dress and undress, and in different stages of the physical exams. There was no privacy, not even partitions. There were so many of us that it took ages for the line to move forward enough that you finally reached the eye doctor, or the hearing doctor, the foot doctor, the dentist, and all the other doctors that we had to be examined by. It seemed like an assembly line and we were the cattle being examined.

At noon, they gave us a lunch break and a meal ticket, and told us to go get our lunch at the USO Club down the street in Oakland. After lunch we had to go back to the exam hall and continue with the physical examinations. The examinations said who was and wasn't physically fit enough to go into the military. The guys that didn't pass any part of the physical exam were escorted out of the auditorium, sent over to the USO Club, and told to wait there for their return ride back to their hometowns. All RA guys that passed their physicals were escorted to a room forty at a time and were sworn into the military.

After our physicals, at the end of the day, all of us draftees were lined up again. At that point, an Army Sergeant went down our line and started counting. I thought to myself "This guy can't count," because he counted by saying "One, one, one, four, one, one, one, three, one, one, one, two, one, one, one, four, one, one, one, three, one, one, one, two," and so on.

Afterwards we were told to line up according to our number. That's when we found out what each one meant. The Sergeant said to us, "All the 'Ones' are Army: 'pissed-on.' The 'Twos' are Marines: 'shit-on.' 'Threes' are Navy: 'babies,' and all the 'Fours' are Air Force: 'crybabies.'" After we found out what branch of service we draftees were in, we were sworn in.

Most of the draftees went to the Army and Marine Corps, and a lot of those guys were complaining about not being able to go into the Navy or Air Force. The "volunteers" (the enlisted) though, had the choice of joining any branch they wanted to. They had a choice, we didn't. They could even choose what kind of job they wanted to do in the service (MOS).

I didn't want to be there, and I didn't know anything. I had no expectations about anything there, and I thought, "I guess I'm lucky, I got the Army." After I was in the Army, though, I found out the Army and the Marine Corps weren't good places to be in, especially if your MOS was the Infantry, 11B (11-Bravo) – which I didn't know at the time.

When everyone's physicals were done, we were issued meal tickets for dinner and told to report back to the Processing Center in one hour. Once we finished eating and got back to the center, that's when they told us which fort we were being assigned to, for Basic Training. They also told us what commercial flights we were going to take to get there.

They grouped us according to the forts we were being assigned to, then put our groups on buses and drove us to the San Francisco Airport – where all of our groups boarded the different jet planes which were taking us to our forts of assignment. Thirty of us were going to Fort Lewis, at Tacoma, Washington. All the others went to different bases in different states.

TO FORT LEWIS WASHINGTON
November 1967

My group was going to Fort Lewis, and to get there we had to fly into Seattle, Washington. We finally boarded our plane at about 11:00 p.m. This was the first time I'd ever been on a plane. I thought it was cool, but I was a little scared and apprehensive at the same time. Looking back, it must have been the same for other draftees and enlistees, too. We were all so young and baby-faced, we must have looked like innocent kids to the stewardesses.

The stewardesses were smiling as they pushed their serving carts down the aisle, asking us if we wanted a soda to drink, or a package of nuts to eat. They were all young ladies and very pretty. Their uniforms were elegant little miniskirts that looked professionally cleaned, with crisp creases and lines. It was all put together in a way that made the stewardesses seem appealing, especially to us young guys.

They were all so nice in the manner that they presented themselves. They were smiling and talking to us. When they spoke to us it felt like they knew us, and it made us feel comfortable. It was fun. It made me forget what I was doing there. After a couple of hours the pilot announced over the intercom that we were landing in Seattle, Washington.

A light came on that read "Fasten Your Seat Belts." The jet made a hard right bank toward the airport, you felt it in your seat. You could hear the landing gear going down and locking in place. The plane began slowing down and it bounced up and down a little bit as it hit some turbulence. The wheels screeched when they hit the runway then the engines roared. The plane's speed dropped and everyone was jerked forward a moment. We slowed and finally stopped. Then the pilot said, "We have landed in Seattle, Washington." It was about 3:00 a.m.

After we got off, we went into the airport USO where we waited for another bus to pick us up. There were about forty of us guys from different states, waiting for the same bus. Since the flight was late in landing in Seattle, they rushed us to Fort Lewis (40 miles from Seattle) by bus. As we came to the main gate there was a big sign that was lit up and it read "Welcome to Fort Lewis Washington." As we passed the main gate we went a few miles in and we stopped by this long wooden building, it was about 4:30 a.m.

As we got off the bus a Drill Sergeant was standing there hollering at us telling us all kinds of shit and yelling at us to get in line. Then they ordered us to march inside the building and there were lines of desks where we should line up by. Then we were told to sit down near the desks. Then they gave us all pencils and paper and told us to write a postcard to our fathers and mothers telling them that we'd made it safely to Seattle, Washington and to our base at Fort Lewis, in Tacoma, Washington. They had us fill out paperwork for our Personnel File ("201" File), payroll and insurance, and our next-of-kin notification (which was our name and address, and next-of-kin on a document in case we died while on duty).

Then they gave us IQ tests, and some other tests and asked us what kind of hobbies we liked. I should have never put down I like hunting and fishing. I didn't know that as a draftee, this would put me right in the Infantry.

After that we got all our shots and more physicals that included blood work, then we got our hair cut. When they were done with our heads, we were bald as cue balls. It made us all look different and kind of funny. By this time we'd been up a day and a night, and were into our second day of being awake and we were still on the go. Being up all night doing this and that, we were really tired and sleepy and hungry by now.

When they finally fed us breakfast, it was powdered eggs and powdered potatoes, at the mess hall. It tasted bad and we didn't like it. A powdered eggs and potatoes breakfast was definitely not a home-cooked meal. It was 8:00 a.m. now. After breakfast we were herded over to the supply warehouse where we got our clothing issued to us: this included our Class A's (dress uniform or "wintergreens"), fatigues (work uniform), caps, boots, dress shoes, socks, T-shirts and other underclothes, and a canvas duffle bag. The duffle bag was for all our clothing and once all our clothing was in it, it weighed a ton.

When we finally got to our barracks, Company C-11, our other Drill Sergeant was standing there, nice and quiet-like, then he went ballistic, hollering, "You boys will be men when you leave here! I will be the one and *only* one that can make you or break you! Your life will be a living hell until you leave here! When you leave here, you will be men – good enough to stay in this man's Army!"

He kept his promise. It *was* a living hell for three months of Basic Training. I never had so many aching pains in my body. I never knew the Army was so brutal. The training was punishing, I was pushed to my physical and mental limits. My civilian self was stripped away piece by piece, and in its place I became a well-disciplined soldier who could do my job in "this man's Army." I left Basic Training feeling good about myself physically and mentally.

Our graduation ceremony from Basic Training took place in January 1968, in the snow, on a leveled-out graveled parade field. We were marched in formation from our barracks to the parade grounds about a mile away, where temporary bleachers had been set up to seat the visitors who'd come to watch the graduation ceremony. To my surprise, my Mom and Dad were there. I didn't know it at the time, but they'd driven 12 hours from Stockton to Fort Lewis to watch me graduate. What a lift that was! It made me feel good to see them.

My Mom and Dad were so happy to see me too. They'd driven a long way just to see me for a few hours. I was the baby of the family, and I knew Mom and Dad missed me and loved me. They'd done the same thing when my older brother Selzo graduated from Basic Training at Fort Lewis, the year before. I asked them about my brother and how was he doing in Vietnam. All they said was that he "was doing ok, over there." Mom and Dad didn't say much more about it because they weren't happy about the fact that their two boys were both in the Army, with one already in Vietnam and the other in training for Vietnam.

I didn't know at the time that things were really heating up over there. Basic Training meant we were kept isolated from the rest of the "world" in every respect. We hadn't even been allowed to go into the PX (Post Exchange) without being escorted through it, by one of our Drill Sergeants, and then we were only authorized to pick up essential "personal hygiene items."

We could buy shaving cream, razors, deodorant, toothpaste, shoe polish, Brasso, etc., but no candy, no soda, and no chips – nothing that wasn't used to keep ourselves clean, polish our boots, or shine our brass. The worst part about walking through the PX was seeing all the sweets that we weren't allowed to touch let alone to buy, and just to make sure we didn't think about touching the stuff, those aisles were taped off.

But taping off the aisles didn't stop us from smelling or seeing the stuff and seeing it made us want it even more. It was pure torture. No candy, no soda, no TV, no radio, no newspapers, no nothing, just training, training, training. But while we were training, things in Vietnam had started to heat up, and the NVA (North Vietnamese Army) and the VC (Viet Cong) were about to launch their Tet Offensive.

If I had known about this stuff, I would have been scared to death more, but I didn't know because we were all in the dark about it. Anyway! While all this stuff was going on "over There," I thought the Army would assign me to a different Army base for my AIT (Advanced Infantry Training), but the only thing the Army did was send me right across the parade field to another set of barracks.

I still can remember all those kids that came from different states and they talked different and had different accents. It was kind of funny how they sounded when they talked. Then I found out some of these kids were more prejudiced in their ways. This one big white kid kept picking on me. Because I was Native and I was small, I guess! He thought I wouldn't fight him. So one day we started fighting in the barracks, it was in the morning and we were still in our white shorts and T-shirts. Then the Drill Sergeant got hold of us. He said you guys will finish this in the bullring. I didn't know what he was talking about, all I knew I was mad at this big white kid and finally got tired of his bullshit. He would say a lot of negative things about my Native heritage and call me names.

The Sergeant had all the guys from our barrack form a circle outside the barrack like a bullring. All the guys were still in their shorts and T-shirts too but our sergeant had us dress in our fatigues and meet him outside. It was cold and freezing outside and there was still snow on the ground. He brought out some boxing gloves. He told us put them on and to go at it inside the bullring. All I knew I had to keep on fighting even when that white guy kept knocking me down. After that the white kid didn't pick on me anymore. I think we both found out in this man's Army you do or die, they're not going put you in the corner like little kids. I even have pictures of me being in the bullring. Even though he got the best of me I wouldn't quit. The Sergeant had to break the fight up. Like I said that white kid didn't bother me anymore. I knew if I quit I would have never lived it down. Like Dad always told me, be strong even when the odds are against you. Life is not fair to anybody and that's how you make it in life.

REPORTING FOR AIT
February 1968

My orders said, "Report for AIT. Advanced Infantry Training at Fort Lewis, Washington, Barracks B-11." *Fort Lewis, Washington!* I knew it! I thought, "This is the shits! A draftee doesn't stand a chance!" I got mad at this so-called "Army," they put me right into the Infantry! What made me even madder was that I could have spent more time with my parents.

I had to wait two weeks for the other guys to come in to start AIT. Two weeks I could have been with my parents or even one week would have made me happy . . . shit, I wasn't greedy. "They" knew my parents drove from out-of-state just to see me for a few hours. I thought that was chicken shit of "Them." "They" didn't make it any easier for me.

Boy, if I thought Basic Training was bad, AIT was worse. The training was more intense. Every Army soldier, regardless of MOS, is an Infantryman first, and a Technician second but 11-Bravos are Advanced Infantry soldiers. We are the specialized combat Technicians – the combat soldiers – that the Army depends on to fight its wars. We're the frontline soldiers, the ones who're usually the first to engage, fight, and aggress against the enemy.

We're the ones people call the "cannon fodder." Which means expendable. All Army personnel go to Basic Training to complete Basic Infantry Training, but combat soldiers complete Advanced Infantry Training to become 11-Bravos, the Army's definition of a true combat soldier that can kill or be killed.

I had to remember more and learn more soldiering skills. As an 11-Bravo, there were more specialized combat skills I needed to learn and remember: maintaining combat equipment and web-gear, reading terrain and aerial maps, using a compass, knowing the different weapons of destruction that we, and the enemy, would use. We also learned: our explosives devices, our radio, the PRC-25 ("Prick-25"), call signs, the military alphabet, and a lot more and even First Aid in how to treat our wounded. I even learned how to go into tunnels and search out the enemy and identify booby traps inside the tunnels.

The exercises were tough: push-ups, sit-ups, jumping-jacks, running all the time and doing pull-up bar every day, in the morning, on the way to breakfast, lunch, and dinner, and extra pull-ups whenever the Drill Sergeant felt like it.

Between the exercises, extra duty as punishment, and the Drill Sergeants' constant hollering, it was like a living hell. But I had it just a little bit easier because I ran track in high school. Track already gave me more confidence, stamina, strength, and the ability to accomplish objectives, when you ran track you were on your own, nobody could do it for you, and you did it by yourself. I ran the 880-yard dash and the three-mile event in cross-country. Also because I went hunting and fishing with my Mom and Dad I was used to being outdoors. I was in better shape than most of the guys there and I like the outdoors.

TWO-WEEK LEAVE, BEFORE I LEAVE FOR VIETNAM
April 1968

After finishing AIT I got orders to go to Vietnam. My orders said to report to Vietnam on April 27, 1968, and to leave the States on the April 26. Out of our Company of 120 guys, only 30 went someplace else instead of Vietnam. They gave us a two-week leave to go home and see our parents before we left to Vietnam. We all went to the airport and went on different airplanes. Because we were from different states. I thought I might be with some of these guys I had AIT with. I might meet them in Vietnam. It didn't happen. It would have been nice if we could have been together over there.

When I got home I tried to keep busy and tried to keep my mind off of going to Vietnam. Then all my friends came by and said hi and how was it being in the Army and things like that. Things didn't seem the same to me anymore. My friends acted different to me, I guess it was me. They were still innocent kids, I guess I changed in the way I thought now. Because of the training I went through. I didn't know it affected me and the way I felt now. I was home watching TV with my Mom and Dad, the news came on, they started talking about the war going on in Vietnam. I shouldn't have watched the news on TV, a lot things were happening at that time.

I didn't know it was that bad, they didn't tell us all this stuff was happening. They said it was bad, but when you watched it live on TV, it really scared the shit out of me, it made me upset. I really didn't want to go. It was really happening to me, I'm really going to war, and I didn't really want to believe it.

I wanted to tell my Mom and Dad that I didn't want to go to Vietnam. But I didn't want them to get upset and make it harder on them. So I tried to act like everything was ok with me. But it wasn't I was scared as all hell. It's not like the movies, you can't feel things for real in a movie. You feel all these different emotions that you never had before and it was hard to deal with it when you never dealt with it before.

My brother just came from Vietnam. He was stationed Stateside on the East Coast. Before I left I called him and he told me to be safe and to take care of myself. He said it has gotten a lot worse since he left and things are going to be a whole lot worse by the time you get there.

I told him I know, I'd been seeing it on TV. I'd try my best to stay alive over There. It's for real that I'm really going to war. But in the back of my mind I didn't want to believe it. It can't be happening to me, it was scary. Then I went to see my ex-girlfriend before I left. She gave me a Dear John letter when I was in Basic Training. I couldn't do anything at that time. Boy only if she knew how it messed your head up. But that's life, ha! You take it and move on.

I told her it was better for her and me anyway, she wanted to give back the things I gave her when we were together. That was nice of her. I didn't want the stuff anyway but I took it back. But I still liked her but I couldn't do anything about it. I just had to take it in and deal with it, that's the way things go in life, you take it in and deal with it one step at a time. But I got over that too! (In time!) I'm glad she didn't do it when I was over there, it would have been a lot harder for me.

But what I didn't get over is that they stole my car at 99 Speedway when I was on leave. I couldn't believe that my '55 Chevy with my 327cu. engine and new paint job, the tuck and roll interior and wide tires all around was gone! What a car! I couldn't do anything about it. The only thing I could do was report it stolen. I found out later, there was a big car theft ring going on. They used a tow truck to steal the cars with. I remember seeing a tow truck next to my car. I thought there was an accident, it was them stealing my car.

Like they say shit happens for a reason. I found out later this made me a lot stronger for what was going to happen to me in a war zone. I found out life has a lot of different roads. Some are hard and some are easy and some don't go anywhere. So deal with what you got and hope for the best. Then I went to see my teachers at my high school before I left to Vietnam. Then I went to see my track coach Don George. I told him if it wasn't for his training I would have had a lot harder time in Basic Training and AIT.

He was glad to hear that. I asked him if he would like to write to me and he said he would. I didn't know it till I got his first letter that he was Lieutenant Colonel in the Air Force.

I couldn't believe he was a Lieutenant Colonel, we used to call him "little fat man," that's the nickname the guys on the track team gave him, who knew him real good. If I would've known what he was back then in his time in the service, I wouldn't have called him "little fat man." He was a real nice teacher and coach, he helped a lot of us kids that weren't fortunate to have things.

He would go out of his way to help you. Later I can remember my Second Lieutenant asked me who this Lieutenant Colonel was. I told him and he said he must really like you. I said yes he did, he's a very good person.

The night before I left home, my Mom made me a special dinner. Home-cooked Indian fry bread and all that went with it. It smelled so good while Mom was cooking it.

Then me and my Dad started talking, he told me you are a man now and you are going to become a Warrior. Just do what you were trained for and use common sense when you are doing things out there and you will come home. And be strong and our God the Creator and our Ancestors will be with you.

But it was a long night for me, there was a lot on my mind back then. It was hard to talk about the unknown, I really didn't understand why I was going off to war. I had no idea why we were there in Vietnam and what kind of people I would be facing. I had no idea what their culture was and what they looked like. I felt so uneasy about going over "There." I wanted to tell my Dad how I felt but I didn't want to worry him and my Mom about how I felt inside of me. Before I knew it, it was time for me to leave.

ON THE AIRPLANE TO VIETNAM
April 26, 1968

Here I go to Vietnam. Dressed in my wintergreens uniform looking good and it was a cold winter night so far. My Mom and Dad took me and drove me to the Oakland Depot Departure Station. It was about 6:00 p.m. It was sad for my parents and me. As my parents drove me I could hear the tires going thump and thump on the pavement as we were going down the highway.

It was cold and dark, that night as we were going. I was staring out the window looking at the lights and thinking of what might happen to me in Vietnam. Then I could see the lights of the town of Tracy. I'm doing the same thing again like when I got drafted, going down the same highway through Tracy. Then as we went through the pass still on the same highway it made me think about my ex-girlfriend. Boy this is bullshit I didn't need this shit! I have enough on my mind. Other than that it was a quiet ride to Oakland, there wasn't much to say. What can you say to your son going off to war?

They must have known I was scared because I was real quiet and I might have looked scared to my parents. So we finally got there to the Oakland Depot Departure Station. As we were going through the gates there were kids holding protest signs, I didn't really pay attention to them, I was in my own thoughts. I noticed my Dad pulling over to this big warehouse where other cars were parked. We said our goodbyes, but my Mom started crying and my Dad's eyes got full of water, all I could say was I have to be leaving now. Don't worry I'll be back soon and maybe I can get another car again and fix it up. It made them smile a little bit.

But I felt like shit it broke my heart to see my parents like that. I couldn't do anything about it. It was so hard to leave them like that, in that kind of pain. It was hard for me to put a smile on but I tried to act like everything was ok with me. But it wasn't ok I felt bad inside and scared as all hell to be leaving.

I put my duffel bag over my shoulder and turned around towards the warehouse and went inside the Departure Station, this Sergeant said you guys line up here, we'll be loading on a bus to go Travis Air Force Base to get on a jet after you guys report in. So there was about 30 guys in my group from all over the country that flew in to Oakland from other states, we loaded our duffel bags and we got on these buses.

As we were riding the bus you could see the entire city lights of San Francisco in the distance, I was thinking of my Mom and Dad, how they felt inside, and if I would ever see them again, what a feeling to have.

I felt so sad inside and alone, that was my first time that I cried to myself for my Mom and Dad. I didn't know I had these kinds of feelings inside. I guess I'd never gone through this before. The bus took us to Travis Air Force Base where we got off and went inside the airport terminal on base to show our orders and paperwork.

We had to show we had our orders, shot records and our paperwork for our physical, dog tags and our IDs and to check in our duffel bags to go to Vietnam. We had at least 100 more guys leave that night. It was a lonely ride, I didn't know anybody, it was real quiet.

I remember what my Dad told me before I left. Be strong and God the Creator and your Ancestors will take care of you. Just be strong in what you have to do over there and try and do your best. Listen to what they tell you and always use common sense. My Dad served in the service so he knew what he was talking about. But he didn't talk about it much, I will find out why after I come back from Vietnam. We took off on a commercial flight from Travis Air Force Base.

We had to land in Alaska before we went to Vietnam. I remember how cold it was in Alaska. We had to run though this hallway made out of wood about 300 yards to the other terminal to board another plane, it was below zero.

We ended up picking up more kids to go to Vietnam. They had been waiting at the terminal for about an hour. It was strange there, there was no civilian population, just working personnel at the terminal, we were isolated, it felt real strange in that environment, we were all dressed in our wintergreens. It looked like a green sea moving in the terminal.

We all looked so sad and lonely and young and scared. It was not like my first airplane ride when everybody was happy and talking and laughing. What a different feeling, nobody was happy here! We all got on two different commercial airplanes to go to Vietnam.

The plane was full now and we flew straight to Vietnam. It was a long flight, I think it was about 18 hours or more in the air. We were tired of being on the plane, some were sleeping in their seats in different positions. It was still quiet on the plane, there wasn't much to say, everybody was in their own little world just thinking of things.

Remembering things about home and how it's going to be when you come back home. That people would be thankful that we served our country. I found out that was not going to happen when I came home. Then the pilot announced we'll be landing and he would be turning off the main lights and putting the night lights on in the plane and fasten your Seat Belts when the light comes on that reads "Fasten Your Seat Belts." Then the night lights came on in the plane and the plane started going down. We are now starting to land into Saigon, Vietnam. Then you started thinking about how it's going to be in Vietnam. What are we going to do? Or what we're going to see. How we're going to take it, or can you handle it, all kinds of thoughts run through your head at 100 miles an hour at that moment.

As you look out the window you could see there was something going on. There were flares going off in the sky and in the distance there were these red lines coming from the sky landing on Mother Earth. Later on I would know what I was seeing, it was a battle going on and the red lines were tracers ("bullets") flying in the sky. I was scared as all hell. I didn't know what was going on. I just wondered what the hell I was doing here.

So, I tried to focus on the pilot giving us instructions again, so that I wouldn't keep thinking about how afraid I was. The pilot announced, "Close the blinds on the windows, we'll be landing in a few minutes." Then the light read "Fasten Your Seat Belts."

I can remember the stewardesses looking at us, like something was going to happen. The looks in their eyes, were like my Dad's eyes when I left. Their eyes were glossy and that sad look on their faces. They even look scared.

Then you could hear the landing gear lock in place and before you knew it the wheels hit the runway, then the roar of the engines, it was a little rough landing. Then the plane came to a halt. We stopped on the runway. The pilot announced that we have landed in Saigon, Vietnam. I guess we had to wait for the all clear sign to move.

Then we started moving again down the black top. What are we doing? We stopped again! Then the pilot announced there are buses here to pick us up. Then the stewardess opened the doors and the heat, the smell just rushed right in. It was awful it was hard to breathe the smell and the heat – it was 11:00 p.m., but it had to be 100 degrees or more.

Then the stewardess said it's time to leave the plane, the way they said it, the way they looked at us was sad and they didn't smile this time. Their faces had that scared look. Like I said it was real different this time. It was hard to explain it back then. They knew some of us won't be coming back home.

We must have looked so innocent with our baby-faced look. With that scared look on our faces too. It must have been hard on them to see us that way.

To unload us to our death and knowing a lot of us won't be coming home the same way. Seeing so many young kids going out there at the same time. I couldn't imagine how they felt inside. It had to be a lot of stress on them too knowing what they had to do. To leave us that way.

Vietnam: In-Country

April 1968-October 1968

In-Country
April 1968

As the plane stopped I could see green military buses were on the blacktop waiting for us. The stewardess stood by the doors to the plane. She told us to come to the door and go down the stairs. I thought I was in the land of OZ. I couldn't believe what I was seeing it was the land of hell everything looked different everything was green. You felt the heat and that smell, it was hard to catch your breath. You could hear explosions going off in the distance and see flashes of light in the sky. That stopped us in our tracks for a moment. Then these guys told us to hurry up and get on the bus and move it. Their voices were in panic mode. We got on these buses that had wire mesh on them. It was hot! We were still in our wintergreens from Stateside, that made it hotter and made us really itch a lot more.

They told us to hurry up and get on the bus. We didn't really want to leave the plane but we did. We followed orders like it or not. The training kicked in. Then the military bus driver told us to keep our heads down, they've been shooting at the buses lately. There were four buses waiting for us so we left in a convoy with four MP jeeps with 50-caliber guns on them. There were two in front of the convoy and two in the back of the convoy. While we rode the bus you could hear the gunfire in the distance, it was one hell of a scary ride that night.

All I could think of was about my Mom and Dad. Wishing I was back home again. They took us to the 90th Replacement Center in Long Binh that night. That's where we would find out what Unit we'd be assigned to. It was a long night, they took us to a hootch for us to sleep in. A hootch is like a "barrack." We lay on the floor in case we got rockets or incoming mortars. The hootches had sand bags stacked around them about three feet high to give us some kind of cover from incoming rounds. There were 20 men in a hootch. We really couldn't sleep with all the noise going on. We all lay as quiet as we can be and scared to beat all hell.

Then morning came and they fed us breakfast. They took us to the compound and lined us up in formation and it looked like we would be leaving in groups. Then I asked one of the guys why the groups have different numbers of guys, 20 here and 30 there and so on. He said we were replacing the dead. I thought to myself, people are dying left and right here. Then reality set in! Life can end real fast here, this is for real. I'm in a war zone and no place to hide and no place to run and you're stuck here in it like it or not.

I was already scared, and hearing this shit now made it worse. I just didn't know what was going to happen to me next. My first day here they already called five groups to go out. They fed us lunch, it was a long hot humid day and it rained off and on throughout the day.

Well I guess I'd be staying here tonight again in the 90th Replacement. It was late and starting to get dark. They put us in formation again and picked 20 guys from the compound to pull guard on the bunker line. I was lucky I didn't have to go out there on the bunker line that night.

They took us to this building where we would stay for tonight. I met a few guys there. All we talked about is what state or town you were from, things like that. But we didn't talk about what was going on here. We heard enough bad things that are happening out there.

We went to eat dinner, the food was bad and the water tasted like chlorine and the food tasted funny. Then we came back to our hootches. They had cots in them this time. They are the same thing as a bed, they gave them to us so we could set them up and to have something to sleep on. It was another long night again and the nights seem to get longer here each time.

The next morning we ate breakfast, it was bad too. It tasted like it had chlorine in it. The food didn't look good. The fried eggs looked like they were floating in water and the powdered eggs looked like Jell-O. The bacon wasn't cooked all the way and the biscuits were hard as rocks. So we ate what we could eat. It didn't take long before some the guys had the "GIs." The runs.

Meeting the Wolfhounds in Cu Chi
April 1968

So that morning we lined up again in the compound in formation where I got my orders to report to the 25th Infantry Division at Cu Chi Base Camp. To report to, Alpha Company, 1st Battalion, 27th Infantry, Wolfhound.

It must be a good Unit! One of the guys said to me, they only asked for five of us, then I found out we were the last of the group of 38 guys that had to be replaced, it didn't look good for me.

They flew us five in a Chinook helicopter which was taking supplies to Cu Chi, our main base camp. It was a big base that we could see from the Chinook helicopter. We landed at the airport on base. The runway was dirt, it had a lot of helicopter pads with green sand bags as high as the chopper around them like a horseshoe, it was to protect them from incoming rounds. There were about 30 or 40 pads along the runway.

The trucks came in and took the supplies from the Chinook helicopter and this Sergeant in this jeep asked who was going to Alpha Company, 1st Battalion, 27th Infantry. I said I was Private Maes. I was nervous and the only one that was going to that Company. He looked old and beat and tired and his clothes were covered in red dirt and the sweat was coming down his face. I found out later he was the same age I was! He took me to my Unit where our compound was on base. So the other guys were picked up and went to their different Unit compounds on base too.

It was late in the evening and the mess hall was closed. The Sergeant gave me a box of C-rations for dinner. He took me to an empty hootch. The Company was out in the field. Doing their job protecting our main base.

There were about 20 cots there. They were all covered with dust and everything else that was there. It looked like nobody had been here for months. It didn't feel right being here. It felt like it was haunted. I felt so alone and scared and uncertain of the future. I went to the CQ (Charge of Quarters) and I asked the Sergeant on duty, are there any EM (Enlisted Men) around? He said everybody is out in the field. Then he said if you like you can stay here until you're ready to hit the sack.

We talked about where I was from and where he was from and that he was back here because he got wounded about two weeks ago. That he was on light duty and he'd be going back out in the field in a few more weeks. That he was only 19 and was in-country six months so he was my age. He said tomorrow morning he'd take me to the mess hall to eat and to my one-week jungle training class. So I went back to hit the sack. I couldn't really sleep with all the different sounds going on and being scared and alone and uncertain of the things to come.

Then morning came! Then me and the Sergeant went to the mess hall and ate breakfast. It was a small building and a few other guys were there. The food was the same, it didn't taste good or the water. It just had a funny taste. I know they put chlorine in the water to kill the bacteria. I guess because they cook with the water you get that chlorine taste too. Then the Sergeant drove me to my class in a jeep. To the other side of the base camp where we did our jungle training. There I met guys from different Companies. I was supposed to do one week of jungle training but they added three more days of training for me. To show me how to go into tunnels and check them out. I didn't need that kind of training. It was bad enough to be in the Infantry. The Sergeant said because I was Native, I would be good in doing that type of work. Boy I didn't need to hear that kind of bullshit. That's all I needed is to put my life more on the line. Now we're all done with all our training in Cu Chi Base Camp and I guess I'm prepared to go to war. They already gave us our jungle fatigues and our weapons. Then told us what to expect out there in the battlefield and what kind of booby traps to look for in the jungle. I didn't know there were so many different types of booby traps out there.

And then they took us out on a night ambush and tried to show us what it feels like to go on a real night ambush and how it is to operate a Prick-25 radio at night. How to set your Claymore mines up at night. At the same time to get us used to the weather out here and our weapons at the same time. To me it wasn't training it felt real, the fear of war was present. I just can't believe how hot it is here. You sweat just standing there or even just sitting. The flies, mosquitoes, and ants are big out here and can they bite!

The humidity is real high and it rains before you know it. You get all wet and within an hour, you'll be dry as a bone because of the heat. Boy just being here and how everything looks is so strange to me and the fear of the unknown is so real to me.

Everything here is green, the vehicles, helicopters, airplanes, sand bags and everybody in green jungle fatigues everywhere you look is green and even C-ration cans are green and your T- shirts, shorts, and towels and so on. This was not like the Emerald City in the land of OZ. There's nothing beautiful about this place.

Boy what a scared feeling it is. To see it for the first time and how strange everything is. Now I can tell I'm really in a war zone and I can feel it. It's like being on a different planet, it is so strange seeing it all and feeling it all at once. I didn't know I could feel so scared and nervous at the same time, and alone. That it was going to get worse as time moved on. I just can't believe I've handled it so far. I don't know what is keeping my head together. It's so much to take in at once. I am trying to understand myself, why my body feels so nervous and my mind running away with so many different thoughts. I just hope I can keep control of myself in this hellhole!

I finished my one week of jungle training, and a half a week of tunnel school. I was ready to go out into the field into combat. I was scared shitless. I still didn't know what to expect out there. Even with the training they gave me. All I knew, I can get killed out there. It was my time to go out in the jungle somewhere in Vietnam. I felt so alone out here! I'd meet somebody and the next thing he's going to a different place than you are. It's kind of hard to make a friend out here. Things are always changing here from one moment to the next. They issued all my equipment to get ready to go out in the field. I didn't know how heavy all this equipment would be. Everything was extra, two of everything, water and grenades, Claymore mines and a belt for the M-60 machine gun then ammo, 20 magazines of 20 rounds per magazine for my M-16 rifle and so on. I didn't know when I was going out to my Company. It was just a matter of time for me to go. It seems everything is done at the last minute around here.

MY FIRST DAY WITH THE WOLFHOUNDS
May 1968

The next thing I knew, it was the middle of the afternoon, almost the middle of May, after about two weeks in Vietnam. They told me to get my things, and said, "Get ready to go out to your Company." Boy! When he said that my stomach tied up in knots and at the same time it scared the hell out of me. Then the Sergeant waited for me to get my equipment and then he took me in a jeep to the helicopter pad. He told me good luck hope to see you later. But that look on his face was trying tell me something. I just couldn't tell what it was. It bothered me the way he looked at me. Then I noticed I was the only one getting on a helicopter. It was just me going to my Company out in the jungle to resupply it! There were guys unloading the supplies off the truck, and loading the chopper with ammo boxes and C-ration boxes, and water to supply my Company. I got on the chopper and it lifted up blowing dirt everywhere, and I could hear the blades on the chopper cutting through the air and making that popping sound as we went up in the air. I couldn't believe what I was feeling and seeing for the first time. I was flying on a UH-1 Huey helicopter for the first time – it was great!

I was near the open door where you could see everything. As we were flying over the base I could see how big Cu Chi Base Camp was, and it was *big*! It looked to be about three miles wide and about five miles long or more. It had a big dirt landing strip and all kinds of helicopter pads, and all kinds of buildings and dirt roads. It looked like a small town. Then the bunker line went around the perimeter of the big base camp, with lots of concertina wire in front of the bunkers and guard towers. There were about 40 guard towers or more around the perimeter with five bunkers between each tower, and four main gates around the perimeter.

As we flew higher and further out away from Cu Chi the land looked so beautiful, like I was on a vacation. It felt so safe up here, about 2000 to 3000 feet in the air. I wasn't scared anymore. The rotor blades chopping the air sounded like drums to my ears. And the cool wind in my face, and on my pants legs flapping in the air. Then smelling the sweet fresh air, it felt so good and safe up here. I felt like an eagle flying in the air, what a moment to feel as free as an eagle.

What a beautiful ride this was! We'd only been up in the air for about ten minutes so far. But the guys – the Door Gunners – had a look on their faces. Something like the Sergeant had! Then they put their face shields down and were talking to the pilot on the radio and before I knew it they started checking their machine guns. We made a hard right bank. Then we started coming down real fast toward the ground where my Company was, First of the Wolfhounds.

The Crew Chief raised his face shield and said, "This is going to be a Hot LZ (Hot Landing Zone)." I really noticed the look on his face . . . it looked like he was going to see death. It was scary to see his look! I didn't know what he meant by "Hot LZ." I found out later. It meant the Company was under fire. The men had been taking fire from the tree line next to the canal and were making their way out of the rice paddy to the tree line.

Then I noticed bomb craters all over the ground, trees were blown apart and smoke was coming out of the tree line. Guys were lying down and hiding near the tree line along the canal. These guys looked real ragged and dirty, their skin look burnt, their clothes torn, long hair, beards, they hadn't shaved for a month or more.

I just couldn't believe this! Is this really happening to me? They didn't train us on how it felt in a real war zone! They tried to, but the reality of war is hard to teach in any training class. Your life isn't at stake in a training class.

It's a lot different when you know you might lose your life at any moment. The only way to understand it is to be there in it, and if you've never been there you're not going to understand. I've been there and I still don't understand it . . . why things happen the way they do.

There was so much pain and suffering back then. How awful things looked, and things that I'd never seen before and felt. It just made me sick to my stomach. The Crew Chief said, "Get ready. We'll be going in, then you get out as fast as you can so we can get the supplies out, and we can get the hell out of there." He pulled his shield down and both Door Gunners started opening up with their M-60 machine guns as the chopper was moving up and down and sideways because of the turbulence. I couldn't believe how rough of a ride it was, coming in and everything was happening so fast!

We landed in the rice paddy out in the open about 100 yards behind my Company. I jumped off the helicopter and these guys started running to me and hollering at me to get this, and that, and keep my head down. Talk about being scared shitless. I was. My legs didn't want to move. I was shaking, and tears were coming down my face, and the smell was horrible. I couldn't believe what was going on, and what I was seeing for the first time, and how loud the gunfire and explosions were, and the Company guys screaming and hollering at each other and at me.

Then the same guys started throwing bodies in the chopper. The bodies were our men! They were all blown apart! The guys were throwing them in the chopper they didn't even have a chance to put them in body bags. This happened in just seconds, and I couldn't believe what I was seeing, and I couldn't believe I was helping them throw the bodies on the chopper that way. I couldn't believe how warm their blood felt on my hands. Their bodies were still warm and the heat of their blood was a real contrast to the cooler air of the higher altitudes. The chopper had descended so fast that my hands hadn't had a chance to warm up to the much hotter jungle temperature that we were in now. The bodies were still draining blood and it was smeared everywhere. The bodies were still relieving stool and urine, what an awful smell. It was on the helicopter floor-plates, and on the men who were picking up the bodies and throwing them into the helicopter. And it was all over me on my arms, hands, face, and fatigues. But there was no time to think about it at the moment. Things were happening way too fast. I was doing things because I'd been told to do them, and I was moving on pure adrenaline, instinct and training. I was following orders to a "T."

At that moment I thought I was going to die. I couldn't believe how young they were. You could tell most of the guys were new guys in-country. They didn't have a suntan yet and their clothes still looked new like mine and their boots still had a shine on them. Then this guy said, "Come with me." We ran from the open rice paddy to this mound of dirt and we lay down by it. I could hear bullets snapping over my head. Then he said to me, "Stay here!" Then he took off. I was really shaking, scared and confused. I thought to myself, "I hope I don't die here." I heard the chopper taking off. I knew it was leaving because the blades were making a whopping sound, and I wanted to get back on it and go home. I wanted my Mom and Dad to take me away from "Here." I was crying for them to help me keep it together out here in this madhouse.

I didn't know what to do, so I stayed there like he said. Then some other guy came by and said, "Come on with me." All I knew was that we were moving up closer to where the battle was going on. It was scary and crazy as all hell, and I was still confused. I didn't know anybody and nobody even knew me, or asked me my name in case I died.

They didn't know who I was. I felt so alone. There was nowhere to really hide, and nowhere to go or run to. I was stuck "here," like it or not. I thought this was my last day on Mother Earth. I couldn't believe how my whole life went by so fast. I guess I was still in panic mode.

I thought about home, my Mom and Dad, and about how they would miss me. I just knew I had to keep my shit together, or I wouldn't make it home. Things were happening too fast for me. But I knew to keep my head down, and follow orders to the "T" if I wanted to stay alive.

Then it started getting dark. There were guys around me, and the battle was still going on, but no one knew me they never asked my name and I didn't know them. I felt isolated, alone, and unwanted, in spite of everything that was happening around me. Being alone is really hard on a guy. You just can't believe how it makes you feel inside. Being alone and terrified, in a strange place, with guys dying around you, feels a whole lot scarier than just being alone. Then this guy, a young Mexican-American kid, a "three-striper," said, "I'm Sergeant Bones. You'll be in my Platoon in Alpha Company, 3rd Platoon, 2nd Squad."

Then he asked my name, and I told him, "I'm Joseph Maes. But you can call me Joe." It made me feel a lot better about myself, and it felt like somebody cared about me. I thought, I'm not alone in this hellhole. Somebody knows me by my name, now. I won't be a John Doe. I knew I had my dog tags around my neck, but if I got blown apart like the other guys did, they still wouldn't know who I was, unless I put one of my dog tags on my boot between the laces. Which I did later on.

Then he asked me, "Can you speak Spanish?" I said, "No, I'm Native American." He said, "Cool, I never met a Native American before." After asking me these couple of questions, he moved off to check on the rest of his Squad and I was alone, again, with a bunch of strange guys I didn't know. I can't believe how confused I was that day. But now I know some of my training did kick in and I followed orders, like it or not.

I did what I was ordered to do, and what I was taught to do. What we did in training paid off. It was the little things that saved your life or your ass out there. If you freeze or hesitate, you can get killed and that's why you follow orders to the "T," even though you can't move. Or you don't want to go. You have to be strong and take control of your body and your feelings and do what you have to do to survive.

I'm trying to get over the shock. I'm still shaking from what I've been through, and hoping I can get through this shit from now on. It was a long, scary afternoon for me. I just can't believe I'm still alive in this damn place and that I made it this far, today. I just hope it's not like this every day I won't make it the whole year if it is. But I didn't know that things can get a whole lot worse being a Grunt.

I thought this day was bad enough. The more time I spend out here, the harder it gets as time moves on. I just can't believe I'm still alive. I still have blood on my hands and fatigues and even urine and poop from this afternoon. This must be a bad dream. This can't be real. I look at my hands and fatigues again, and there's still blood on them, it wasn't a dream. I didn't know that we were in the Hoc Mon area about 20 miles from Saigon, next to Highway One, which went to Cu Chi about 25 miles West-North on Highway One (we Native Americans put "West" before "North," because we face West when we do our blessings). Back then I didn't know where the hell I was! I was scared just being here. It was so hot being out here. I was sweating to beat all hell. It had to be over 100 degrees and the humidity was real high. My arms hurt and my back hurt from lifting and pulling all the supplies off the chopper and carrying the dead and putting them on the chopper. I just wonder where I got all that strength to do that. Where did the time go? It's late now. It's starting to get dark. The firing has stopped now. It's kind of quiet. I'm just waiting to be told what to do next. I'm scared to beat all hell!

FIRST NIGHT AMBUSH
May 1968

That day wasn't over yet. I heard my name being called! Sergeant Bones said in a soft voice, "Joe! It's time to eat. We'll be going on a night ambush tonight. Here's your C-rations for tonight! And a P-38 to open it with. I'll bring the rest of the stuff you need to take on patrol tonight."

Boy, I just looked at my little box of C-rations with my head down. I could smell the other guys' C-rations when they opened them up. I didn't feel like eating, the smell made me sick to my stomach and I was still in shock and shook up from this afternoon. I was so tired, and all my emotions were drained out of me. I still had the blood from the men's bodies on my fatigues, and on my hands and arms. The more the blood dried up on my fatigues, the stiffer the fatigues got. And the blood on my skin was getting sticky. But my face was sweating and sweat was pouring down my face, and my hands were sweating and the blood started washing off my hands. I just couldn't believe what I'd been through. I looked up at Sergeant Bones. He must have read my face with its fear and hopelessness because he said, "Don't worry, we'll take care of you out here. We're all brothers out here, and we all act as one out here in this damn place. It's ok to be scared out here. Just follow orders like you did out here today. You did a good job for being a new guy."

I didn't think he knew who I was, or what I was doing under fire. He made me feel good about myself, and knowing he had his eyes on me comforted me. He said, "Most new guys don't make it under fire on their first day. We usually end up loading them right back up on the chopper. It was your lucky day, today, and I hope your luck keeps going for you. Things will happen, and we have no control over the outcome. It's just pure luck that things happen for the good."

This was my first day with the Wolfhounds in the field and under fire. The guys in my unit said I'd been "baptized in hell." I'm now a true Wolfhound, and a true Grunt at the young age of 19. I'd been baptized in battle, and blood. My Dad will be proud of me today, and my Ancestors too. I've been under fire, and in battle, and I am a true Warrior now. I can wear an Eagle Feather with pride when I get home, and hold my head up high in our Pow Wows as a true Native-American Warrior defending our people and our nation. The most honorable thing for a Native-American male is to become a true Warrior. A Warrior that has shed blood for the tribe and its people. He's defended lives and been prepared to give his life in protection of our people. "Eagle" for us represents strength, honor, sacrifice, and "Spirit of the Circle of Life." And only those who've experienced the strength of the "Circle of Life" have earned the right to wear a Feather as a true Warrior. I am now a true Warrior in the Creator's eyes of the spirit world and to my Native people. Also being a Wolfhound and for us Natives the Wolf symbolizes direction and leadership and also embodies protection and destruction and also symbolizes strength, endurance, and intelligence. I will find out that I possess all the Wolf powers of leadership, strength, endurance, and intelligence as I walk through the path in the battlefield of hell. Because six months from now I will make E-5 as a Squad Leader in the Platoon, a true Warrior of intelligence and leadership.

Boy, if it's like this all the time, I'm not going to make it. I'm completely drained, tired, homesick, and scared. I'm so nervous and tense. This day is getting to me. Can I keep up with this shit? It's only been my first day with my Company. It's been only five or seven hours since I've been out here. I just don't know if I can keep this up for a whole year night and day. It's so sad seeing the guys from our Company that got killed earlier today and loading the bodies in the chopper that way. We threw them like cordwood onto a pile, bodies piled one on top of each other, and the blood was all over everything. It was awful to see and to handle such young men that way. But really they were just young kids like me and so many of them. I just can't believe I helped load them up that way. I guess I was still in shock! Panic mode! I still had their blood on my hands and on my clothes. I didn't know I could do that! It happened so fast I guess I didn't have time to think about it, then. I just did what I was ordered to do, like it or not.

It seemed like the guys didn't care about the dead. But they did. There just wasn't time to give the bodies the respect they deserved. There wasn't even time to put the dead into body bags. Every second counts in a battle. I learned real fast how quickly you have to get your shit together, in order to stay alive, like it or not. If you're lucky you might get a second chance to live another day.

I found out later that you have to do what you have to do and that's the way it was even if you didn't like it. You do what you have to do to stay alive out here. That's how my first day went, out in the field, in-country with Alpha Company, First of the Wolfhounds. And that day began in mid-afternoon! I didn't know back then, that May of 1968 was the beginning of the Mini Tet Offensive. I wound up in five more Mini Offensives that year, full NVA and VC Battalion Offensives trying to control entire districts of territory. I didn't know I would be in so much shit in Vietnam. Later I found out May of 1968 had the highest casualties for US troops in the Vietnam War. I also found out later that for the whole war, only one Division had more men KIA (Killed in Action) than us, the 25th Infantry Division, "Tropic Lightning." That was the 1st Cavalry Division. We had even more men killed than the 101st Airborne, the "Screaming Eagles"!

For the next three months, day after day, and night after night, we were in some kind of contact with the enemy. The Main Tet Offensive of 1968 began with the Vietnamese "Tet" (New Year) in February of 1968. Then it slowed down a little bit. The five Mini Offensives happened (after the Main Offensive) throughout the rest of 1968, and some of 1969. During the Main Tet Offensive and in May the Wolfhounds lost a lot of men, at least now during the Mini Tets we weren't losing so many young kids.

How did I make it? Only the Creator (God) or the Great Spirit knows what I've been through and how I made it. I know my Creator and the Great Spirit will help me through this hell on Mother Earth. Sergeant Bones introduced me to the rest of 2nd Squad from 3rd Platoon and our LT (Lieutenant) who was the oldest guy at the age of 25 in our Platoon. He said we'd be pulling a night ambush tonight, in the area where we'd been receiving enemy fire, about 600 yards down the tree line where it meets the canal.

Sergeant Bones said, "We'll be doing a night 'L' ambush." Then he said, "Joe, you'll be walking point tonight." I looked at him and thought, "Are you crazy! And for being my first night out in the battlefield?" Then he said, "All FNG (Fucking New Guys) walk point when it's their Squad's turn. 2nd Squad from 3rd Platoon is moving out first tonight." Then I found out why it's better for a new guy to walk point. He'll be more alert, and more on the ball. I never felt so scared in my whole life and I felt so alone being here. I had no choice in the matter I just had to follow orders. I knew in my own mind I had to think positive and not negative and do the best I can do out here to survive.

Like they say, "It's better to get wounded or killed early . . . that way you don't have to suffer as much, and it gives the 'older guys' a better chance of getting home alive." The 'older guys' meant those guys that have been in-country longer than you, and on a Line Unit for at least six to nine months, or more. The older guys have already done what you (the FNG) are about to do…they've been through it already. Now I know what "That Look" is. I could see it in their faces and eyes. "That Look" is the look of a thousand-yard stare you get on your face and eyes, a look that comes from being in battle for so long, and from looking for the enemy for so long, from pure mental and physical exhaustion, and from seeing your friends wounded or dying, and from having to endure the physical and mental punishment that a Grunt in battle has to endure.

I guess we all have to put our time in as point man, like it or not. I already had 20 full magazines of ammo for my M-16 and a full canteen of water on me. Sergeant Bones then brought me a belt of M-60 ammo of 100 rounds for the M-60 machine gun, a Claymore mine, four grenades, a LAW (Light Anti-tank Weapon), two smoke grenades (one red and one purple), ten more full magazines of ammo for my M-16, and another full canteen of water. Anyway, it was time for the Platoon to move out. I can't believe how heavy this load is that I have to carry! And I can't believe how dark it is out there on the trail. We move as a silent column one quiet footstep after the next into the pitch black of the unknown. And I'm at the front of it!

Sergeant Bones told me, "If you see anything out there moving, shoot for the kill. The only thing out there is the enemy. Your training is over. It's for real, from now on. You shoot for the kill, and ask questions later." I will always remember what he told me that day. They were words of wisdom – Grunt wisdom.

Here we go. I was at the front. Everything was quiet in our area. None of us was saying anything. I was the point man but I didn't know what I should do next, so I looked back at Sergeant Bones for some guidance. He pointed down the trail towards the blackness. Then pointed with his two fingers to his eyes to tell me to keep *my* eyes wide open. I can't believe how nervous I was walking down that tree line along the trail, on the bank of the canal, in the dark for the first time. I was shaking like a leaf! I can't see what I'm stepping on. The ground is not even. There are dead leaves and broken branches on the ground. I am just hoping the enemy wouldn't hear me stepping on that stuff. I'm scared as all hell. I could step on a booby trap at any time. Or we can be walking into their ambush, I just don't know. I just hope I can make it to our night ambush location without getting blown apart or killed. All I know is my eyes are wide open, and I can hardly see anything in front of me. I feel so alone being up front. I am about 30 feet in front of the rest of the column. It seems a lifetime away from everybody.

This isn't like going deer hunting. I feel like I'm the deer who's being hunted. The "deer" out in that blackness in front of me don't have doe eyes and racks on their heads, they shoot back. These "deer" have weapons, and are called NVA and VC and they're waiting to kill you. They're out there moving around, resupplying their units, setting up ambushes and waiting for you to step into *their* kill zone. We are trying to do the same thing to them.

It was a weird feeling – doing this at night for the first time. You know the enemy is out there waiting for you, to ambush you at any time. Your hands start sweating while you're holding your weapon, your forehead, too. Your heart starts pounding. It pounds so hard it seems everyone can hear it. Your lips and mouth go dry and all you want is a sip of water. But you can't drink anything because you're moving, and you have to suck it up and keep heading forward to your night ambush site. Then your legs feel weak, and you're shaking and so scared you want to cry. Your gear feels so heavy, and your web-straps are cutting into your shoulder. You just have to deal with the pain, and the stress, and keep on moving. At the same time, every muscle in your eyes and ears is straining to see and hear what's in front of you, as you're walking, and all the while you're thinking, "This could be my last step on Mother Earth."

Crazy thoughts go through your mind as you're moving. "Are they going to be loading me on a chopper tonight, or tomorrow, all blown apart, like the guys I saw earlier in the day?" "It seems like I've been walking for hours." "I could be home eating a home-cooked meal." "I could be sitting in a car with my ex-girlfriend." My brain is sending out one thought after another as fast as it can, in my head. It's my brain's way of trying to calm me down, and keep me in the present, in the "moment," so I can deal with the fear, and so I can pay attention to what I have to pay attention to. Now I know what my Dad has taught me is working. When I used to get hungry or I had some kind of pain when we went deer hunting my Dad told me to always think of something pleasant to take away your hunger or pain, it really works if you have the strength. It's mind over matter. The simple things in life that my Dad and Mom taught me in real life are really working for me out here in how to survive. At the time when my Mom and Dad taught me this stuff I didn't think it would help me in any way. Boy was I wrong, now I can really feel my love for my parents out here in this damn hellhole. Boy! I can't wait to see them again.

The night is pitch black, and the sky is clear and the stars look real big as I look up for a moment and look back down. In the distance near the ground, I see flashes of exploding lights like fireworks, from the ground up towards the sky, and red tracer-lines streaming down from the sky, towards the ground. The tracers tell me that a helicopter gunship is working over the ground area. It's firing its mini-guns at the enemy. There are no sounds yet, just an explosion of bright lights and tracers. A few split-seconds later, though, I hear bombs exploding and gunfire going off in the distance. All the gunfire has different sounds to it, I hear mini-guns, M-16s, AK-47s, M-60's, and M-14's all mixed together. It's a racket of noise. There's a battle going on, and I'm glad I'm not over there in that area. It looks like it's a couple of miles or more away from me.

The Moon is starting to come out now. I can see a little better now, it makes me feel a little bit better. But then, they can see you better too. You're damned if you do, and damned if you don't. The clouds are moving across the moon, and the shadows of the clouds are moving on the ground. It looks like things are moving out there! Boy that made me nervous! And it scared me all to hell, even more. It could be the enemy moving out there. You just don't know what's really out there.

You really have to think, and make sure you make the right decision before you start firing. Because when you do, you give away your position. You better be damn sure the enemy is out there when you start firing. People will die by your mistake. If you make a mistake, it's going to cost you or somebody their life. If you don't fire, they'll shoot you. If you fire, they'll shoot you. You're damned if you do damned if you don't. The main thing is to not give away your position. Boy, it's really something to be doing this for the first time. I never felt so much fear in my whole life, knowing death is just around the corner and the unknown.

I just don't know how I did this shit for a whole year, day in and day out. I should have gone crazy. I finally made it to the end of the canal where it meets the other canal. This is our ambush location, it's by the canal and the column's getting ready to set up for tonight. I'm tired and drained, but I'm wide awake and scared shitless.

We laid out our Claymore mines, down each end of the bank, facing the canal and towards the opposite bank of the canal. I still don't know what I'm doing from one minute to the next. All I do is what I'm told to do or by their hand signals. There's a rice paddy next to the bank. It's full of water. We can't lie on the bank where it's dry, because we'll be exposed. So we all lie down in the rice paddy full of water, where we won't be exposed. There's tall grass on the dikes and banks. The banks are along the rivers and canals, the dikes make up the grids of the rice paddies. But both the dikes and banks are mostly the same height. The guys in my Squad said it had been raining the past few days! It's monsoon season, the rainy season and it will rain constantly for the next three to four months.

Now we are waiting for the enemy to come down the canal, or on a sampan (boat) . . . or walking along the dikes . . . or along the next dike over from us . . . or from either end of this dike. It's starting to get real cold. We were lying down in the water, in the rice paddy and there was a cool night breeze. Our wet clothes made us colder. Lying there, waiting for the enemy, it was something else. It seemed surreal, and thoughts crossed my mind, "Is this for real? Am I really living this way?" This is not the way to live a normal life. This feels like an out-of-body experience. Here I am, freezing my ass off, in the middle of a rice paddy, halfway across the world. This isn't what you see in the movies. This is not a comfortable atmosphere! You don't feel and see all these details in the movies! This is real life and it's sure as hell different from the movies, it's living hell.

I'm trained to fight but no one's ever trained us to sit here waiting for a firefight and the unknown keeps me on edge. I have to control my thoughts, so I don't lose my confidence in my own abilities to perform my duties. I have to keep fear from invading my thoughts, but it's always there peeking around the corner of my mind, waiting to take over my actions. Letting fear control my actions will keep me from fighting, from shooting the enemy, and will put me and my buddies in danger. And I don't want that. I've seen my friends lose it because of fear . . . they can't respond . . . they can't fire their weapons . . . they panic and run towards the enemy . . . they don't think of their safety, or that they have to save their buddy. I've been scared shitless, and in their shoes and almost lost it, and the fear of "losing it" is always there. But knowing that I can be killed or that I have to kill someone pushes my adrenaline to the edge of my tolerance. Adrenaline and fear are always existing side-by-side in me, and it's a constant struggle to "maintain." There's fear every second, every minute, every hour, every day, and every night. At any moment, it can make you or break you.

Battle is a soul killer. Each time that you have to prepare to be killed by someone, and each time you have to prepare to kill someone, is like a death to your soul and to your mental well-being and spirit. Battle and Waiting-for-Battle are "deaths" that haunt you till the day you die. Battle and Waiting-for-Battle are living deaths that take away all your innocence, and all the happiness you have in life. What's left of you after that experience feels like nothing more than a dead shell that's going through the motions of life. What you are, afterwards, is just a dead shell that's missing out on the things that life has to really offer you.

Here I am in the night of silence lying here next to the dike in the rice paddy. My head is right against the dike and I'm watching the canal. I'm soaking wet because we have to lie hidden in the water that floods the rice paddy. It's so cold that we're all shaking and our teeth are rattling. The Moon is full and bright, and there are a few clouds in the sky. I notice movement on the dike!

Something or someone is creeping along the top. It's a snake! It's the first time I've ever seen such a large snake! It's slithering out of the water from the rice paddy. It's moved onto the top of the dike about ten feet from me. It's about five or six feet long and it's curled itself up into a coil in front of me. Earlier I saw big rats and they were as big as two-month-old Labrador puppies. Seeing the rats and the snake scares me, all I need now is for one of them to bite me. I know rats carry rabies and the snakes carry poisonous venom in them. The rats like walking on top of the dikes, it's dry there. The snakes like hunting for the rats on top of the dikes. It's real weird lying here waiting for the enemy to walk up to us so we can spring our ambush. I'm watching the snake and I know the snake is doing the same thing waiting there all coiled up, ready to ambush its meal. This is just another one of life's ironies!

It's weird how life is and how things work out. I can't believe I'm doing this, it's so weird watching this snake doing its thing waiting for its meal to get close enough for the kill. The snake looks like it's dead, it doesn't move at all. Its eyes are wide open just staring, and not moving, they look so big and yellow. Just staring down the dike and completely still except for its tongue. Every time its forked tongue flickers you could see it moving in the moonlight.

The snake was an imitation of us, waiting there to spring an ambush. Before I knew it, it was gone. Boy! Where in the hell did it go? Oh great, now I have something else to be afraid of! I know I'm not the only guy watching the snake. We look at each other in the understanding that we're all seeing the same irony behind the snake lying in wait. All we can do is watch and not move around or we would give away our position.

I look over to one of the old guys. He is one of the guys who'd been in-county for about four months. He is my age. He looks beat, tired, suntanned, and has that thousand-yard stare that looks right through you. I can feel that there is no compassion for me in that hard stare. That stare scares me, it seems to me that his stare is telling me he doesn't want to know me, doesn't want to get close to me and doesn't want to deal with me. And it seems that his stare is saying to me that I am going to have to deal with this on my own. He looks at me and all he does is put his two fingers to his lips to show me, not to say anything. I can see he is freezing his ass off like me. He is shaking like a leaf. We all are! What a night so far. It's been a miserable cold night so far, and not being able to move around to keep warm, makes you even colder. You just have to suck it up and take it! You do it the best way you know how, in your own way. It's mind-over-matter now. I'm only 19 and I've never suffered so much in one day, and now it is night time and when does the suffering end? This is my first night out here with my Platoon on a night ambush. I don't know if I can take it anymore and the night just started. As time goes on it gets worse, the pain from my body hurts more and more.

How the time just drags on, waiting and waiting. You're lying there shaking because it's so cold. The water smells real bad and your hands look like raisins from being wet so long, and they hurt so bad because it's so cold and wet. I'm holding onto my weapon and that cold metal on my hands makes my hands feel colder and hurt more.

I was freezing. There was a cool breeze and I could feel my face getting colder. The outside temperature was about 80 degrees, but it felt more like 40 degrees. Here I am, lying in this frigid water. Not moving a muscle, trying to stay still and keep quiet. My body is shivering just trying to keep itself warm just my face and head were above the water. The rest of me was completely underwater. I could feel a little temperature shift. The air moving across my face felt cooler. I must have sensed that the weather was about to change because I looked up towards the sky. I could see a lot more clouds starting to block out the Moon. I felt a drizzle touching my face. Then it started raining, real gently for a while, the drops tapped on my helmet. I can see the lightening in the dark, off in the distance. Then before I knew it, it started pouring down real hard on us. It was a cold rain, I could hear the raindrops on my helmet. By now the drops were thumping so hard on my helmet that the noise never stopped. I wanted it to stop raining so hard, it even got colder because of the cold rain and my body was hurting more and more.

The tapping and thumping on my helmet sounded louder and louder. My head started throbbing and throbbing. I thought Mother Earth and my Ancestors and the Heavens were mad at us! The rain is bouncing off the leaves on the bushes and shrubs all around us, and the sound is like thunder around us, like the sound of a thousand horses running through a canyon. Even the raindrops splashing on the water and onto to my face sounded so loud to me now I can't escape the rain and the noise.

The rain won't stop. The rain is hitting the rice paddy water and splashing up all around us. My face is getting bombarded by big fat drops of water pouring out of the dark skies. It's being bombarded by big fat splashes of water, they're ricocheting up off the paddy water as I'm lying there with my head barely above the water line. The rain keeps coming down. I start to get an awful headache my head feels like it wants to explode and I'm so damn cold my bones hurt, more now.

I want to get out of the rain. But there is nowhere to go. You have to stick it out. I'm about to go nuts. I pray to the Creator and Mother Earth and to the Heavens for it to stop raining. I almost can't take it anymore I even hold my helmet high over my head and try to stop the sound of the rain coming down. But that doesn't even help.

I have such a bad headache. The rain drops pounding on my helmet make it worse! I want to scream! But before I know it, the rain starts coming down real light. Boy am I so happy for that, now all I have is an awful headache, and I'm freezing my ass off. It's so damn cold and wet and I'm shaking to beat all hell lying in the water in the rice paddy, by this stupid dike. Then I look down the dike, I see the dark silhouettes of the men lying down. The water reflects off their wet equipment and helmets, it shines in the darkness. I can see a mist rising off their clothes. The cold rain and the heat from their bodies mixes and makes steam come off them. The scene is disturbing and scary! It seems hollow without beauty or life. It looks like dead shadows against a wall, and seems like a vision of death.

Boy I didn't know that the force of Mother Earth could do this to me. This was the first time that I was ever forced to do something like this on my own. I just can't believe this is just the start of things that I'm forced to do out here on my own and see for the first time. When you can't move around, you can't take shelter, or you can't get up for hour after hour, it gets to you real fast. You just have to take it, and deal with it the best way you know how, on your own. Nobody can do it for you, you're on your own out here. But the only one I can thank is the Creator and Mother Earth for helping me get through it so far. I just can't wait to see the sunrise come up tomorrow. To feel the warm Sun on my body . . . what a luxury that's going to be from now on, to see the next day. If I live to see the sunrise, the little things in life will be so important to me, now.

I just can't believe it! It's the simple things in life that are so important to me now. To have dry socks, or something to sit on, or just cool water to drink, instead of the hot water out of your canteen. I just can't believe what sorts of things I've had to do without, in this war. How you just miss those little things in life when you don't have them. When I used to go hunting with my Dad, if it rained we got out of the rain, if it was cold we bundled up. If we got tired of sitting in one spot, we moved around. But not now. Right now, at this moment, it's a matter of life or death, and I have no choice but to lie here, freezing, shivering, and without moving, hoping and praying that I live to see the sunrise.

It's about 0100hrs now (1:00 a.m.), and I am still shaking from the cold breeze. I tap the guy next to me on the shoulder. I whisper to him I wanted to use the bathroom, he looks at me and says, "Go in your pants, we've all done it!" I say, "Ok." My lips are shivering from the cold, and I'm thinking to myself, "Is he kidding me? I can't do that! It not right." But when it got later, I can't believe how bad my bladder starts to hurt inside of me. I can't hold it anymore. So all I can do is go in my pants, like he said.

What a relief it was! For a moment, it felt so warm. What a luxury to be warm for that moment. I can't believe it, I don't think it's wrong to go in your pants now. I wanted to be some place warm, not out here suffering in the damn cold. That's when I found out you do a lot of things out here that you wouldn't do in civilian life. It's not right. But you do what you have to do to stay alive in this damn place. It's not like back home in the States, you don't have all the luxuries of life out here. You have to deal with what's in front of you right now, and a lot of things that you never had to deal with before. Life is not fair to anybody, especially in a war. The rules of life out here change so fast from one moment to the next, it's hard to understand the outcome on how things happen.

Now I know one of the things that made these guys smell so bad. From the moment when I first saw these guys 12 hours ago I realized how awful they looked and smelled. Now I know I'm starting to look like them, and I'm going to have to go through a whole lot more shit to get where they're at.

It scares me to know that's what's in store for me out here, and what might be coming up next. I'm not looking forward to that at all. I just don't know if I can make it, and if I can handle this kind of shit all the time. The more things I go through, the worse it gets, and the more scared I am. The more I want to go back home to the States. This is only my first night out in the battlefield. How much worse can it get out here?

My stomach has started growling. Now what? It's growling real loud now. I can't believe what the hell is happening to me, now. My stomach, it's starting to hurt. I am so hungry! I want something eat – now! But I know better than to open my can of C-rations and eat them. The VC will hear me opening my can of C-rations. Sounds travel a long way out here, especially at night. Also they can smell the food at the same time. And that would give away our location, and they would know where we are, if they were in the area out here. Then I knew if I was one of the guys they would have beat the shit out of me for opening my C-rations and for me not having common sense.

I drink some water out of my canteen, the water's warm. I try to stop my stomach from growling! It helps a little bit. It's now about 0500hrs (5:00 a.m.), and my stomach sounds so loud to me. Now I know why Sergeant Bones handed me my rations earlier in the evening before we went out on patrol and said, "Eat." He knew what I'd be going through right now how hungry I'd be at this moment. Boy how I wish I'd eaten them. But back at that time, I'd just seen my first dead bodies, and I didn't think I could've kept anything down . . . my stomach was too upset at the time. Boy, I wish I'd eaten then. I'm starving. I really don't need this shit. I don't know if I can take it anymore. Life is not fair over here. All I want is to go home to my Mom and Dad. It's been a long night so far, and I can't believe how the time just drags on. Seconds seem like minutes, and minutes seem like hours. I'm just hoping to see the Sun rise in the morning, and to feel that warm Sun on my body. It's been a long night and I haven't slept at all. My mind's been running a hundred miles an hour trying to keep my sanity intact.

Earlier, yesterday, I'd been dropped into the Hot LZ. It should've been a routine drop. But wasn't routine – not at all, I was dropped off in the middle of a violent firefight. I was terrified the whole time coming in, then and afterward. It was traumatic. Moment after moment of terror which had stretched my nerves to the breaking point, I couldn't calm down enough to get any sleep, or even to eat without wanting to throw up. Now I am starving my ass off wishing I'd eaten when I'd had the chance.

All of a sudden I was startled from the thoughts in my head by an explosion. It was a Claymore mine! Another one went off, then another, and another. The guy next to me squeezed his handle to his Claymore mine, and it exploded! Then I heard people screaming, and moaning, and crying. The first explosion blinded me for a moment, and my ears were ringing. I felt the blast from the explosion then I could smell the burnt gunpowder. Suddenly the guy next to me whispers, "Don't do anything, don't fire your weapons yet or your Claymore mine." I was scared shitless and shaking like a leaf, in the water. My hands hurt so bad being so cold I could hardly hold my weapon. I did what he said. We listened to what was happening on the other side of the canal. I tried swallowing to see if I could stop the ringing in both my ears, and it helped a little bit.

We knew we'd killed some of them, but how many, we didn't know. It was hard to see anything out there in the pitch dark. You could hear them though. They were running away from us. You could hear the water splashing as they ran away from us across the rice paddy on the other side of the canal. You could tell by all the noises they made that there were a bunch of them. We still didn't know how many were out there, or how many we killed. The VC didn't shoot at us because they didn't know our location or direction of fire, and they didn't know how many of us were out here.

They moved away from the kill zone and us. Based on all the noise they made, we figured they had maybe 25 guys, about a Platoon size. If they'd come across the canal we would have been in a firefight for sure. I was so cold and wet my teeth were rattling in my mouth, and my hands were so cold they hurt. At least the ringing in my ears stopped ringing. We waited for daylight to come. Sunrise was at 0630hrs (6:30 a.m.). We had an hour before sunrise. We could still hear moaning and crying from the enemy on the other side of the canal.

A few minutes passed then I heard 155 mm artillery percussion in the distance. A few seconds later, I heard the rounds whistling in. Then the rounds exploded in the area where moaning and crying was coming from. The explosions were close to us. I'd never been so close to artillery explosions before. The ground shook under me, I felt the concussion and heat from the blast. I thought one might land right on top of us. I was trying to crawl into my helmet I was so scared! I was scared shitless and was trembling as I was waiting there. If one those rounds landed where we were at, we'd all be killed for sure.

The rounds were close, but they were landing on the other side of the canal, on the banks and dikes about 50 to 100 yards out from us. You could smell the burnt gunpowder from the explosions, drifting towards us. Boy, I was shaking like a leaf. In training, we were never this close to exploding artillery, I just can't believe how different we do things over here. The unknowns can really scare the hell out of you. I guess our LT (Lieutenant) called in for some artillery rounds. About ten rounds came in. He did it to make sure the enemy was dead and wouldn't be coming back to our location. It looked like our LT knew what he was doing, I'm glad of that. Half an hour later, close to sunrise, we heard another of our ambush sites open up with their Claymore mines and weapons. A battle was raging. Based on the sound of the M-16s and M-60 machine guns firing, they must have been opening up on what was left of the VC Platoon.

The guy next to me said, "That's why you don't open up with your weapons, unless you have to. It depends on the situation you're in. Opening up at night gives away your position, and you end up in a firefight. They opened up and now they're hoping for the best, in surviving the battle."

That's why the other VC or NVA didn't fire at us, they didn't know where we were, and they knew they were in a kill zone. It had to be a Platoon-sized unit. Our other ambush site hit what was left of the Platoon we didn't kill. I didn't know we had another ambush site about a mile and a half, or so, away from us.

It's almost daylight! It's time to move out and check the area. They told me to walk point again and move across the canal to check it out. Boy, I was not ready for this shit. I never did this before! I was scared shitless to cross that canal. I didn't want to do it. But I didn't want them to think I was a chicken. So I did what they told me to do like it or not, I did what I was told.

The canal was about 50 yards wide, and I didn't know how deep the water was. I moved into the water slowly. My legs muscles were cramped and hurting from lying still all night. They didn't want to move, but I got them moving anyway, one leg, one step at a time. The water was waist high and cold out there. I was almost to the other side of the canal when I heard a chopper flying. Now I see it. It's coming down the canal. It's a gunship checking out the area, I guess my LT called them in to give us cover and support. I feel a little better, now. Knowing we have support from the air. We didn't know if we killed all of them, yet. I feel like somebody can put a bullet in my head . . . it seems a long, long way to the other side. I feel so alone in the canal, wading across to the other side. I can't believe my stomach is growling so loud, and my heart is pounding so loud. I can't believe this! I'm sweating to beat all hell, and I'm cold, and in water up to my waist, and my equipment feels so heavy to me now. Boy, I'm scared shitless doing this shit! I'm only 19, and I have no choice in what I'm doing. I was drafted into this shit! I'm too young for this shit. I'm not even old enough to vote yet, and here I'm doing this shit not knowing if I am going to die any second, now!

The things you think of when you're doing this shit. The chopper is flying over my head, again. It's flying back and forth along the bank of the canal making that popping sound as it passes by. The sound's fading as it moves away from me. Now the chopper's coming back. It's in a firing position. It's lower, now, about 40 feet from the ground. It's flying steady and level, at a 30-degree downward angle, with its nose pointing towards the ground. I can see the pilots. They're ready to fire the mini-guns and rockets at any movement from the enemy. The water's so damn cold and it smells like shit, and I'm stepping in nothing but mud. The mud sticks to my boots when I pull them from the water, one foot at a time. My boots feel so heavy under the water, pulling them out of the mud takes a lot of energy. My leg muscles are still cramping and hurting. From not moving all night. If I get wounded, I'll drown for sure with all the equipment I have on me. One way or the other I'll die. The sweat is getting in my eyes and burning them it's hard to see in front of me, and all that green grass on the bank can be hiding anything. My lips are dry, and I've got no saliva to swallow, and I'm really scared shitless moving across this damn canal.

I'm moving closer to the bank on the other side of the canal, and I see the grass and how green it is. I never saw such tall grass, it's beautiful and as tall as me. It looks like the enemy could be hiding in there, ready to put a bullet in me. The things that can run through your head at moments like these. As I get closer and closer to the bank, I feel like a target I know a bullet is going to find my head any second. I've got a twitch in my eye and my neck. I can almost feel the bullet penetrating into my skin and through my forehead. What a way to die with your head blown off. Alone in the middle of nowhere. The closer I get to the other side of the bank, the more scared I get. The more scared I get, the more nervous I get and the shakier I get. I'm staring so hard my eyes are watering. Or am I crying? All I know is I'm putting one foot in front of the other, and I'm moving closer and closer to the other side.

I miss home, and I miss my Mom and Dad. What if I get killed . . . what will happen to Mom and Dad? How will they take it if I came home in a coffin and all blown apart? But I have to keep moving towards the other side of the bank to make sure things are safe for the other guys to come over.

I'm finally at the other side now. I never knew my emotions could make me feel so tired and so drained out. I can hardly pull myself up onto the bank. I'm so scared and nervous, that I can't stop shaking and sweating my ass off to beat all hell. I'm standing up and on my feet, and my legs are shaking and weak. The chopper's flying over my head again, making that popping sound as it flies over me. I can see the pilot! He has his face shield on, his face shield is green. I can see his eyes! Why are they so wide open? Is he afraid? Do I look afraid to him? Is he seeing me being afraid, or is he seeing something that I can't see yet, is the shit about to hit the fan? I must look the same to him, not knowing what's going to happen next.

I keep moving one foot at a time, in front of me, as I walk along the top of the bank, now. The water in my boots is sloshing around because my boots are too big for me. All I hear is, "squish, squish," with each step. Water is running down my pants legs and dripping off me, everywhere. I see craters where the artillery rounds landed. The vegetation and earth on the bank are all blown away in a rough circle pattern on the bank where the rounds landed. Smoke is still coming out of some of the blown-out trees and vegetation around the area. I smell death in the air, a ton of Mother Earth has been blown up and out of the crater. Anything living when it hit is blown up, animals, bugs, snakes, trees, plants, and people. The fish are dead, and floating in the canal. Even the dirt looks dead, chunks of it are lying scattered everywhere. The ground looked like it had been scooped up and turned upside down. The explosion left a ridge around the hole.

There are 11 enemy dead in front of me, and four wounded VC. They're barely alive, and barely moving. I move their weapons by kicking them away from them. I check the rest of them to make sure they're dead and not just playing dead.

Blood is everywhere, and body parts are scattered all over the ground and equipment. We really messed them up with our Claymore mines and artillery rounds. Now I know what a kill zone can do in an ambush. Boy, what a mess it is. I'm horrified by what I just saw. I guess that's why the NVA didn't stay there, they knew they were in a kill zone.

You can tell these were NVA, because they're dressed in uniforms. They have brand new weapons on them, AK-47 rifles and RPGs. Scattered around all the destruction is enough ammo, weapons, and rice to resupply a Company. I finish checking the area around me and I give the all clear sign with my hand, to the guys on the other side of the canal bank.

The scene is horrible, and part of me is numb from shock at seeing all this. The other part of me is on autopilot checking the dead, giving the all clear. I don't know how I stayed in control of myself. I wanted to run away from all this horror, to someplace safe, where I didn't have to look at dead, burned, pieces of bodies. I feel traumatized by what I see in this moment.

At that moment, my childhood died, and my innocence with it. My feelings – my emotions – went numb at that moment, and to this day I feel like most of them never came back. I feel like I will always be in limbo – my soul lost to the "Me" I was before that day. I will always be confined in my pain and thoughts of that moment. Looking back, I didn't realize that I said goodbye to the real me on that day and my first day with my Company. I'd gone from boyhood to manhood. That was the cost of being a true Warrior.

DAYBREAK AFTER THE AMBUSH
May 1968

The chopper was still flying over my head making that popping sound that faded away as it went by and down the canal bank, again. It kept sweeping around the area and keeping cover for us. Then the rest of the Platoon started to move across the canal. The guys started to come over in groups of four at a time. Boy, I could see that scared look on their faces, too, as they waded across the canal. They were expecting some round to fly through the air towards their heads, too. Even though I checked the area, it's never safe around here. Some of the guys came towards me, and the rest of the guys started searching the area around us and down the river banks. Making sure everything was clear and there weren't any enemy still in our area. You just never know where they were out there, they seemed just to come out of nowhere and everywhere. They could come out of hidden fighting positions, spider holes (the entrances to tunnels) and bunkers, and any number of other places that you didn't know about.

Sergeant Bones came over and said, "You did well today, for being an Indian!" My Dad always told me that if they knew you were Native American, then you're going to hear a lot of comments. Now, that's all I need to hear, ". . . for being an Indian!" Ha! I just brushed it off.

"We Natives are not dumb," I thought to myself. We know how to think for ourselves, and we know what a hard life is all about! We are used to doing without. Poverty is nothing new to me and my people. I'm just glad that my Mom and Dad taught me how to survive out in the wilderness, and to be strong in my Native ways. Sergeant Bones really is a nice guy, and he likes me even though I am Native American. When he tells me to do something (even though I don't want to do it) I do a good job every time. I know I'm keeping everybody alive and myself too, and I believe Sergeant Bones appreciates that. I follow orders to the "T," and I know how to adapt and overcome in situations without anybody telling me what to do next. That included being out in the battlefield. I've tried to do my best in every situation I was put in even though there were times when I didn't want to do it. I know a lot of my abilities have to do with my Mom and Dad, and the way they raised me. They showed me how to hunt and survive out in the wilderness and how to be strong in life. We always tried to hunt downwind so the animal wouldn't smell us. In the forest, we moved real quiet and didn't move abruptly when we were hunting. Animals will notice you when you move real fast. I learned how to live in the elements and to be strong and protect myself from the elements. But here in Vietnam, you have to endure the elements. You have no choice but to stay in the elements. I've learned real fast how to be strong, adapt, and overcome any situation on my own out here. Sergeant Bones has taught me a lot about being out here, in Vietnam, too! And how to stay alive in this damn place. I've learned real fast from him.

The chopper flew over again, making that popping sound as it went by, the noise brought me back to the present. I told my Sergeant that I was bleeding around my waist and I felt weak. I didn't know why! He smiled at me, and said, "Take off all your gear, and lift your shirt up." So I took my gear off and raised up my shirt. I had some kind of slugs all over me. I didn't know what they were. They looked like a bunch of little snakes on me. I was scared. I had blood all over me, and I was numb around my waist. I didn't even realize that they were sucking out my blood! Some of them looked so big and fat, and some of them were falling off me because they'd fattened up on my blood.

Sergeant Bones told one of the old guys to light up a cigarette and burn them off of me. Then that old guy said, "You Indians must have good blood, to have so many leeches on you!" Leeches? What? Is that what the hell those things are? The old guy took 30 to 40 leeches off me. Then Sergeant Bones called for our "Doc," our Medic. Then Doc came over and put some kind of ointment on me so I wouldn't catch an infection in the openings where the leeches had been.

This is how it's going be from now on over here, we take care of each other out here, no matter what the cost is, we all have a job to do, as long as we do it right, we all have a good chance of making it home alive . . . or one way or another. No one has a choice of what you're going to do out here. You do what they tell you, and hope for the best.

Our LT called in a Dust Off to pick up the two wounded NVA. We called in for another chopper to pick up the rest of the NVA equipment and weapons that they left behind, along with the paperwork and maps that they had on them.

All that stuff went back to the main base camp at Cu Chi, so our Intelligence Units could study the maps and documents. When the chopper came in, it brought us a resupply of ammo and water.

We destroyed five 100-pound bags of rice that the NVA had been carrying. The rice had to be destroyed in place by throwing it in the water. The equipment that we captured, and the rice we destroyed, could have resupplied an NVA Company for a month or so. We left their bodies there. Maybe the gunship would get some more kills, tonight, when the NVA tried to recover the bodies.

This is my first day and night of hell with the Wolfhounds, 3rd Platoon, 2nd Squad, Alpha Company. That's how it is, then! Kill or be killed. That day was one of my better days. I didn't know being a Grunt would mean that I would be going through so much trauma. Most every day and night we were in some kind of shit. Being in Vietnam was a hell of an experience. I didn't know that every day and night, there, was going to be a repeat of my first day and night in hell. Like they say, "War is Hell, no matter how you look at it." WHAT A LIFE TO LIVE, AS A GRUNT AT THE AGE OF 19!

I know I did a lot of praying to the Creator, to the Heavens, and to my Ancestors. I prayed to come home, alive, in one piece. That's what helped me get through a lot of the things that happened out there – praying, and hoping for the best. I said a lot of things to the Creator that I wouldn't think to say to my fellow man. That was the way of life in the battlefield. I prayed a lot to the Creator and to the Heavens and the Spirit World to keep me safe and alive out here. I also ask Mother Earth not to be so hard on me. Mother Earth was so strange over here to me. It's not the same as back home. The plants, trees, and vegetation are so different and the people are strange. Later I found out that they live a simple life, like we did on the Reservation, and they respected their Ancestors. This was my first month in Vietnam.

HEDGE-HOPPING
June 1968

Sometime in the month of June, 1968, we'd been working the swamp and jungle and a lot of rice paddies around the Saigon area on the West side of the city. It had been a month and a half, about fifty days, since I'd been in-country. We'd been doing a lot of Eagle Flights, hopping from one place to another. We Grunts call it hedge-hopping. Rice paddies are surrounded by canals, trees and vegetation are always growing along the canal banks. From the air, the canals, trees, and rice paddies look like little grids ringed with hedges. We'd been doing two to four hops a day, hopping from rice paddy to rice paddy – hedge-hopping.

Going into the rice paddies out in the open to land was a living hell. Because you didn't know what to expect. Landing in the middle of those rice paddies left you completely exposed and highly vulnerable to the enemy. If the enemy's there, "They" could see you, but you have no idea where the hell they're hiding. That meant death could be hiding in wait, ready to mow you down at any moment. And the anxiety of knowing that the unknown is out there, waiting to take you down, is terrifying. Rice paddies leave you out in the open where you have no cover, and it's a long, long, long way to the tree line. You never know if the enemy is in the tree line, too, exactly where you're moving to. And you can't run, because you don't know what's out there. And you have to wait for the LT's orders. Then you have to walk in the direction he says, and pray that there isn't a line of bunkers with the enemy in them waiting for you, with guns aimed at you, ready to open up on you from that direction. You can feel death breathing near your neck, and your heart's racing, but your feet are still walking. And if the LZ is hot and "They" start firing on you, there's no time to pause, you have to move quickly and charge to suppress the fire "They" are pouring down on you. And you have to move forward, so the rest of the Company can move forward behind you. And you have no choice in the matter. It's move forward or die. Once the choppers leave and it's all quiet, and we're all on the ground, and nothing's happening, we feel so relieved. We made it out of the choppers without getting killed but now we have to move into the tree line, one step at a time.

You just can't believe all the thoughts that go through your mind, trying to get to that tree line and how tense you are, and how scared. You start shaking as you step closer and closer, sweating to beat all hell. Then you get so nervous that all you can do is cry to yourself, and hope nothing happens to you. You take it one step at a time, knowing it could be your last step on Mother Earth. At any moment you could step on a mine or booby trap. You feel so uncomfortable moving towards the tree line. Your eyes are straining to see what's hidden in front of you. And you're concentrating so hard on what might be out there, that you start to imagine feeling a bullet penetrating your head. It feels so real in your mind that the center of your forehead crinkles up, and your eyebrow twitches every so often. Your lips are dry, and sweat is dripping into your eyes, and the sweat burns so bad you can't see, and you keep blinking to try to see clearly, but your eyes tear up and you can't clear the watery sweat out of your eyes, and you can taste the salt from the sweat getting in your mouth. Then you're gripping your weapon so tight your hands are sweating. You can hear you heart pounding in your ears at one hundred beats a minute. You're walking, but your heart's pounding like you're running. The tree line is so close, now, you're almost in panic mode, and before you know it you're in the trees. Can you believe I'm doing this every day?! We made it – I made it this far without getting killed. We made it to the tree line!!!

Now, it's time to start patrolling the area along the tree line. It's another hot day, you can feel the heat on your clothes and on your back. Sweat is pouring down your face and your forehead, and running down your body. It's been raining off and on, today, and I just can't believe it! One minute you're soaked through and through, and within an hour you're dry as a bone, at other times you're soaked through and through for day after miserable day. I just can't believe how many days I've been here. And I'm still alive here! It feels like I've been here for years, but it's only been a month and a half. We've been losing guys almost every day mostly firefights or booby traps. I'm walking point again and I've been lucky, so far. I have to walk down this river bank along the tree line, to check it out. I'm scared and uncomfortable doing this, walking point again. We're here to find the enemy or any enemy bunkers or tunnels and supplies along the canal. I just don't need this shit anymore. At any time I can step on a booby trap and get killed, or shot and messed up.

It's noontime and we've already been walking a mile down this bank. Boy, is it hot. I've been sweating a lot, and my back is sore. My web-gear is cutting into my waist, and my backpack straps are cutting into my shoulder. My feet hurt from walking so much, my feet were wet, and now they're dry. The leather and canvas on my boots is dry and hard, now, and they're uncomfortable. I can't stop, because I'm walking point.

I feel so alone up here walking point, and I'm scared shitless. I feel like I don't know what I'm doing, it's a lot different during training. Training can't put the fear of death in you. You know in training they can't kill you. But out here in Vietnam, death is right around the corner every second of every moment and that can really put the fear of death in you.

There are a lot of spiders and ants in the bushes and trees. There are so many different kinds of plants and creatures around here. Some of the plants are beautiful, and the colors on the little creatures are brilliant. Some of the creatures are so huge and ugly, that they look scary.

The creatures here are a whole lot different, than what are in the States. Boy, can those red ants and black ants bite! And the mosquitoes, they're so big that they sound like dive bombers when they buzz by you. Boy, these mosquitoes really suck the blood out of you. Every time I squash one of those monsters, blood spurts all over the place. I hope I don't get malaria because of their bites. They bite right through your clothing. Thousands of them flying around here, especially around the river banks and rice paddies. I want to drink some water, but I can't yet, we're still moving and I'm walking point I have to be on guard 24/7.

Will I be able to see any booby traps on the ground, with all this vegetation around us? Will I see one before I step on it, or trip one off because I'm having to move through this vegetation? Every time I have to move some damn vegetation out of the way, I keep thinking that I'm going to touch a tripwire. So far I have found seven booby traps. Now, I'm looking down, and all around. Stop! What's that! There's something different in the vegetation ahead of me. I'm real scared for a moment, and I'm straining my eyes to see what's in front of me! I raise my hand to stop the patrol, I hand signal the guy behind me and point to where I'm going to go check out the vegetation. He's about 30 feet away from me and he stops. He signals back "ok" with his hand, we don't talk much when we're on patrol. We give lots of hand signals.

I move forward towards the brush, and I'm scared as all hell. I can't believe I'm doing this on my own. I guess I want to protect the guys in my Platoon. My heart is pounding! I'm sweating to beat all hell and my eyes are wide open. I bend over and use my weapon to move the vegetation aside. There's a hole in the ground! I open up with my M-16! Then I grab a grenade, pull the pin, and throw it into the hole then I hit the ground for some kind of cover! I don't want to get hit with back blast or fragmentations from my own grenade. I'm scared shitless! There's no return fire. I get up and move forward to see if there are any enemy in there, I'm shaking to beat all hell, but there are no enemy. It's a bunker – a freshly dug bunker! I go inside to check it out, but the bunker's empty. I'm sure glad of that I can feel myself breathe a sigh of relief! We find five more empty bunkers along the canal about ten yards apart as we move up the bank of the canal. I'm scared as hell each time I come up to one. No matter how many times I come up to one of these bunkers, I'm still scared as hell! I'm so scared I feel like I want to piss in my pants, I don't know how I push myself to do this. I think a lot has to do with each of us working as a team to keep each other alive. We have no choice but to do it. It's all about survival!

If there had been enemy in the bunkers, I would've been dead meat. If we had been in the rice paddy, out in the open walking toward that tree line, we would have been right in *their* kill zone, in *their* ambush. The bunkers were set up along the tree line, and had plenty of cover from all the vegetation in the area. If the enemy had been there, we would've been dead meat! That's why we like walking down the banks of the canals, instead of going across open rice paddies, from canal to canal. Lots of times, though, we have to cross the rice paddies out in the open, like when the choppers drop us off in the middle of rice paddies. That's when we're at our most vulnerable time out here. You just can't believe how much pressure it puts on us Grunts. You feel like a sitting duck. When you have to be out in the open, walking to a tree line or canal bank. That's when you start thinking that somebody's going to put a bullet in your head. And that thought stays in your head every second, of every step, until you get to the tree line or the canal bank. Checking these bunkers is stressful, too, because there could be enemy inside of them waiting to kill you or booby traps waiting for you to trip them off and blow you to pieces. Then there's the stress itself, plus the heat, all the sweating, and the nervousness it all adds up when you're doing this type of work. Being a Grunt just sucks the life out of you.

My LT said, "Take a ten-minute break." Boy, I'm thirsty. I'm going to take a drink from my canteen. Ugh, my water's hot, and it tastes like iodine from the purification pills I had to put in the canteen, earlier. And it's murky. Our break's over, and now our LT wants me, and a few guys, to go into the canal. He wants us to find out if there are any enemy caches hidden under the water, in the canal near the bunkers.

We cut some branches and make some long sticks, so we can probe under the water with them. While we're probing the water, the rest of the Platoon secures the area. They're looking in the bunkers, and vegetation for caches, and spider holes. The guys need to make sure there're no enemy hiding in any tunnels. If the guys don't look for spider holes, then an enemy may start shooting at us from one of those things. If the enemy is in the spider holes, it'll be like getting shot by a sniper but instead of getting shot from the trees, we'll be shot from holes in the ground. And because spider holes are hard to find, it takes a few hours to search the canal where the bunkers are. The canal is waist deep, the water is warm. It smells, and it has a lot of leeches in it. While we're wading around in the canal probing it with our sticks, we see a few water snakes, and those things scare the hell out of us, too.

The mud sticks to our boots, as we're moving through the canal water. As we're probing, we find three new AK-47 assault rifles and four ammunition boxes all still wrapped in wax paper in a hole dug into the side of the canal bank. The hole was about six feet long, and four feet deep, and two feet high. Just above the water line and covered by long grass hanging over the entrance like a curtain. If we hadn't been actively searching for holes, we might never have seen the damn thing. The enemy was real sneaky! They make the grass look like it was growing there naturally. The top of the canal bank is only about four and half feet above the waterline. The top of the canal bank right over the hole is covered with bamboo, with dirt piled over the bamboo to hide it. The bamboo adds support to the canal bank, so a person can walk above the hole, without caving in the bank. The grass roots are like glue holding everything together and that hides the entrance to the hole at the same time. You had to be actually in the water to find the hole. The enemy's pretty smart to think of that. Those little bastards! And that hole was just big enough for one of those "little people" to hide in it. If the enemy had been there we would have been dead for sure. To make sure the little people couldn't use it, we blow up all the bunkers and spider holes in place, and blow the hole in the bank to smithereens.

Now, it's time to move out and down the river bank about a half a mile, or so. It's about 1800hrs (6:00 p.m.), and the Sun is still beating down on our heads. We get word that it's time to take a dinner break, and eat our C-rations. We have to get ready to move to our night location in about a half-hour. So it's time to check our weapons and gear, again, for the night ambush. We open our C-rations and eat. I want to write home, but I don't feel safe and I'm too tired, anyway. And we still had to bury our empty C-ration cans so the enemy can't make some kind of weapons out of them.

We were told we'd be setting up an ambush near a blown-out bridge approximately one-half mile from here. It looks like it's going to be another long night. I can't believe how much I think about home, and my Mom and Dad, and wishing I was home. And away from all of this hell.

I sure don't like doing this type of job. I hate it! I don't want to be here. I was drafted. I didn't join to be over here in this damn hellhole. It's sure not like the movies. In the movies you don't feel the environment, the pain and suffering, the heat, cold, or the smell or taste of death. You don't feel how scared you are or how time seems to last forever and what it is to face death every day and night and every second in this damn place.

The way I see and feel time depends on if I'm facing death or not. In the middle of a night ambush or in a firefight, time never feels the same. I'm a Grunt, and I'm always on edge waiting, waiting, and waiting for the first signs of a firefight to start. That's when time drags on and that gives my mind the opportunity to think negative thoughts about life and death. How will I die? Will I get shot? Will I get blown apart? If I'm blown apart, how will I live? But when the first explosions or shots start in a firefight, things happen too fast to keep myself focused on all that's happening. Battle is a crazy mix-up of sweat, chaos, and confusion. I'm panicking, screaming, yelling orders, and firing my weapon and it takes what seems forever before I begin controlling my emotions and reactions, to focus on my job as a Grunt. Grunts – we get on with the job of fighting the battle, so that we're *responding* to battle rather than reacting to battle. But in the middle of a battle, time feels like it's never moving fast enough. So I do what I have to do, like it or not. This Grunt – me – is two people. One person is the innocent, baby-faced kid who's been dropped into the middle of this bloody hellhole. And the other person is what I've become, a hardened Grunt, the point man, who's forced to give life and death orders to other Grunts while the firefight's all around us. I'm walking point, today. My decisions can be life and death. The whole Company can get killed, and I can die, too. If I'm not doing my job right. Everyone depends on me, knowing that puts so much pressure on me. Knowing I could be the first to die puts even more pressure on me.

Boy, I'm glad I don't have to walk point, tonight, though! 2nd Squad is moving out first, tonight. I'm in 3rd Squad. Boy, I need a break from walking point all day! I'm bushed. I feel so lost in my emotions, being here in Vietnam. I'm sad. I'm tired. I'm uncomfortable. My body is not my own. It's been punished from lack of sleep, by stress, fear, and pain. It's been pushed to its limits. I just want to go home. I want to be safe, again. I want to be home in comfort. Home, with Mom and Dad and safety.

Boy, I hope the other guy knows what he's doing. He's a new guy too another one that's only 19. I guess he thinks the same of me, too. When I'm out front, I bet the other guys are glad they're not up front walking point. We all hope we're doing our jobs right, over here. No amount of training can prepare you for the reality, the mind-numbing fear of death, the brutality of combat, and the gore of broken bodies. No training will ever prepare us for the constant battle we fight within ourselves, to simply control our emotions in these firefights. One moment I want to take off and run, the next minute I'm fighting the urge to run! I buckle down, and do my job, I have to. None of us wants to be "the coward." We depend on each other to stay alive. It's getting dark, but there's still enough light to see. It's time to move out, and down the canal bank. What a day so far. It's been a long, long day. There's about half an hour of daylight left, and 3rd Squad has moved to the rear of the Platoon, now.

We're quiet. We don't talk much to each other when we're on patrol. It's hard to believe, but it's true. All we do is think . . . and think . . . and think! I think about home . . . wishing I was home. Where all the good things are. I flash-back to the things I did when I was home, hunting, fishing, hanging out with friends. I flash-back to my high school days, and the sports I lettered in. I wrestled, ran track and cross-country. I can see myself running around the track, and up and down a hill, I see myself pinning my opponent, and suffering through a pin-down. That was the good life. Home. And sports. Then working with my Dad and Mom out in the fields picking walnuts, grapes, cherries, onions, and so on, when he got laid off his regular job as an electrician. Now, all I think of is being away from all this shit out here. It doesn't seem like the good life was just one year ago. Right now, it feels like a lifetime ago. None of us talks about this "thinking" we all do out here. Our thoughts are our own and too personal to share. If we did talk about it, it would make us more homesick and maybe it might break our confidence of being out here.

I don't know what the other guys are thinking about, but I know they're thinking. Everyone does. We think about anything that will keep our mind off the danger we're in. We don't talk about what we're going to do next, or what might happen at any time. We're thinking, but we always keep working. We're looking down for any booby traps we might step on, or looking up into the trees for any booby traps we might trip. We're listening for the sounds of the enemy, it could be anything out here it could be a twig snapping. Or somebody's canteen water sloshing or metal clinking against metal, somebody's equipment shifting. Maybe a noise like a grunt when somebody's exerting himself. Our ears strain and wait! for sounds that don't fit into the normal sounds of the jungle. Our noses are working too. Smells can come from the jungle that tell us a man is hiding and waiting. We smell his sweat, and the rice and fish he eats, even the smoke he cooked his food in. They can smell us too. So we have to be real careful we don't use soap and deodorant when we go out in the jungle. We only get to do that when we're back at the main base camp. I'm smelling the air, and the plants, the dirt in the ground, and then my brain comes back to reality. There's a smell of death. And my nerves get tense. A moment passes and nothing happens. We keep walking and thinking.

Even as we're thinking and walking, our bodies are working hard to keep us as safe as possible. Sweat is pouring off my face, down my neck and back and into my pants. My underarms are soaking wet. I feel tense. My muscles ache and my feet are cramping, all the equipment I carry weighs on me like a ton of rocks. And my body hurts in every place the equipment touches me, and the sweat just keeps pouring off me. I pray to the Creator every day, every step. I pray to the Spirit World to keep my spirit strong in what I'm doing. I want to get out of this place, alive. I don't believe there are any nonbelievers in foxholes.

We each of us, inside pray to get out of here every day and every night. The pressure of looking for the enemy day after day and night after night has me worn out emotionally, physically, and spiritually.

We have been walking for a while towards the sunset, I know we are going West because us Natives know that the Sun goes down towards the West, and the Sun comes up on the East.

It's dark now. We're still moving down this river bank. We should be getting close to the blown-out bridge. We'll get there, soon. As long as we don't run into "Charlie." Charlie is our word for the VC. I hope we don't run into them out here before we get there. We don't have much cover here by the river bank. With the rice paddies next to us we're still exposed, we'll all be in one hell of a fix if we do run into Charlie.

I feel a little relaxed, now that I am not walking point. I'm at the rear of the column with the other Squads in front of me. But when I look ahead, I can't see much – the men's silhouettes are blocking my view, and it's too dark to see much of anything else. I hear their movements, too. Shit, someone just stepped on a twig, and that's someone's web-gear shifting. It's terrifying not knowing what's in front of me! When I'm walking point, I can see, hear, and smell what's out in front of me, but it's terrifying walking point. You never know what you're walking right into. Being in the rear though is just as scary. I can't see what's in front, behind me, or to my sides. It doesn't matter if I'm walking point, or walking at the rear, I'm damned if I do, damned if I don't. I'm still trying to see what's in front of me, behind me, on both sides of me. Boy, can it get any scarier than that? Something can happen at any moment and I wouldn't see it or hear it! Boy, how time just drags by.

I'm looking all around me, trying to see if the VC are out there hiding somewhere, ready to ambush me. Maybe they're in the trees, ready to put an AK round into me! We're still moving. It's real dark now. The column has stopped I think we made it to the blown-out bridge. We're all kneeling down, waiting for Sergeant Bones. He walked up to the front of the column. We're waiting and waiting, I placed the stock of my M-16 butt-down on the ground so I can brace myself against the weapon. I'm taking some deep breaths, trying to relax. I settle one knee on the ground and look up, between the trees, the leaves, and the branches. I can see a few stars twinkling. For a moment, I feel a sense of peace. I look towards the horizon and I see flashes of light, which means artillery is exploding, the peace is gone. I've come back to reality. My body hurts, I'm tired, exhausted, hungry, and thirsty. I don't want to think about the "what can happen." I need to relax a little! I'm so tired of holding back my emotions, feeling inside like I'm moving toward panic, then stepping back from the panic. It's so hard to stay sane – in my emotions it's like I'm physically walking through mud up to my hips. Expecting that my next step will be on solid ground, only to find that mud goes on for miles. There's a constant battle raging inside my own head, between controlling my emotions, and wanting to fall into a pit of despair, hopelessness, and loneliness. I've only been here a month and a half. Only 51 days, it feels like 51 years! I can't believe I'm still alive. I've made it this far.

Sergeant Bones finally walked back to the rear, where we are. Boy, how time drags when you are waiting for someone to tell you what to do next. The waiting is getting to me. Bones tells us we'll be doing another ambush near the dirt road that goes North and South to the bridge. The head of the column will be positioned about 100 yards away from the bridge. With the rest of the column positioned along the road going South. He tells us the head of the column is facing the bridge North, the center is facing the road West, and the column's rear is facing down the road South away from the direction of the bridge. My Squad's at the end of the ambush, that means we're facing down the road. We have four M-60 machine guns. We place an M-60 at each end of the column. One is facing the bridge and the other facing down the road. The other two M-60s are spread out in the middle of the column, facing the road. We line up our ambush along the dirt road. We're in the tree line about 40 yards from the road. There's good cover in the tree line. Now we're setting up our Claymore mines. They are facing out towards the road, and we're placing a Claymore mine behind us towards the trees, in case the enemy tries to move in behind us, since we don't know which way the enemy will be coming from, we have to cover all our loose ends. So now we're just waiting. Waiting to see what comes down the road, tonight, or from behind us. It's just another night of being scared to death!

We take turns sleeping. Or trying to sleep. When it's your turn to sleep, you stay awake and can't get to sleep. But when it's your turn to stay awake, all you want to do is sleep! We're damned if we do, and damned if we don't. Every ambush is the same. It's crazy, there are moments of terror and fear, moments of hard work over and over, moments of repetition of pressure, stress, and anxiety, and pure physical exhaustion and lack of sleep. No one really sleeps all we can do is try to get some rest.

Boy, it's another cold long night of shaking in my boots. I just can't believe how long the nights seem to be out here. When I can't move to keep warm, how miserable I feel and how scared I am all night. I'm nervous and lonely. All I can do is think. Think of things, good and bad. How good it was when I was home even though I was poor, there was so much love in my family I never felt alone. And how bad it is over here in Vietnam. I think about life. How important it is to live, now when my life is on the line, every second of the day and night. But we've made it again to see another sunrise! I just can't believe how good it makes me feel to see the Sun rise above the jungle. Every day it comes up, it feels good. No enemy came down the road last night. Boy was I glad of that! It was a long night, and it was still stressful. I really feel the pressure on me, when there are a lot of unknowns out there especially at night.

It's time to move out again. Bones said we'd be sweeping along the road about 50 to 100 yards from the road on each side (I started calling the Sergeant "Bones." That's what most of us call him at least those of us that aren't brand new anymore). We're headed to a burnt-out village to find out if we can locate any enemy in the area. Or their supplies. It would be a lot easier to walk on the road. But we know it would be a lot easier for the enemy to ambush us there, too.

We move forward about a mile and a half from the bridge. It's a rough walk along the side of the road about a hundred feet from the road. The roadside is all piled up with dead trees. Our LT gives the order to take a break in place, and to put out our defenses, and get ready to eat. I ask Bones, "Why didn't we eat at the bridge? We already had our defenses out?" Bones answers, "The VC can put mortar rounds on us. They might already have the area marked off, and we can get ambushed by them too. So that's why we moved out."

Then I ask Bones, "How long has the LT been on line?" He replied, "Four months already." I say, "He's a pretty smart LT." Bones says, "Yes he is!" I ask Bones, "Sarge how about you? How long have you been here?" He says, "Ten months, so far." I answer back, "Boy, I wish I had ten months in like you." "Joe," says Bones, "you have to put your time in like everybody else here and hope for the best. We all are doing the same, hoping for the best. Just put your time in from day to day, and night to night. And try to make it home in one piece."

Then Bones says, "Joe, for you being a new guy, and a Native American, you've been doing ok. Just try to keep your shit together, out here. That's all I ask of you. We all lose it, at one time or the other. We just don't know when it's going to happen. Shit just happens. Some guys lose it, and don't come back to their senses. So keep your shit wired up tight out here."

When you have so much fear in you, at some point you're not going to perform your duty correct. It can last a few seconds, or a few minutes, or you can lose it completely and not recover. Out here, you just don't know when it's going to happen. It just happens. When it does, you're put on a chopper and flown out of the field. And all we can do is hope that you come back to reality. I've never seen such a blank face on a young kid as when he loses it. Some kids run, blindly. Some just stare out into space. Some start mumbling to themselves, and some get the shakes or jitters. Looking at the face of a young kid that's just lost it, it's like looking at myself in the future if it happens to me. I see my own innocence in his young face, and I *know* that we're too young. My face is his face, my eyes are his eyes, his fear is my fear, and I know we shouldn't be in the middle of this insanity. Seeing his face scares me, because I know the same thing can happen to me at any moment and it terrifies me! We're in a man's situation, but we're still kids, him and me. I'm haunted by my memories of those young kids. I see their eyes to this day.

We've eaten our C-rations and buried our empty cans and boxes. Now, it's time to move out again. Thanks to the Creator, we didn't encounter any enemy on our ambush. It's kind of funny how things work out, here. I hear a gunship shooting in the far distance, and explosions going off, and smoke coming up from the tree line about five or ten miles away from us. I know the enemy is around here, someplace, and ready to kill me, too. But they weren't in this vicinity last night trying to kill me and for now, I'm safe.

I just wonder who is "in the shit" and what new guy is getting baptized in hell, and what kind of hell he's going through for the first time. We've all been there. It's hell in the day, and it's more hell at night. And we know it won't end until we get back home to the good old USA.

We have to head North to an old burnt-out village a couple of miles away, and set up an ambush, there. It's in the opposite direction from the battle that's still going on behind us. We can't see the flashes from the explosions anymore because our backs are to them. But we can hear the gunships with their bursts of automatic fire. And the sound of rockets going off. From the sounds alone I can tell that our gunships are prepping the area so our guys, the Grunts, can move in and assault the enemy. I hope we make it to the village. I hope we don't run into the VC or NVA.

I hate doing this. We can get ambushed any time, now, because we are moving around so much. I can't help thinking about the ambushes I've been in, and the ambushes we've sprung on "Them." I can still see how they look after we've killed them in the kill zone. It messes with my head. The feelings and sights are too much. It's the same emotional feelings every time I see "Them" in the kill zones. I just don't know how I live with these images in my head, day after day. I start feeling anxious and panicky, and my mind wants to think of all the "what if's" that can happen to me. I have to calm myself down, and take my mind off my thoughts. I do that by thinking of other things, not the "what if's." Sometimes I do that by looking at the way the guy's canteen, in front of me, is bouncing around on his hip, or the way his rifle strap sways when he walks. I have to make my eyes see a movement I don't normally pay attention to. Or make my ears hear a noise I would normally ignore like the sound of a Grunt's web-belt shifting, or the soft clink of metal touching metal, as he's shifting his weight from one leg to another. These sounds, from the Grunts around me, are safe familiar sounds, they're sounds that break the madness and keep my mind from going into a panic. Waiting for the unknown to happen. It's unbelievable. My imagination runs away from me during those times. It's exhausting. I know the other Grunts go through the same emotions, we feel each another's anxiety. We don't speak about it, but we communicate it anyway. Our body language does the talking for us! The far-off look in our eyes, the narrowing of our eyebrows, and the lines on our face, the turned-down corners of our mouths, and our cracked dry lips. Our jungle fatigues look worn and dusty, hanging off our bodies. Most of us have lost a lot of weight. We're dirty and tired! Our fatigues are all stained with salt from our sweat. We sweat so much it fades our fatigues into different shades of green under our arms, on our backs, and where our packs and web-belts sit against our bodies. Our shoulders stoop a little and our feet drag an extra millisecond along the ground. Red dust kicks up into the air with each step we take. That red dust floats up and gets in our eyes and mouths, dries out our lips and makes us thirsty and colors our lips. Like red chocolate stains.

The enemy didn't stand a chance in the kill zones I've seen. I just hope the same thing doesn't happen to us. I don't want to be caught in a kill zone. I know in the back of my mind that it can happen at any time. I still have a whole long time to go! The odds are not in my favor. At all. All I can do is live from one day to the next, hoping and praying to the Creator for the next day to come, and for me to see the Sun and Moon rise each day and night.

Most of the old guys have either been wounded or killed. Sergeant Bones has been wounded twice. I wonder how he can still be out here and take it. It can happen to him, again, at any time. Boy, he must be under a lot of pressure and stress and being a short-timer must make it more stressful.

I wonder how I'm going to get wounded. Will it be in the arms, or in the legs? Or will I get killed in an awful way, and sent home in a body bag? Will my Mom be able to see me in an open casket, or am I going to be in a closed casket? Boy, the things I think about here in Vietnam, just walking my next mission one step at a time. My life keeps flashing by in my mind.

It's just a matter of time before I get wounded or killed. I have a good chance of one or the other, since most of the old guys have been wounded, some of them two, or three or even four times. We don't talk about how many die out here. It's too painful for us. It's bad enough to get wounded, like most of these guys have been, but they're also lucky to be alive even if it means being back out here again, in the bush. None of us wants to be back out here in this hellhole. Also I found out there are ten new guys in our Platoon, some of them have one or two weeks ahead of me being out here. My first day out with my Company out of the six bodies I loaded up on the chopper that day, four were new guys who'd only been on line for about five days. I guess it was my lucky day that day like Sergeant Bones said.

The odds don't look good for me on an Infantry Line Unit in 1968. I have a real high chance of being a casualty. But the odds of being wounded are in my favor, over being killed. I don't like the odds. But I guess it's better being wounded than getting killed. These are the things I think of. When I'm out here with my Line Unit on patrol. Almost every day I do the same things: try to stay alive while moving out to my next mission. I can't believe I live on pure survival instincts, it's not for God and country, or all that other patriotic stuff I hear. I live one day to the next! I just can't believe how much pressure is out there in this type of environment. It's a living hell to be out here, at the age of 19.

I wonder what our next moves will be, once we get to the burnt-out village? I'm just a Private First Class. We PFCs know how to take orders and follow them through, one at a time. We're not told much the Sergeants point to us and say "go this way" or "go that way." That's all we need to know as Privates, and that's all our NCOs tell us. But we Privates know one thing, we'll be the first to fight, or the first to die.

I can see the village now, on the other side of that rice paddy. The whole Platoon has stopped in the tree line. Waiting for our next orders. Sergeant Bones has passed the word down for me to come up front to let me know I'll be crossing the rice paddy to the village. That means I'll be walking point again. I hate it when he calls my name out, it sends chills up my back. It's about 200 yards to the village. The other Squad's new guy and I have to cross the rice paddy, together. We'll be 50 feet apart, walking to the other side. I've never seen this new guy, I wonder if he's walked point before? We have to make sure that it's safe for the rest of the Platoon to move out across the rice paddy, so our Unit can get to the village.

Boy, the village looks so far away. Looking at it from across this rice paddy. The Sun is reflecting off the water. I can see the water sparkling in between the rice stems. The stems are about a foot apart in the water, and the water is still and clear. Boy, I really don't like what I'm having to do! I really don't need this shit! The new guy and I start walking across the rice paddy to the other side. The water stinks like shit! It's ankle-deep. Now it's knee-deep. The mud's sticking to our boots, and every step stirs up the water into a foul-smelling dark liquid as we walk across the rice paddy. The fertilizer used by the local villagers is nothing more than human or animal shit. It gets spread all around the rice paddy, mixed with dirt, and left in place. But with each step I take, the stink rises up into my nose and makes my stomach upset. My legs feel heavy from the mud I'm dragging along on my boots.

I'm so scared, I'm sweating and shaking to beat all hell. And if that's not enough, the sun's beating down on my helmet. My head feels like fried eggs in a frying pan. It has to be 100 degrees, or more. Mosquitoes are buzzing around my head, landing on my arms and face, and biting me right through my shirt.

My boots are making a popping sound with every step. My boots are sticking in the mud and water, and when the suction finally lets go of my boot, it pops. It sounds so loud to me, and my heart is pounding so fast. The Sun's glare on the water blinds me, and makes it hard to see in front of me.

If being blinded from glare, and making loud popping noises isn't bad enough, they can see us coming! All that noise I'm making makes me feel vulnerable and nervous out here. Now I'm shaking, I can't believe how nervous I am. I'm praying to God the Creator that I make it to the other side, before I get killed. I just can't believe how far it is! Now, it's only a couple 100 yards away. That isn't that far. Boy, it seems like it's 100 miles away, today. I just don't know how I've pushed myself to do this shit day after day, and night after night.

The other new guy is about 50 feet to my left side. We are halfway there. He looks so scared, too. His eyes are wide open. We glance at each other every now and then, and I can see the whites of his eyes. Like the rest of us, dark shadows around his eyes show that he hasn't had enough sleep. I can see sweat dripping down his face, and "that" scared look at the same time.

I must look the same to him. We keep moving across the rice paddy. We keep putting one step in front of the other. It's so damn hard to move through this mud and water, I hope I don't step on some booby trap that's hidden under the water. I'd never see it, and wouldn't know if it was there until I stepped on it. I know things can go wrong at any moment!

Being out here in the open makes my scalp itch. Here I go all over again with the same thoughts! I can feel a bullet going right through my helmet and into my head at any moment. I have a twitch above my eye, and I feel the skin on my forehead tighten up, and I know I'm tense. This is one hell of a feeling, imagining that a bullet will rip a hole right through my head and splatter my brains all over the place! I've seen what a head shot does to brains. The bullet makes a small hole going in and coming out it blows the whole back of your head off and splatters your brains everywhere. When you see it for real it will never go away in your mind. It's going to haunt you till the day you die.

I can't believe the pressure my mind is feeling. The closer we get, the more pressure I feel. The closer I get, the easier it is for the enemy to put a bullet in my head. I just can't believe I'm doing this! This feeling is awful, but I have to endure it. I don't know if I can make it to the other side. My nerves are getting to me! I'm really shaking, the closer we move in towards the village. But I keep moving in. It's so hard to put one foot in front another, right now.

We've finally made it to the other side! We check out the front flank, the first row of hootches. The hootches kind of remind me of a Native American adobe house that my grandparents lived in because their walls were made of mud and grass put together. We hand signal the all clear sign, the rest of the Platoon starts coming across the rice paddy. They come over in groups of five. I bet the guys coming across, right now, feel the same way we did when we crossed all that open ground. Even though we checked everything out, things can still happen. It's never safe out here. Things happen when you think it's safe. Boy, it's hot, it has to be 105 degrees. The Sun reflecting off the water makes it hotter. We all can feel the heat rising off the water. Even worse, the glare made it hard to see while crossing that rice paddy, and not being able to see in front of us made the crossing terrifying. I kept thinking I was going to feel a round going into my head.

TUNNEL RATS AND SPIDER HOLES
June 1968

Now that we've all made it to the other side, it's time to check out the whole village. We check to see if anyone's been here, lately, and look for hidden enemy supplies. We find a few spider holes along the outside of the village by the rice paddy we just crossed. One had a tunnel in it. The enemy hides in spider holes and ambushes us from them, so we have to do something about them. These types of spider hole entrances were flat on the ground like a manhole cover. But instead of covering the holes with steel covers, the VC covered them with different types of natural camouflage and made a natural manhole cover by building a bamboo frame that they packed real solid with dirt. Then they planted vegetation into the dirt and let it grow naturally. The plants grew fast and rooted themselves into the dirt. Then the plants kept growing throughout the bamboo structure. The end result of all this work made a cover, hard as a rock that camouflaged so completely into the plants around it, you couldn't see any line between the man-made object and the plants around it! A full-size man could stand on top of the cover. And never know that he was right over the entrance to a whole tunnel system.

After we located the tunnel, the LT calls me over, and tells me to get ready to check out the tunnel. I take off all my equipment, web-belt and canteen, pack, helmet, and M-16, and strip down to my fatigues only. The LT hands me his .45 automatic pistol, and a flashlight belonging to the Radio Transmitter Operator (RTO). Now I'm ready to go in and check out the tunnel. I'm scared shitless! I didn't want to go to school for any tunnel training. But the Army sent me. And now, I have no choice. I do what I'm told to do. I'm at the point that I don't give a damn anymore. I feel like my life isn't worth anything anymore. My odds of getting wounded or killed are pretty high. I feel hopeless. I know that my odds of being a casualty are better than my odds of getting in and out of this tunnel alive. I've only been stuck in this shithole country for less than two months, and I've already been through so much crap – and I still have ten more months. Only the Creator knows how much more crap I have to go through! All I know is, I have a job to do. I'm in constant fear. Now, I'm at the point where I'm just going through the motions of doing my job.

Before going into the tunnel, I check the flashlight. It's an "L" shape. It's an OD (Olive Drab) green military flashlight that has different lenses stored in the back of it. I change out the red lens in the flashlight for a clear lens, and put the red one into the lens compartment in the back of the flashlight. Then I check the .45, and make sure it's loaded and ready to fire. I tuck my bayonet into the side pocket of my jungle fatigues. I walk towards the tunnel and I stop in front of it. I visually check the outside of the tunnel entrance to make sure it looks clear for me to enter. I kneel down and look into the entrance. Then I call two guys over and tell them, "Hold my ankles, I have to probe the floor before I go in." I scoot head-first into the spider hole, while the guys hold my ankles and keep me from falling in.

Luckily this hole isn't too deep only about four feet. Sometimes these entrance holes are deep enough that the VC dig out hand-and-toe holes in the sides of the walls so they can climb in and out of holes that are longer than they are tall. I hang upside down while I use my bayonet to probe for booby traps on the floor and the sides of the wall. I have to be careful, because the VC place booby traps along the inside walls of the entrances. So when a Grunt puts his hand along the wall to support himself . . . Boom, he's just triggered some kind of explosive device! The Grunt, and maybe some other Grunts, become casualties. So I hang upside down scanning the walls feeling sweat pour down my face, and into my ears and eyes, with my blood pressure pounding in my head more and more and probing the floor with my bayonet. Once I decide there are no booby traps, I holler for the guys to pull me up. They pull me out by my feet. I struggle to stand up and my blood goes rushing from my head, for a second I feel like I'm going to tip over. Then one of the guys that pulled me out hands me a towel so I can wipe all the sweat off my face and neck. Now I'm ready to go in feet first. I sit on the edge of the hole, and I make sure I've got my flashlight and bayonet. I drop my whole body into the tunnel. I feel my feet hit the ground. It feels so cool, I can't feel the heat above ground anymore. I can smell Mother Earth, and she smells sweet. It's hard to move around, and I feel closed in. I don't move until I calm myself down, and my eyes adjust to the dark ahead of me. But I'm scared to beat all hell to be in here.

It takes me about ten minutes before I can start crawling through the tunnel. I turn on the flashlight, and start checking for any booby traps, other entrances, supplies, or the enemy. I'm holding the .45 in my right hand, but I have to lay my flashlight down on the ground keeping the light pointed down the tunnel, while I gently run my left hand over the top of the dirt. Checking for trip wires or solid objects that may feel like a trigger for a booby trap. My .45's still in my right hand. I've got an iron grip on it. The ground here is clear, there are no booby traps. Then I get into a prone position because I've got to move farther into the tunnel, and the tunnel is only about two and a half feet to four feet high. Once I'm lying on my belly, I reach ahead of me to probe the ground there. I run my hand over the dirt then I grab my bayonet and gently probe into the ground with it, feeling for anything solid like mines or tripwires. Or entrances that may be hidden in the ground. Once I make sure the ground ahead of me is clear, I grab the flashlight and bayonet in my left hand and crawl forward on my belly, using a low-crawl to inch myself forward by my elbows and toes, one foot at a time. I'm still holding the .45 in my right hand and pointing it down the tunnel. I keep repeating the same process: place the flashlight on the dirt, light pointing down the tunnel, run my hand over the ground, probe with the bayonet, crawl forward – point the .45 down the tunnel, place the flashlight on the dirt, light pointing down the tunnel, run my left hand over the ground, probe with the bayonet, crawl forward. Again and again and again. It's pitch black in here except for the flashlight. I feel like I can't breathe, it's so closed in, in here. My memories and thoughts are racing through my head. Now I feel like I'm hyperventilating I have to calm down and breathe slow and easy. Take nice deep breaths, Joe. I'm terrified! Creator, get me through this, please! Just get me through this!! Control your emotions, Joe. I'm a damn spotlight with this flashlight, any VC can see the light if he's in this tunnel, and use it to know where to shoot at me! I feel like I'm descending. Now the tunnel's turning towards the left. Now, I'm coming back up.

I don't know how I managed to handle my fear of the unknown down here, but I completed the job of checking the tunnel. I'm so relieved! I can't believe I've actually done it! I don't know how long it took me to crawl this 200 feet, underground. It feels like it took about half an hour, maybe more, it seemed like forever! So far the tunnel's been clear, but I see an opening up ahead, and there's a little bit of light coming through it. What's on the other side of that opening? Is that daylight I see? Looks like it. And this opening? What is it? It's a tiny bunker! It looks like it's underneath a hootch. I crawled from the tunnel, into a bunker located beneath a hootch in the village! That is daylight! I see a hootch entrance. The bunker runs inside the hootch. I'm inside a hootch! Now, I'm crawling out of the bunker and standing inside the hootch. I'm looking around the hootch and I'm so relieved, everything is clear!!

I yell out to the Grunt crawling behind me in the tunnel my backup guy and let him know that everything's clear. I'm relieved that I made it this far! My heart's still pounding a little, but mostly I feel a lot of relief! Nothing happened to me crawling through the tunnel or coming up out of the bunker. I'm still here!! I step out of the hootch and see the rest of our guys searching the village area, and securing it. My LT gives us the order to blow up the tunnel and spider holes. We place C-4 in about five spider holes as well as the inside of the tunnel, and blow them all up in place. It's time to move out again. It'll be getting dark in a few hours, and we need to set up another ambush again. I don't know where we're going yet, not until Sergeant Bones tells us what to do next.

Sergeant Bones tells us to take a 15-minute break and eat dinner. Afterward, he took off to find out what our next move was going to be. Boy! I sure needed this break, so did the rest of the guys. It gives me time to rest, change my socks, and drain my boots. My boots still had rice paddy water in them, and I needed to let them dry a little, before we move out again. I placed my helmet, strap down, on the ground so I could sit on it. I relaxed a little and got myself back together after that stressful tunnel experience. The guy that had walked across the rice paddy with me, sat next to me and we opened up our boxes of C-rations. As we ate, he asked me, "How long have you been here?" I said, "I've been here about a month and a half, so far."

I asked him, "Why're you asking?" He said, "I thought you'd been here a lot longer. You've been walking point all this time, and then you went down into that tunnel. I've been here four weeks, and the first time I walked point was when we walked across the rice paddy." I thought to myself, "What the hell is going on? It's bad enough that I (a new guy) had to go down into that damn tunnel, but now I find out I'm a new guy who's been walking point since I got to my Unit a month and a half ago!"

When Sergeant Bones came by later on, I asked him, "What's going on? The new guy just said that he's been here four weeks or so, and hasn't had to walk point yet until today?" Sergeant Bones answered, "His turn hasn't come up, yet. 3rd Squad – your Squad – has been taking point for the past month or so, then 2nd Squad will do the same. Then 1st Squad, and so on. 3rd Squad still has a few days left to do on their rotation. Today, we put another new guy to walk with you, so you wouldn't be alone crossing that rice paddy. You'll be doing the same for him when needed."

The Sergeant continued talking, "We know how hard it is to walk across a rice paddy, like you did. Any more questions?" "No, Sarge!" I replied. "And by the way," said Bones, "you did a good job going down that tunnel."

Now I felt guilty about asking him that question. I felt about as big as an ant. But, hell, I needed to know. He was right, though, in what he was saying, and what we were doing. Like he said, he'd been here ten months already. And he knows what the hell he's doing. He's lasted ten months, so far, and that was good for him – in a way. He still has about two months left on his tour, and sometimes shit happens.

I can tell just by looking at the Sergeant that he's been through a lot. Boy, with only two months left, I bet he must be scared as all hell, too. But he doesn't show it. I just don't know how he does it. I will find out, later, I guess because the more time you spend out here, the harder you get. The way I look at it, life will be a whole lot different as time goes on. The things we're going to do, hear, see, smell, and feel, will haunt us for the rest of our lives.

We just got word that it's time to move out, again. So here we go, on another mission, hoping for the best. As beat and run-down as we are, we've got to go. There's no way of getting out of it when you're a Line Unit. We still have a job to do, like it or not. It's the life of a Grunt. Pushing ourselves to the limit of life and death until one of us breaks or we make it home. A lot of times we push ourselves beyond our physical and emotional limits. I have to wonder how we made it through a firefight, or how we're going to make it through the next battle. I guess it's just pure luck, sometimes, that keeps us alive from one day to the next.

Sarge told us we'd be going on another mission, riding on the choppers again on Eagle Flights. That means we're going into battle with ten Huey's and four escorting gunships. Ten choppers flying in formation make one hell of a scary sound. The rotor blades chop the air in a thundering rhythm, while the engines howl and strain with the blades rotating. The sound is like a pounding beat across the sky like giant war drums . . . Boom. Boom. Boom. Boom. Every time I hear the choppers coming to pick us up, my stomach knots up, my body tenses. I hear the low Boom, Boom, Boom in the distance and I suddenly want to panic, but I choke down fearful thoughts, and replace them with thoughts that won't break my will to get on board the choppers. A few moment pass, and now the low Boom, Boom, Boom sounds like it's about to split the sky. The Eagle Flights are coming in to load us up. They look like a bunch of eagles coming in with the skids on the chopper looking like claws reaching out. They're right over us, and now the noise from the engines and blades is so intense, it's like thunder, and so near, it sounds like DEATH rejoicing in taking us to hell! The Eagle Flights land, pick us up, and carry us off. On a one-way trip straight into hell. I'm an emotional wreck. The muscles in my legs, my arms, my neck, my back, and my face feel like rubber bands ready to snap. My mind is struggling to keep my sanity – I'm walking a tightrope between sanity and the insane asylum! No one can imagine the terror that ripples through your body in waves once the sounds of those choppers first hit your eardrums, as low noises in the distance. For every foot closer to the LZ the choppers fly towards you, the huge vibrations from the blades beating the air and engines screaming at full throttle start running through your body. You not only hear death, you feel it, too. With every beat that pounds into your soul.

We're airborne now, and for a few precious moments I feel no terror as I look out into the distance below me. The air smells sweet and clean. The humidity is almost nonexistent as the winds beat through the chopper. It helps us forget where we are for a just moment. But that feeling doesn't last. We're descending, now, and I feel my terror starting again. My body tenses, again, and in my emotions I'm back where I was when I heard the first beats of the choppers in the distance . . . Boom, Boom, Boom, the blades cut through the air.

I don't know if I can take this anymore. I have no control in what I'm going to do next. I'm told what to do and I have no choice, I just follow orders. Like it or not. So far it's been going ok for me. I just hope my luck keeps working. I know my whole life can change in a split second out here. It's hard to believe it's only my second month in-country.

GOING TO HELP THE MANCHUS
July 1968

I have 283 days left in Vietnam. I've only been in-country about three months so far, 82 days. We just finished a mission, and we're getting ready to go to a pick-up zone for a routine mission out in the jungle. Our LT says, "Take a break, the RTO just told him he got a call from HQ." When he comes back to us, he says, "Things have changed. We're going on a different type of mission. A Unit's in trouble – the Manchus."

Boy, that's all we need, some more shit to go into. A Hot LZ. I just got through putting an X on my helmet to mark off another day I'd been in Vietnam. A few months ago, I drew a short-timer's calendar on my helmet. It was a three-dimensional cross with 365 numbered squares on it. Each day that I'd been in-country was marked off with an X, beginning with day 365, which is one year. Then counting backwards. That way I'd know how many days I have left in-country. I didn't need to know how many days I'd *been* in-country, I want to know how many days I had until I left for home. Each day I spend here just seems to get longer and longer. The more time I spend here, the longer it takes for time to go by.

I just used my P-38 to open my C-ration cans: pears, stale crackers, peanut butter, and beef stew (Oh, yummy, beef stew chunks with nice little layers of cold lard on top of the stew that gives you the runs when you can't heat it up and have to eat it cold). I put my P-38 back on my dog tag chain, and start warming my food with a piece of C-4 explosive. I want to keep my fingers and hands, so to make sure the C-4 doesn't explode when I light it, I roll the C-4 up into a little ball first. Once that's done I light it up, there is a light blue and green tint as it burns. I hold my C-ration can over it, and watch my food heat up. The sequence is important. If I put a C-ration can on top of the ball of C-4, then light the C-4, I'm liable to get my hands blown off. The C-4 only has to get compressed a tiny bit, and it'll combust and explode when you light it. After these past few months here in the field, I know better, now. Going hungry one time like I did my first day in-country is enough to teach me. That I better eat something before we go on another mission. It just might be a very long, bad day.

Boy, what a difference now that Sergeant Bones has gone back home to the good old USA. That was a few weeks ago, he was so happy and sad at the same time. I didn't understand why he was sad. I will find out later when I make Sergeant and have to leave my guys behind. We have a new Sergeant, this is our second new Sergeant, the first one didn't last too long. He tripped a booby trap on one of our patrols out there in the jungle. That was about a week after he got here. I guess he wasn't lucky enough. To me, it's all about luck. I don't care how good you know your job, shit can happen to you.

The LT just said this is going be a Hot LZ. I know what that means now. That means we'll be flying into a firefight. The Manchus are in trouble. They've engaged the enemy under heavy fire, and it's not going well. When we fly in, the enemy will be shooting at the choppers as we try to land in the LZ. That means we can die before we even touch the ground. Shit, that's all we need. This is not good, at all! The guys know it's not a good thing but it has to be done to save the Manchus' lives. There's nowhere to run, nowhere to go, and no choice in the matter. Looking around, I can see some of the guys. Every one of them is eating. They learned the same lesson I learned, too, eat when you can. Because it might be your last meal. Looking at their faces makes me wonder if I look the same: their faces are beat and tired, their clothes are covered with days of dirt and sweat, they look like they've been spending time on the "Green Mile," forever. At least someone who's actually on the Green Mile knows that their execution is set for a date and time, but we Grunts never know when our "execution" can happen. We just know that we have to keep putting one boot in front of the other until we go home or the Creator calls us to the Spirit World.

Some guys are writing home to family, friends, or girlfriends. Some are giving notes to their buddies, in case they don't make it through this mission. Keeping a buddy's note is a sacred task. It's something we all take serious. We always hope that we can give the note back. To the buddy who gave it to us. A note given to you by a buddy has a special meaning. It's personal, not a telegram, and we keep the promise that's implied when we put the note in our pocket. We know that the note's words speak more lovingly to our buddy's kin because it's the buddy speaking his final words directly to his family. We know that those words will give comfort to grieving loved ones.

I'm scared to beat all hell, and trying to keep it together out here. Can it get any worse than what it already is? I don't know anything about the Manchus, who they are, or what they do. The LT briefed us about the situation we would be going into. "Be prepared, this is not going to be a joy ride," he said. "The Manchus landed in an NVA or VC village, on a road that runs right down the middle of the village. Out of ten choppers going in to the LZ, three were shot down on the LZ. We don't know how many guys made it out of the choppers, before the remaining choppers had to escape from the LZ. Some of the Manchus managed to disembark, but they're in bad shape and they need help as fast as we can saddle up. The only good thing about this, is that we've already been resupplied, and we're ready to go."

The LT continued, "We'll be going in, two choppers at a time. We'll be landing in a little rice paddy about 200 to 300 square yards, and located near the Saigon River, where the village is." The LT said, "Break's over, it's time to saddle up and move out." Our break lasted all of fifteen minutes, and it's been a damn long day so far, and it doesn't look like it's going to end anytime soon. We have to head out to a bigger clearing, about a half a mile from here. That's the pick-up zone. Our current location isn't big enough to pick up the whole Company all at once.

After what seemed like a long time, but was only about 15 minutes of patrolling through bush and vegetation, we finally made it to the bigger clearing. It'd been hot and muggy all day, so far. It took another five to ten minutes to secure the area. Just as we finished doing that, we heard the Eagle Flights come in. Here come our choppers! Shit, I'm sweating a lot. It's this damn heat. When does it end?

We pop red smoke to give our location and identify ourselves to the choppers. If the Pilots don't see the color of smoke they expected from the smoke grenades, rising from ground, then they won't land. If it's not the right color, it can mean Charlie popped smoke trying to lure the choppers in to their area for an ambush.

While we wait for the choppers, we all take a knee. It's important to make ourselves as small as possible to make sure we don't take a chopper blade in the upper body. And just as important, we want to keep from getting blown down to the ground by the fierce wind and turbulence whipped by the chopper blades. We are all kneeling, and spread out in groups of seven, on the ground. I can feel how tense I am. I'm already stressing out. I bet the rest of the guys feel like I do.

I hear the choppers coming in and look up towards the sky. I'm stressed out, but I can't help feeling a sense of awe when I see the choppers. There's something graceful and powerful about how they move. All that ugliness that we're about to head into, but I still have time to see a vision of beauty in what's taking place. The choppers move together like a ballet of eagles. It's graceful. Watching the choppers coming in feels like watching great eagles floating and gliding through the heavens, with the chopper skids looking like eagle claws and their sharp eyes scanning the ground below. In preparing to land, the choppers become eagles whose wings catch the air currents, and their tails scoop towards the ground. With feathers rustling in the wind, the eagles drop to earth suddenly and gracefully. Ready to seize their victims with their two steel skids that look like claws!

The Huey choppers approach the LZ, ten in a staggered row. Four helicopter gunships, two on each side of the rows fly alongside the choppers. The noise at first is soft, pleasant to my ears. I'm still watching the formation move in, and now the noise is increasing. As the Eagle Flight moves in to land, the noise becomes a deafening roar of engines, and propeller blades chopping the air. The four gunships peel off left and right, to circle low above us. I can see the Door Gunners – face shields down and their M-60s at the ready – scanning the LZ perimeter. They're our protectors in this harsh environment. It only takes one enemy to knock out a chopper. I feel my fear rise inside my body. My chest tightens. I'm nervous. I'm back to reality, again.

Boy, I don't like knowing that this is going to be a Hot LZ. My stomach is upset. I feel chills running down my back, and across my body. I really don't need this shit. It reminds me of my first day in-country. That day was a living hell! Hard to believe it was only about three months ago. It seems like a lifetime, I don't know if I can take it anymore. We move into position, here in this big clearing, waiting for the choppers to land. But we've still got to watch that jungle that's just behind us. Anything or anyone could be in there, just itching to fire on our position. I feel like a sitting target here! There are ten groups of us Grunts, seven per group, waiting here, staggered in a line hoping some gook doesn't blow our heads off. That's how I thought about them now, the NVA and the VC, when they're trying to kill us! We have to keep an eye on that perimeter behind us and hope nothing goes wrong.

Here come the helicopters, flying in a formation. It's time to pop a purple smoke grenade. We have to identify ourselves to the choppers, and signal it's safe to land. It's the CO's responsibility to make sure the smoke grenade is popped. Since he's coordinating with HQ and the Forward Observers. What a sight, watching the choppers come in all at once! They're approaching the clearing in a long staggered line, staggered the same way we're staggered on the ground. The formation moves downwind from the smoke, and flies into the wind for better air lift and smoother touchdowns. The landings are so perfectly staggered with our line that each chopper is right in front of each group of men to the side of us. The choppers are kicking up a lot of dust. As soon as they land, we're all running towards the cabin doors. I hear the sounds of my boots pounding the hard ground, my gear bouncing on my back, and the buckle on my rifle strap clattering against my magazine. With every step I take towards the chopper. The smell of smoke from the smoke grenade and the dirt kicked up by the choppers is sticking to the sweat on my face and in my nose. I taste dirt and salt mixed with my sweat. The dirt is dry. It smells stale and all the whirling dirt makes it hard to breathe. The dirt's in my mouth, my hair, and my eyes. The more I do this, the harder it is to do.

We all board the choppers. What a sight we are, choppers landing in lines, everyone running in step towards the cabins! The sounds of our feet beating the ground, the rhythm of our equipment hitting against our bodies. These are actions we executed without spoken commands or wasted movements. It was military clockwork, we did this same maneuver so many times, we didn't need commands or wasted movements.

We load up, seven men per chopper. Our whole Company is moving out, now. Wait! What the . . . ! Why in the hell are all those extra piles of ammunition and C-rations stacked in this chopper? Oh, fuck, we must be going into some real bad shit! What other reason would there be for all that ammo and those rations? Crap, the Crew Chief is telling us the extra ammo and rations are for *us*!! What in the hell are we flying into? It must be real bad out where we're going if we've got to have all this extra stuff! It means that we'll be in a fucked-up hellhole for a long time!

GOING INTO A HOT LZ
June 1968

Just a few minutes pass before we're up in the air, and flying Southeast towards Saigon. The village we're headed to is about seven to ten miles away from the outskirts of Saigon, near the Saigon River. The city's shape is in the distance, in front of our formation. We've been flying for about ten minutes, but it seems like a lifetime. The choppers are turning left, Saigon's position is moving to my right, now it's to my back. A few minutes ago, I could see the shape of the city, out in front of me. Now, I'm looking down at the Saigon River. The river moves through the landscape, and I try to focus on the beauty, below.

Yes, this is me getting punched by the guy that kept picking on me. I was knocked down a few times, but I kept getting up, the Sergeant finally stopped us from fighting and that guy never bothered me again.

My Mom (Josephine) and me at home on my two-week leave after getting out of AIT from Fort Lewis, Washington, just before leaving for Vietnam. Mom was trying to smile, trying to hide her true emotions, I was not smiling because I was scared as all HELL.

My first day with the Wolfhound Unit was in May. I'm standing in front of the Wolfhound County sign in Chu Chi, our main base camp.

These are the guys in my Platoon that survived being out in the field. You can see the different tans on the guys, the ones without a tan are FNGs, the guys with a tan were the "old guys."

This picture was taken in July after 73 days of being in the jungle with no rest, baths, or change of clothes or peace of mind until we got into our main base camp. After being out in the field, we lost 31 of our fellow Wolfhounds. This ceremony was done on our Stand-Down that lasted only three days in Chu Chi Base Camp.

Here I am with Milky my buddy. He carried the M-60 machine gun, he put his hand on top of my head as if I were a little kid. He got wounded a few months later, to this day I don't know his outcome.

To try and keep myself from feeling the fear that wants to climb up my throat and take control of my body, but it doesn't work. I can see black heavy smoke filling the air, with swirls, like it's curling and dancing. Smoke and balls of fire, orange and red and purple, light up the jungle floor and afternoon sky. If I didn't know the terror there was down in those flames, they would seem beautiful. They are lighting up the jungle with colors. The action is heaviest in the jungle and along the river banks. It was an F-4 jet dropping bombs and napalm near one of the villages by the river, and a ball of fire exploded upward. I see smoke rising from the explosion, into the cracks of the sky between the jungle and the village. I'm looking, but not believing what I see. A huge battle is underway! Helicopter gunships are firing their weapons. Heavy artillery is pounding the ground, and air support is flying in. The gunships, artillery, and air support are all working together. It's like it's a dance, so coordinated it's amazing, in and out of the kill zone. I know, without even thinking, that men are dying down there in awful ways.

I can't believe we'll be landing down there in a few moments! I'm scared shitless. I know, without a doubt, that some of us will be killed or wounded. I know it! There's no way around that fact the odds are against us! I'm so damned scared. I'm trapped! There's nowhere to run, nowhere to hide, nowhere to go. All I could do is jump out of this bird, but I don't want to commit suicide – it would be an easy way out of this mess. I want to live but I don't want to die down there on the ground, either, with my body blown to hell. I'm a draftee. I'm here through no choice of my own. I'm 10,000 miles from home, incarcerated in a foreign country, with no hope of escape. Where would I go? How would I hide? All I can do is follow orders, try to suck it up, and hope for the best. I'm praying to the Creator and the All-Mighty Spirit, help me keep it together! Get me though this shit. So I can live another day.

I'm sitting on the floorplate of the helicopter, with my feet hanging out the door, and I'm hanging onto the door post with my arm. To my left is the Door Gunner. Both his hands are resting on the butterfly grip (the handles) of his M-60. The Gunner is looking out the door. Scanning the ground below us. He's got his headset on and he's listening to the battle chatter coming across the radio systems. His face is tense. The more battle chatter he hears, the more his expression changes. I turn to look out the door. While I'm looking, out of the corner of my left eye, I see the Door Gunner lower his face shield. I look over at him, he looks over at me. Our eyes lock for a second, and he answers my unspoken question with one motion of his arm. He puts out his arm and points downward, giving me the sign to get ready to go in.

Boy, when he does that, my heart drops and chills run down my whole body. I can't believe I have this cold, chilled, feeling. I'm sweating and my hands are cold. I can feel my heart pounding! My heart is pumping so hard, I hear it throbbing in my ears! What the hell's going on with me? I've got to keep it together! I just have to! I look at the other guys' faces. I can see terror and fear in their eyes, sweat's pouring down their faces, their eyes are wide open. All I see are the whites of their eyes. Everybody's got dark shadows under their eyes. Their eyes look like those of raccoons. Boy, now I'm even more scared! I know I must look the same. I just can't believe I'm doing this and that these guys sitting with me in this helicopter are feeling the same terror as I am. All we can do is hope that we make it out alive from that hellhole below us.

I think, "We must be going straight down," so I let go of the door post I'm holding onto, to hold onto my rifle. Then the chopper makes a hard left bank, and drops down, fast. The wind is blowing in my face. I feel my stomach jump into my Adam's apple. Talk about tightening up your ass, while trying to stay in the chopper at the same time. I almost slide right out of the chopper, 1,000 feet above the ground. With my feet still hanging out the door, and both hands still holding onto my rifle, without even thinking it I'm keeping my hands gripped on my weapon. It's my lifeline in this war, and I can't lose it by dropping it out the door! But it's a fucking struggle to stay in the helicopter. I'm sliding out the door, all I can do is flatten myself backwards towards the floor, away from the door, as flat as I can go! Once I'm flat against the floor plates, I stop moving forward. At the same time, the chopper levels out and I'm able to get my balance and stay in the chopper. Shit, that experience was another unexpected, unknown obstacle I've had to overcome in this war!! The chopper keeps descending, and as we drop, I look at the guys next to me. I can see they feel the same as I do, I can see it in their faces and in their eyes. There's so much fear in all of us. They're as scared as I am, and they're trying to keep it together, too. Our chopper is one of the first two going into the LZ. The gunships are alongside us, giving us protection as we enter the LZ. Man, people just don't know how it feels being forced to face death. Unless they've been there.

Suddenly, the Door Gunner is hollering at us saying the chopper won't be touching the ground. I can hear the fear in his voice, too. Instead, we'll be hovering over the ground and we'll have to jump out. Boy, this is going to be the shit! When the Gunner started hollering, our emotions ratcheted up. At the same time, our training kicked in, we got ready to do battle. We all took our safeties off our weapons. I guess the shit is really hitting the fan, out there. The Door Gunners opened up with their M-60 machine guns, as we were going in.

The gunships were doing the same firing their weapons, as they went in with us. The noise is hell. It makes me jerk, and before I know it, I'm hearing soda cans crunching or popping sounds. What the hell is that? As we come into our LZ, I see an ARVN compound to my left. An ARVN compound is like a little South Vietnamese Army fort. It's supposed to provide protection for the Vietnamese village in that area, and there's a Platoon-size group of South Vietnamese Army soldiers staying at the compound. I'm in the group of two choppers landing first. The Command chopper is to my right and is the second of the two choppers landing first. Only 20 yards separate us. To the right of the Command chopper, about 250 yards away I can see smoke where napalm has been dropped.

I jump out of the chopper, into a rice paddy still flooded with water. Now, I understand why the choppers aren't landing! The wind from the chopper is spraying rice paddy water into our eyes and all over us. We're about five feet off the ground. I jump out, hit the water, and get my feet stuck in the mud, for a moment. It only takes a total of 20 to 30 seconds to unload the supplies and for everyone to jump out of the two choppers. They take off, and two other choppers move in to unload their guys. Before my chopper takes off, though, I get up as fast as I can. I take a moment to get my bearings and figure out what direction I'm supposed to run. Just then, I see the guys from the Command chopper running towards a tree line, 50 yards to our right. As fast as I can, I struggle to get to the tree line, I manage to run through the mud and water. Mud is sticking to my boots. It's so hard to move through this type of shit! Every step I take through this muck, takes so much energy and effort my feet and boots are getting bogged down. That's all we need – more shit to be in!

I see water splashing in front, and all around, me. I know the splashes are bullets hitting the water. I can't believe I made it, I really made it to the tree line! Guys are hiding behind the trees. They're from the Company we've been ordered here to help in securing the LZ. I can't believe how scared I am! I'm breathing hard, trying to catch my breath. And trying to stop shaking. Everybody is firing towards another tree line, where the smoke is, about 200 yards away from us, on the edge of the village. I do what everyone else is doing and start firing my weapon toward the other tree line. I can't see the enemy all I can do is put more fire power out there. We have to stop the enemy from firing into the LZ.

I can hear explosions, and guns firing. I look back. I can see that some of the guys jumping from the choppers don't make it to the tree line. I knew it – some of us wouldn't make it! As bad as things are, the choppers are still coming in. They have to unload the rest of the Company, as guys get off the choppers, they're picking up and dragging the wounded guys over to our tree line. The choppers come in, two at a time, and unload the rest of our Company and supplies. Enemy rounds are zipping over our heads and smacking into the rice paddy water, and guys are falling into the paddies. Things are happening so fast, I almost panic! But I keep my shit together. I don't know how, but I do. My emotions are going crazy. A chopper lands, and guys have to run out of the LZ straight to the tree line, so another chopper can land, unload the guys then move out of the LZ – the kill zone.

The gunships are firing over our heads, now, in front of us, while they fly above our position. Above us, we hear machine guns firing down on the enemy, rockets are whooshing over our heads, too, exploding on the enemy positions. We're pinned down. It looks like we're not going anywhere for a while. It'll be getting dark in a few hours. We're on the outskirts of the village, about 200 yards away, it's hard to know exactly how far away we are. Boy, most of my clothes are dry, now! It's been a few hours since we landed. As I look across the rice paddy, I can see the ARVN compound. I find myself thinking, "Where in the hell are they? Aren't they supposed to protect the village from the enemy??" Part of our Company is moving up to the village. The other part of the Company is staying here to secure the area for the Dust-Off choppers to come pick up the wounded.

I don't have time to think about what's taking place. There's too much going on. Later, I realize that the can-crushing and popping sounds I heard were actually bullets striking and ripping through our choppers as each helicopter approached the LZ. I could have been killed long before I even got off the chopper! I was lucky to make it to the tree line. Dozens of bullets were buzzing over our heads, smacking into the rice paddy water, as we, each of us Grunts, ran towards the tree line! I was better off staying ignorant about those zipping, buzzing noises, realizing they're bullets only makes me feel like DEATH is breathing down my neck.

Here we go again. My Company is moving up to join the other part of the Company still in trouble. I'm in 3rd Platoon, 2nd Squad. 1st Platoon is moving to our left flank, about 100 yards from us. I guess we're going up front to support the rest of that other Company. I'm not walking point this time, that's a good thing! There're still a lot of explosions, and guns firing. 3rd Platoon is moving out in a column, walking hunched over, along and over the defensive tree line. They're moving into place, 100 yards parallel to us, we're crawling on our stomachs up to where the battle's taking place. It's finally dark, and we've only moved 200 yards up this damn ditch. The ditch runs parallel to the road, or trail – it's hard to tell in this darkness. I sure as hell don't want to get on top of this road or trail and expose myself. It seems like three long hours, now, since we crawled the first 200 yards and all we've managed is another slow 100 yards on our bellies. The closest guy to me is only five yards away but that doesn't keep me from really feeling isolated and lonely. We can't talk to one another, we have to maintain silence. We're prisoners in our own minds, in our own emotions and in our own thoughts. No amount of training could have prepared me for this terrifying, lonely, sense of being trapped in my own mind I'm experiencing here with myself and my thoughts. We each have to suffer through all this trauma on our own, without a friend or company, just hoping that our mind survives this horror.

It's late, very dark, and it's a hot night so far. The temperature is between 90 degrees and 100 degrees. I haven't stopped sweating all night. I've got two canteens of water at my side, but I don't dare move my arm to bring a canteen to my mouth – I'm too afraid I'll give away my position if I move. It only takes one half-second to let the enemy know where I'm at, and that one half-second can be the most valuable half-second of my life!

Flares are lighting up the night. I look at my watch. It says 9:00 p.m. civilian time, for us that's 2100hrs. None of us Grunts has military-issue watches. We're all wearing PX-bought Seiko 23-Jewel wristwatches, with metal link straps. Only the Sergeant, then the "Top" (First Sergeant), and the LT got military-issue watches. The rest of us bought our watches at the PX. The watch hands and numbers glow in the dark, so we wear the watches with the face on the inside of our wrists. If we wore the watches with the face on the outside of our wrists, like civilians do, then the gooks can spot us at night and fire at us. We keep the long sleeves of our jungle fatigues rolled all the way down, to cover the watches. I'm taking a huge risk just glancing at my watch, I have to move my hand and arm to push up my left sleeve cuff a little bit to look at the watch face. I cover my watch with my right hand, so the light glowing from the numbers and watch hands doesn't shine outwards. In the darkness, the light shining off the watch face feels like a giant spotlight on my face, making my position easily visible to enemy rifles. When they wear their watches on their arms, with the face on the outside of their wrist, we can spot their arms swinging back and forth while they're walking at night from at least 300 yards away. I know an enemy looking for any signs of our movements and watching in the direction of our positions can see our watches glowing if we don't take steps to keep the light hidden. Looking at my watch makes my heart race and my thoughts go wild! Shit, what if that little action I just took, looking at my watch, exposed my position to the enemy? I half expect a round to tear into me, or an explosion to go off near me! I'm terrified, again, so I lie here as still as possible! I've got to control my breathing, and calm down! I don't want to breathe too hard or too loud, I don't want to move too much. My heart is racing, I'm sweating so much that my rifle feels like it's going to slip right out of my clammy hands. My mouth is so damn dry. All I want is a sip of water. But if I move my hands to get my canteen, then I can be spotted by snipers in the trees. My thoughts! I've got to control them. I feel myself about to panic! POP! Another flare went up.

The flares keep lighting up the night and making that popping sound just before they light up the ground. It's been almost six hours since we landed. We've been crawling slow and low to the ground, to get to our destination. I can't believe how scared I am.

Boy, it's such a long night! But it's only been a few hours. Only a few hours, and it seems a lifetime. I can't believe how time drags on and on, in these circumstances. Seconds seem like hours out here. When things start happening, when the shit hits the fan five hours can seem like a five seconds, and you can't keep track of everything going on around you. I live life in some kind of time warp out here, we all do, during these moments. When shit's happening, time doesn't move fast enough! Then five seconds drags like five hours, and I can't tell up from down, and I can't wait for it to all be over with, I feel like I'm going crazy, but I have to calm down and control my thoughts, and the only way to do that is to pray and ask my Mom for help in getting through this, and do what I have to do. "Mom, I need your help right now, to get me through this, and make it out all right," I'm crying to myself. The act of crying out to my Mom, in my thoughts, helps me calm down. My tears are my inner emotions! This is pure hell all the time.

The gunships are still flying above us. Their rotor blades are making a whopping sound as the gunships cover us, going in and out of the area. The sound is comforting for a moment. The flares lighting up the night sky give an eerie look to the night. It's spooky. Who knows what's hiding in the shadows of the jungle? Can they see us? Will they start firing on us? The unknown consequences are terrifying. Am I laying on top of a spider hole? Are we crawling onto a booby trap? Is a sniper pointing his rifle at my body? I feel like a sitting duck out here!

I hear artillery firing in the distance. It's a single hollow sound, and I know they're firing flare shells in our direction over our heads towards the enemy positions. Next, I hear the popping sound of the shell's metal plate firing off of the shell. The firing of the metal plate expels the flare's parachute and lights the flare. Now, I'm hearing the plate falling to the ground. I know this, because the metal plate is spinning through the air while it falls, causing the plate to spin with a deep buzz. Like the sound fast-moving tires make when cars drive fast across corrugated steel bridges. Hearing the falling plate buzz through the air, causes us to curl into little balls of scared Grunts, like a reflex. We pray that the plate doesn't land short of its target and kill one of us, instead of the enemy! When the plate hits the ground, it hits heavy with a dead thud. The flares are attached to little parachutes that fall and drift to Mother Earth. A flare's main ingredient is magnesium, which burns hot, it sizzles and spits burnt magnesium as it burns. The effect shines out like a strong, bright light, it lights the jungle with a ghostly white glow. It's bright light, like a welder's arc. While falling through the night sky, the flares dance with the breeze, swinging back and forth like pendulums in the air, and leaving smoky white trails zig-zigging across the sky. The trails remind me of snakes gliding across the night Heavens! When I hunted back there in the "Real World," I used to see evidence of a snake passing across my hiking trail, by the "S" patterns the snake left behind. Then I would go on the alert, since I couldn't tell by just the marks if the snake was friend or foe. Here I go again, my mind's trying to calm me down by reminding me of good memories from the "Real World."

The jungle underbrush is full of scary shadows when each flare lights up the terrain. Shadows are moving at the same time as the flares. I can see creepy silhouettes rising up from the jungle floor, it's like the bush fills up with monsters that stretch and grow. Then they disappear back into the darkness when the light moves on to another spot. I feel like my emotions are on a roller coaster ride up one second, down the next, then turned upside down.

It's hot, with terrible humidity! Sweat's pouring out of me. With all the moisture in the air, even the trees seem like they're sweating! There's moisture heavy on the leaves. Some are canoe-shaped leaves where moisture collects. The sounds of battle in the distance are familiar, I'm calm knowing the battle is "over there," not here with me. I'm not "in" the battle . . . yet. But, wait! My body startles, all the sudden, as I hear a sound I'm not expecting! Is that an enemy moving through the underbrush? My nerves tense up as I half expect to die! Is the enemy next to me?! What the hell is that noise? My mind races as it tries to figure out what the source of the noise is! My reflexes go into hyper-drive as I prepare to protect myself against death. I breathe a quiet sigh of huge relief as I figure out the direction and source of the noise. It's those damn canoe-shaped leaves, they just dumped their water onto the leaves beneath them! Their stems can't hold the weight of the water their leaves collected. So they jerked downward and spilled it onto the leaves below them! That sets off a noisy chain reaction through the jungle canopy, of water spilling out and onto the leaves beneath them hitting the leaves with a "Splash!" of water. Then it slows down to a drip . . . drip . . . drip in the quiet night.

My heart rate slows from its skyrocketed beat, I know I'm going to live at least another few moments. Shit, now I have time to think about how scared I really am! Ok, Mom, help me calm down and get my shit together. Thank God! for these few moments when you helped me get my shit together! Mom, I'm always thinking of you, to help me get through these crises. Talking to you in my own thoughts helps me. Even though you're not here, you're back in the "Real World." You always help me get my thoughts together. I told you I was going to come back home, and I'm going to keep my promise, so I'm going to keep talking to you while I'm here. You're my strength, you're the reason I keep going, and keep surviving. I'm just 19 years old and still your baby, Mom. I haven't lived life long enough to depend on myself, yet. I went from your home to this hellhole. I haven't lived long enough to understand life. Neither do most of these kids here, either, we're all the about same age, maybe a year apart. We are fresh-faced teenagers, who have just started shaving, and who are still wet behind the ears . . . all we are is fresh meat for the war. My life was filled with joy and happiness before I came here. Now all I have experienced is trauma. No amount of military training can prepare a young kid for all the traumas of battle. Or war! No one tells you what it's really going to feel like! Because every situation is different and everybody handles it different, in their own way.

The lights from the flares are shining through the canopy, I see the damp leaves shining bright. The canopy shadows are still bouncing from tree to tree, and leaf to leaf. The flares and parachutes keep on falling and the flares get closer to the jungle floor, that makes my mind think of all the kinds of awful things that can happen to me. I think I see an enemy moving there, here, and everywhere but I have to wait and make sure it's the enemy before I fire my weapon. I don't want to give away my position, yet, by firing my weapon. All hell will break loose once I fire, so I've got to be sure that the shadow I see is an enemy. I need to preserve my night vision, so I make sure that I keep one eye closed as I'm scanning the lit jungle, and wait the three to five minutes it takes the flare to burn out before it lands on the jungle floor. Sometimes the parachutes get caught in the tree branches before landing on the ground. When that happens, the flares keep burning, but the shadow movements slow down to a slight jiggle as the parachutes and flares come to the end of their swinging, and the flare finally burns itself out in the trees. At other times, the flares are short rounds, they touch down on the ground sooner than they normally would. Once on the ground, the flare keeps burning, and the shadows aren't dancing around since the flares are not moving. At the same time, the glow from the flare seems bigger and brighter and more scary until finally the flare burns out.

I don't know where we're going. I'm just following the guy in front of me. I hope the VC or NVA don't break through our column as we crawl down this ditch. That would be the shits again! We've stopped moving. It's been about a half-hour I have no idea what we're supposed to do next. No one's said anything. It seems like a lifetime passes when I don't know what we're going to do next. I'm in my own little world, here, thinking to myself, "I've got to deal with my emotions in my own way." The other guys are probably thinking the same things I am. Thinking of home, or their cars (or girlfriends), or their families. I'm thinking of home, and how nice it was back then. How good home was even as poor as we were and how we were treated in the white neighborhood. It was bad, sometimes, but not as bad as this shit! In a way, coming from a poor family made me be stronger. Even the racism made me stronger. I'm able to deal with this shit, so far. It taught me how to control my emotions.

Word has been passed down to the guy in front of me. He's crawling about five yards back towards me. To tell me something. I can tell he's as scared shitless as I am, it's in his voice. There's a tremor in his voice as he whispers that the wounded are being moved to the rear. Now it's my turn to crawl back to pass the word down to the guy behind me. He looks like I feel, too. I see it in his face. He's as scared as I am. We're all scared. I can see it in our faces whenever I look in the face of some other kid! My mouth is so dry, I can barely get the words out of my mouth to tell the guy behind me what I've got to tell him. And my words sound shaky. I wonder if he can hear how scared I am, too? I guess we've made it to our destination. I'm about the tenth guy from the front of the column.

Boy, we can hardly move around in this damn ditch. I don't feel safe at all! I feel like a sitting duck, but it's a hell of a lot better than being out in the open. My eyes are wide open, looking all around me for any little movement that the enemy is there, and my ears are listening for any type of noise that's out of the ordinary. And I'm hoping to the Creator the enemy doesn't break through this column. I can barely see the guy in front of me, or behind me. All I can do is wait . . . and wait . . . and wait. Wait for the next move or the next command and think a lot about what's going on around me and my immediate surroundings. I hear explosions every now and then. And there are guns firing, on occasion, somewhere out in front of me. Bursts of rounds from a machine gun, and casings hitting each other before hitting the ground, and echoing across the night sky. It scares the shit out of me! The bursts make chills run through my body. It's really spooky waiting for the "unknown" to happen. The more time I have to think, the more scared I get out here!

I'm lost in my own thoughts, when suddenly the guy in front startles me by dragging something towards me. It's one of our wounded guys. He hands the wounded guy off to me, then says in a quiet whisper, "Hand this guy down the line. There're more coming, so just keep handing them down the line." I grab the wounded guy around the torso. Oh, shit, his arm is missing! But he scrambles as quickly as he can. To help me move him to the next guy behind me. I don't have to say anything to the wounded guy, he's been passed down through so many guys now, ten at least, that he already knows he's got to help me so I can hand him down the line to the next guy. He's moaning, he's doped up on morphine for the pain. Yet, somehow, he's managing to show courage and strength in spite of his injuries. I half drag him down the line, he leans against me half pushing with his feet, until we both get to the next guy down the line, about five yards behind me. I don't need this crap! I repeat the same thing with the next wounded guy, until all of us on the line have dragged wounded guy after wounded guy, like an endless bucket brigade. Passing wounded guys down the line, one at a time with the seriously wounded doped up on morphine. These guys are all torn up – bad – missing arms and legs! Some guys are big, some small, some of the guys are walking wounded, shrapnel, bullets, burns and they're crawling down the line on their own.

It's about 0100hrs (1:00 a.m.) now, and the wounded sure look bad. Up in front, there's still shooting going off every now and then. I don't know what's happening up the line, but from the looks of the wounded, they sure took some heavy shit! It's spooky not knowing what's going on up front. It's spooky only getting hints of what it is, by looking at the wounded coming in. It's spooky not knowing what can happen to me, and to the other guys around me. I'm fighting two battles: a physical battle out here where my body's at risk, and a mental battle inside my own mind where my sanity's at risk. I'm doing all I can do, just trying to fight the sweat-making fear I feel inside of me. I have all these emotions, but some of them I can't identify, and it makes me feel lost within myself! But I guess I can handle some of my emotions a lot better than most of the guys out here. Because my Dad took me deer hunting a lot and I was used to seeing blood and feeling it when we had to clean the deer. If you ever did a gut-shot wound on a deer in the stomach, it would stink real bad and you had to really wash the cavity out so it wouldn't spoil the meat. But handing these guys with my bare hands was a different kind of emotion.

The things I had to do, then, and see firsthand, and smell, and hear. All the moaning, the crying, the blood, the death, the harshness of the elements will haunt me till I die. It was awful then, and it's still awful now. I don't know how I lived with it then, and sometimes I don't know how I live with it, now, from day to day. It never goes away. It's my constant companion. It goes with me to the store, to bed, and to the best moments of my life. I've had to learn to deal with it the very best way I knew how, on my own, at that time and moment. There are no rights or wrongs to my memories, and experiences of my battles. They just "are." They exist. There's no changing the past. I was crying inside myself while I was trying to fight my own fear, I was tired, but I was still alive, alert, and wondering what was going to happen next. I had to control the fears and thoughts that were running through my mind, or I would have lost my mind out there, that night.

This night seems so long, I can't wait for daylight to come. I'm so scared being out in this confined and dangerous darkness. These "nights of the unknowns" can break you, if you let them. The night still has me trapped. I'm lost in my own thoughts, again, when I'm startled by a shadow moving in my direction. It's the guy in front of me dragging another body towards me. "Don't worry, he's dead," says the shadow, in an exhausted voice. Now, it's time to move the dead down the line, one at a time. The bodies are getting stiff. Rigor mortis is setting in. Some of the bodies are in advanced stages of decomposition, bloating up like giant, overfilled water balloons ready to burst with the slightest puncture. Other bodies weren't so bad. But all of them are starting to smell. These poor guys have been out in the humidity and Sun most of the day! I realize that the bodies are much heavier to drag than the wounded, and more difficult to handle. There are so many dead, I can't keep count. It's been a very hot night so far, it has to be about 90 degrees. I'm sweating to beat all hell, and I'm so tired of doing all of this: the firefights, carrying the wounded and dead, being afraid, being afraid of being afraid and freezing in place, tired of the darkness, tired of being startled, tired of the enemy, tired of being tired, tired of no sleep, tired of watching every shadow. And tired of the "unknown."

I don't know if I can keep doing this shit for the rest of the night, we are under so much stress. This is the first time I've had to handle so many dead bodies at one time. It seems like we've passed dozens of bodies down the line towards the rear, to the LZ. It takes a long time to drag a body five yards. Then crawl back to my original position. I don't want to give my movements away to the enemy. It makes you so tired and beat. I can't tell if one minute passed, or one hour. And none of the bodies are wrapped in ponchos or body bags. They were passed into my hands, the same way they left the world. My hands touched the skin, blood, and bodies of the dead and I wanted to recoil but I made my hands do the work they were ordered to do . . . pass the dead down the line. Though I was alive, my soul felt the pain and suffering the dead had endured, and my heart really hurt for their loss.

We're still under occasional fire. Whenever a round goes off close to me, I tense up. Behind us, at the LZ, I hear the Dust-Offs coming in throughout the night, picking up the wounded and then the dead. The helicopter blades seem solemn and sad behind us, picking up the wounded, then the dead, on round after round of LZ landings. The Angel of Mercy has traded her place with the Angel of Death, and he's spending a long time with us, tonight. I'm 19 years old, and this is almost my fourth month of being in-country, is this what it's going be like from now on? Things seem like they're getting worse every time we go on a mission! I don't need this! I just don't need this!! I don't know if I can take this shit, anymore. I don't want to be here at all! All I want is to get away from here, and go back home and be safe. I want to be back home with my Mom, and my Dad, and my brother, and my friends. All I can do is try to keep it together out here, and hope for the best, so I can live to see the next sunrise. I just can't believe how time drags on and on, out here in a war zone seconds and minutes seem like hours. I've almost come to my breaking point so many times. I want to run away from all this. But there's no place to run, and I don't want to lose it in front of these guys. I don't want to lose face.

ANOTHER DAYBREAK
July 1968

It's almost daylight, the shooting has stopped. As the Sun rises, and the light gets brighter, I feel some sweet relief from this "night of death." None of us has had any sleep. I feel weak from the constant sweating, and worrying about staying alive. I finally have time to drink some water, the water's hot, but damn it tastes great! Word is passed down to us that we'll be securing the area up front, once full daylight is here.

Well, daylight's here, so we're moving up front to secure the village where our guys got ambushed! I guess the CO wanted us to take the wounded and dead out in case we might get overrun by the enemy. I hope they left, I don't need this shit. Every time I take a step I feel like it's going be my last step on Mother Earth. I feel at any moment I can step on a mine or get shot in the head. Here we go, we have to clear out the village. We start searching each hootch, one at a time. Shit, some of the guys just got opened up on! We could hear the firing and explosions going off. We all hit the ground. We hear through the grapevine that a few more guys just got killed, and few more got wounded while they were clearing out the opposite end of the village from us. We're still frozen in our tracks until we get clearance from the LT that we can proceed. We're not trained for hootch-to-hootch fighting, there's a lot we don't learn until it's too late, or almost too late. But like the guys say, "adapt, and overcome any situation even if it costs you your life." It's always about keeping one another alive, and doing the job right, if we want to see another sunrise.

The village has finally has been secured, and we've been ordered to secure the LZ where the ambush happened. We're walking along the hardtop road leading back into the village. There are three choppers in different stages of destruction scattered on the road. Each of them brought down by the enemy, a mix of NVA and VC. The helicopters are spread across an area the size of two football fields. It's gloomy, and tearing up my heart. I'm walking on the side of the road, and I still feel the ghosts of the recent battle hanging over the LZ. My heart and my soul feel heavy with grief and deep sorrow over what has taken place. It's overwhelming, and I can barely hold in my emotions. I fight myself and repeatedly blink my eyes to stop the tears from coming. I know every other Grunt, here, is feeling the same thing. The burned carcasses of the choppers leave dark, burned shadows on the dirt road. And scattered in every direction around the remains of the helicopters are twisted metal casings, craters, and blown-up chopper fragments. There are all kind of pieces of shrapnel from bombs and artillery rounds scattered on the ground, AK-47 shell casings, and M-16 shell casings mixed together in an eerie, torn-up landscape. Jungle, grasses, hootches, and trees for yards around the LZ are destroyed, there are enemy bodies lying around in different frozen stages of death. I see some are lying flat, others are curled into burnt fetal positions, and others are stiff in their spider holes alongside the road. The smell of death is floating over everything, it's burnt flesh mixed with diesel and aircraft fuel, burnt vegetation, the smell of blood, and the burnt sulfur of gunpowder. I smell it in my nostrils. I taste it on my tongue. I want to run to safety, and wash it all off my body, out of my nose, and out of my mouth. But there's no place to go. That smell has never left me.

I don't understand why the choppers tried to land on the road? They never do that! The closer we get to the LZ, the more destruction we see. Blood is splattered or soaked everywhere into the ground, on metal and equipment, and in what's left of the choppers. First Aid bandages, empty morphine capsules, bloody bandages, torn uniform pieces, evidence of heavy casualties are scattered around the entire area. All the equipment belonging to so many young men who got wounded or killed, young men who are not even old enough to drink and vote. The smell of blood and death is thick in the air, and makes me sick to my stomach. But it takes until noon, lots of hours to secure the LZ.

I can't believe it! Our CO was right! The choppers landed right in the middle of an NVA ambush in this village. When we move towards the LZ we move from the jungle edge, towards rice paddies, to crawl along a ditch that was dug between the rice paddies and the ARVN compound. Where the ditch approached the road, it split a big area of open terrain. Before it turned perpendicular to the rice paddies and it ran parallel to the road. Most of the open terrain was to our left, and we'd been receiving fire from our right side where there were some scattered hootches. The village was on the other side of the road, opposite from the rice paddies, ARVN compound, and open terrain.

The NVA and VC had set up fighting positions in a sort of "bracket" set-up. The solid line of the bracket and the main force of the ambush was in and around the hootches on the outer edge of the village, parallel to the road and facing it. The open terrain was straight across from their main firing positions. So the enemy could fire directly onto anything moving along the road or with the choppers, landing on the road! The enemy also had firing positions on the two side legs of bracket, on the two outer edges of the open terrain. The VC/NVA could fire at an angle up across the open terrain, to cut off any retreat for the Manchus, if they tried to move across the terrain back towards the rice paddies and the jungle edge. It was a perfect ambush.

The choppers landed in the middle of a kill zone. I just couldn't help but wonder how they got themselves caught in a classic ambush. An ARVN compound next to this village should have meant the village was secured – free of VC or NVA, instead the village was a hot spot of VC/NVA activity. It appeared that the ARVN stuck themselves behind their compound doing nothing to notify US Forces of the VC/NVA presence. Not only that, but they also failed to provide support of any kind when we were getting the shit kicked out of us! It's the ARVN's job to protect the villagers, and know who's coming or going from the village. From that point on, I hated the ARVN. They never came out of their compound, not once. Not when artillery was blowing up all around the LZ, not when our guys were getting killed and wounded. Not when the helicopters were burning, not even when we were clearing and securing the area! They wore their clean uniforms, and carried their brand new rifles, and never put a speck of dirt on them, here we were with our torn-up filthy uniforms, and our worn-out used weapons, and they had the new stuff. After that, I wanted to kill them whenever I saw them on our sweeps. Every time I saw their stupid little smiles, all I wanted to do was smack them across the face. I'm sure there were good ARVN soldiers, but all it takes is one bad apple to ruin the whole bunch for the rest of us who should have been able to depend on the ARVN.

"What kind of intelligence did the command get, before the ambush?" I thought to myself. "Whoever gave them the report that the village was secured, should have checked out the whole area! He should have brought his ass out here afterwards when we were cleaning up!!! He should have got a first-hand look at the carnage, here, so he could see that his report wasn't quite as accurate as he was led to believe." I was furious! Bunkers and spider holes were laid all through the complex of hootches and surrounding terrain that lay parallel to the road, it was so damn obvious that the VC and NVA had been planning and building their "military" complexes in the village, over a long period of time. My mind was racing and the sweat was still running down my face. I thought, "Someone had to see the construction activity taking place in this village! It's only about ten miles from Saigon. ARVN are everywhere, and their compound is right next to the village!"

The LT said it's time for us to take a break, eat our C-rations, and try to relax for a while. We finally secured the LZ for the entry of the recovery choppers. We're sitting or resting in different positions, along the road, only about 20 yards from the LZ. But we still have to be on guard because anything can happen out here. We've been up all night working our asses off trying to save as many of our guys as we can. We're beat, exhausted, and filthy. I look down at my clothes, and I realize with surprise that my fatigues are shredded at the elbows and knees, and that I'm bleeding in those places. I look at my hands. Dirt and grime are stuck in every crack of my fingers and nails. I feel the filth on my neck and face. My body is still running off of the adrenaline from the previous night and this morning, so I never felt the pain from all those cuts I endured while crawling in the ditches back and forth all night long, on my elbows and knees. I hear Chinooks coming in, and look up, I feel a sigh of relief pass through my body. It seems like they're coming to rescue me. Instead, they're here to recover what's left of the destroyed choppers. A Chinook has its cargo straps already hanging out and hovers over the carcass of a downed chopper. On the ground, guys scramble to and fro securing the straps onto the eyebolts of the chopper carcass. At the same time, other men pick up the bundled cargo nets dropped earlier from the tail of the Chinook, and they unbundle them. Their job is to open the cargo nets, collect any fuselage parts, and pile them into the cargo net for transportation out of the LZ. I can hear another Chinook chopper coming in to the LZ. The actions by the men securing the straps, collecting fuselage parts, and preparing the chopper carcasses look like a well-rehearsed activity. One that each man has done many times before. But it's not a well-rehearsed activity, it's the effort of men who've merged through battle, pain, and frustration into a brotherhood. Through that close-knit brotherhood they can work silently as a team to get an ugly job done that needs to get done.

This is the first time I've seen this, and so it strikes me as weird, like in a surreal way, to see choppers coming in and out, picking up and leaving with destroyed choppers. It's gruesome and sad to see. Men walk with heads down, bodies slumped, and all the movements are happening in a ghostly silence. I feel a heavy sadness hanging over the remains of the battle. I know my own feelings are just like everyone else's. My emotions want to give way to a release of tears, to wash away the pain and suffering I'm experiencing watching all this. But to maintain my sanity, I force my thoughts inward, toward memories of more pleasant days anything but the thoughts of the tragedy right in front of me out here. Suddenly, I hear the approaching whop-whop roar of gunship helicopter blades cutting the air. The gunships move in above the LZ, they circle the perimeter in wide circles, and watch the ground below for signs of enemy in the area. The cleanup of the LZ is happening like a major airport hub: Chinooks are arriving into position above the damaged battlefield and hovering overhead, men are connecting damaged choppers to Chinooks, they're packing and lifting cargo nets, men are policing and retrieving damaged equipment left by both friendly and enemy forces. Chinooks are flying away with the remains of the battle, gunships circle above watching the ground. I feel a mental sigh of relief interrupt my thoughts, immediately afterwards relief passes through my body, as I watch the gunships move to perform their protective missions. The arrival of the gunships makes me feel safer, I know they're able to provide plenty of fire support. The enemy may be "gone" for now due to the overwhelming war materiel on the ground, and in the air. But "gone" may only last until helicopters and men leave the scene. It's about 1500hrs (3:00 p.m.) now, and the last of the Chinooks are almost gone.

Seeing the mangled choppers hanging from the Chinooks makes me feel down and quiet. These emotions are new to me, I don't quite know how to put words to what I'm feeling. It's only with years of time passing that I can understand those complicated emotions better. At the time during and after the battle I couldn't comprehend that my 19-year-old innocence was dying. It was destroyed by war's violence, and would never return, I didn't know, then, that these experiences would impact my life for the rest of my time on Mother Earth. I wondered if I would be able to return to civilian life after these experiences. There was no such thing, then, as counseling for getting back into civilian life. Training for war teaches you tactics and how to survive *in* war but doesn't teach you how to survive *after* war. War takes a young, developing mind and exposes it to horrors and trauma, but nothing exists to help those young minds recover from the experience of war. Part of me realized I was changing, and the other part of me didn't understand the process occurring inside my mind and part of me wondered what I would become when this was over.

Looking at the mangled choppers, I can just tell that people died. I know the enemy sees and knows this, too. I feel the enemy nearby. He is still in the shadows of the jungle, hiding. And I know the enemy sees the Chinooks flying away with the destroyed choppers hanging beneath them, I sense that "He" takes pleasure and pride in the destruction that "He" has wreaked upon us. I know all our men and me, we all did well in bringing the ambushed Company out of the LZ. We risked everything to help these guys out. Our men were trapped, they couldn't get out of the ambush on their own, the situation was desperate. Not everyone steps into a Hot LZ, but we did. We did it to save the men from a hopeless situation and we succeeded. The need to rescue them was real, and I hope they would do the same for us. If it happens to us. I hope it never happens to us. Three months from now, I'll find out, though. That's when my Platoon walks into an ambush. But at this moment, here on the LZ, I realize (from the effects of this ambush) that being ambushed is a "deep shit" situation in which you pray to the Creator to receive backup in time to get your ass out of the kill zone.

We only find 15 dead VC, and seven NVA dead in the area. They must have carried the rest of them off. Just by the amount of new equipment the enemy left scattered across the battleground, we know there were a lot more of them maybe two Platoon-sized elements or more. Seeing what's left of their equipment, and all the destruction, I can't believe that I made it through the night. Last night was a nightmare: my emotions were up and down all night, like a roller coaster! Too many things happening at once, and they're never the same, the different kinds of weaponry fire and artillery explosions in bursts, single shots, rapid fire, close and faraway, zinging and snapping over my head, and bullets cutting through branches, trees, and low-lying jungle vegetation. A snap or zing half an inch to one side or the other might have meant me coming home wounded or in a body bag. All throughout the night I adapted and overcame. Some of my actions were just trial-and-error, some of them were training, and some of my actions were those of a new Infantryman. If I made mistakes last night, I didn't know they were mistakes, I had no choice if I wanted to survive. My 19-year-old mind is trying to deal with my actions and emotions from last night. My actions trouble me, and I hope I did the right things. I'm so tired of being out here, doing this, day after day. I'm trying to keep my sanity intact, but I just don't know if I can anymore.

We just got new orders. I can't believe that we're going to be staying the night here, and pull a night ambush somewhere in this area! Shit, this is going be another long night of the "unknown." It's only 1600hrs (4:00 p.m.), I can't believe people are riding down this road on their bicycles and two- or three-wheeled motor scooters, as if no battle ever took place here barely nine hours ago. I guess they saw the last of the destroyed choppers being taken away by the Chinooks, two hours ago. I suppose to them it means the battle is finally over.

There are too many people . . . I don't like this! I feel fearful again I can't tell if any of them might try to shoot me, or blow us up. It could be another trap in the making. They're wearing black pajamas and straw hats. We've always been told that black pajamas and straw hats out here in the jungle are signs of the VC. A free fire zone only exists from 1900hrs (7:00 p.m.) to 0700hrs (7:00 a.m.). If it's not a free fire zone, that means we can only fire if people fire at us first. But it's only 1500hrs (3:00 p.m.) now, so it's not a free fire zone. I'm nervous, because I can't tell if any of these people intend to fire on us. And if I see someone with a weapon, I wouldn't be allowed by free fire regulations, to fire on him. Only if, and when, he actually started firing on us.

This makes me antsy. The civilians are walking, riding bicycles and motor scooters, on the road. Parts of the road pass through the secured LZ that we're still monitoring. But it does give us a chance to do security checks on the civilians. Before we let them pass through the LZ, we stop random civilians and ask for their ID. "*Can Cuoc*, ID Card," we say to the Vietnamese. The Vietnamese stop, pull out their ID cards, and hand them to us so we can examine the IDs. We study the photos and check the province the person is from. If they're from a province too far away, then our own radar goes up and we have reason to detain them. We contact our interrogator/interpreter to come question the individual more closely, or take them back to Battalion HQ.

Some of the civilians are barefoot, and others are wearing tire-tread "Ho Chi Min" sandals, that are made from car tires or truck tires. None of them are wearing any closed shoes. A few of the people are walking with two baskets dangling on each end of a stick, which they carry only on one shoulder. Some are carrying hand baskets in their arms and hands. The baskets on sticks all have an assortment of items, from live chickens and ducks, to rice and vegetables, and pots and pans, the live chickens and ducks are closed in cages made of bamboo, and even these cages are hanging from sticks resting on shoulders. The ducks look ok, but the chickens are nasty-looking, with wilted feathers, bald spots and sores. The folks carrying baskets on the sticks look funny: their legs are bowlegged, and so their baskets move side-to-side, like a pendulum, even though their bodies, legs, and sticks are in forward motion. There's a kind of graceful rhythm to their walking movements. And the baskets all look heavy. The civilians must be on their way to or back from a marketplace in the area. Stopping civilians gives us a chance to ask an old lady how she carries the baskets on the sticks, and ask how heavy the baskets are. The old lady lets us lift the baskets on the sticks, and we learn that they are damn heavy! She shows us how to lift, carry, and walk with the baskets. There's a trick to it. We learn that the baskets on the sticks go on the shoulder. The carrier then starts a slow pendulum swing, side-to-side, with the baskets swinging side-to-side. Then the carrier starts a slow forward walk, with a slight swinging motion of the torso, hips, and legs, in rhythm to the baskets on the sticks pendulum motion. Then the carrier speeds up with each step, keeping in rhythm to the side-to-side in a forward motion. It's easy once I figure it out, and the odd side-to-side pendulum motion in rhythm with the walking makes the baskets feel like very little weight. I get it, now. The energy of the baskets swinging side-to-side in a forward motion, pulls and pushes the weight forward with little effort.

There are young girls dressed in white pajamas, and wearing straw hats. Some of the girls have sandals, some are barefooted. I was told that the difference between sandals and bare feet depends on how wealthy the girls' families are. How pretty the girls look in white! The boys dress in white shirts, the younger boys wear short pants, and the older boys wear long pants. The children dress in white to go to school. Some children look so poor, you can guess by the way they dress. These children are barefoot. The poor boys wear only well-worn, faded or dirty short pants and no shirts. These boys are dark, they are real tanned, probably from working out in the sun. The poorer boys approach us, walking towards us with their beat up little bicycles. The boys' front fenders of their bicycles hold soda cans in a small basket tied to the front fender, and on the back fender is tied a block of ice in a wooden box. They sell us cans of cold soda for a dollar. They chill the soda in a matter of minutes by quickly spinning the can continuously, by hand, on the block of ice. It's so smart! After only a few minutes, the soda is ice cold. I do wonder where they got their blocks of ice and soda. The only time I saw ice was at our main base camp. A cold soda here on the LZ is great, but we all feel real nervous with so many people around us at once and a huge battle barely ended a few hours ago. We're still on alert status, we're still keeping our guard up in the event we start getting attacked again. As far as we're concerned, the battles are never really over with. Because as long as we're in this jungle, we never know when the enemy might start shooting at us again. We have to stay in a fighting mind-set for our protection, and because of the nature of this war, here, in this jungle. But this civilian environment is something we've never been exposed to, there are too many Vietnamese civilians moving around us. We're always out in the jungle where there are few people. Most of the Vietnamese people we see deep in the jungle look primitive, poor, and dirty. But most of the time, though, most of the people we saw out in the jungle were the enemy, not the poor and dirty Vietnamese.

It was our CO who told us, earlier, that this area was not a free fire zone. "Not a free fire zone" means we can only fire when we're fired upon. Boy, all we need is more shit! We're in the winter months, April, May, June, July, August and it gets dark early, here. Only after curfew goes into effect at 1900hrs (7:00 p.m.) does this area became a free fire zone again. That's when we can shoot anything that moves at night. Curfew ends at 0700hrs (7:00 a.m.). That's when we stop shooting. We're still in a populated area, on the outskirts of Saigon. Hell, this is going to be the shits! My emotions are going crazy in this area, people are walking and motor scooters are moving around two feet by me, I don't know who is friend, and who is enemy.

My Company is lined up and spread out on both sides of the road, ready to go, but I guess we're waiting for the 1900hrs (7:00 p.m.) curfew so we can move out to our night location. All the civilians should be home by then. I just don't get it. Half-a-day ago, guys were dying left and right, here we are, smack in the middle of a civilian population, waiting for night to come or something to happen to us. Shots can fire at any time, and we'll be sitting ducks for a bullet, just sitting here on the roadside waiting for darkness to arrive. I just don't feel like this is a good idea waiting for darkness so we can go on an ambush. I don't know what our command is doing! I hope they do. I can't believe we're actually just sitting, waiting for nighttime. And while I'm sitting here, my emotions are running away from me out of fear. The night is so spooky here, because of the "unknown." I can feel myself reaching panic mode, then trying to calm down. My fear will intensify when we finally have to move out in a night ambush. It must be close to 1900hrs (7:00 p.m.). The road and trails are finally clear of civilians constantly moving around. Here we go. It's time to move out, up the road. I'm back in survival mode. It's getting dark now. The day gives a lot more distractions to allow me to take my mind off my fears. And giving me some comfort from my fears. But the night is full of fear, close, and confining. The day helps me keep my sanity: I can see a cloud, or an insect moving, or the bright green plants. There are thousands of other images to take me out of my fears of death for a moment. But at night there's no protection or distraction from the thoughts of death, which come to life in my mind so easily with the sunset. The night is deadly to my sanity. The dark is like a blanket of death prepared to pounce upon me, and take me with it into more darkness. I feel suffocated by this fear, in the black of the night. And I imagine uglier fates for myself, than what could really be true.

It's completely dark. During the day, we tried to switch our sleep breaks on and off, so we could take two-hour naps. But with the civilians constantly moving up and down the road, a sound nap was almost impossible. Sleep was interrupted by motorbikes and the rattling of pots and pans hanging from sticks, every step a villager took caused the damn metal to clang together. There were mosquitoes and flies buzzing over my head and biting, they forced me out of my already light dozing to swipe at the pests. There was so much heat and humidity, and kids trying to sell me Cokes, and sweat constantly dripping down my forehead into my eyes, making my eyes sting so bad I woke up trying to rub the sweat out of them. And red and black ants crawling up my pants or dropping onto the back of my neck from the trees above, biting the hell out of me and jerking me awake. I scrambled to pull the six-legged bastards off my skin, killing them by ripping apart their damn rugged little bodies.

"Saddle-up" has just been passed down the line. The light's fading and it's getting dark. Shadows are growing, mixing with the darkness. We need to put our equipment back on our backs so we can move out to our night location. We're moving out in a column, now. Death feels too close again, so I move out thinking, "I hate dealing with this over and over, but I'll do it by moving one step, one second at a time, and not thinking much past each step and hope for the best." As we move, I'm praying to myself and to the Creator that this step won't be my last step on Mother Earth. The Moon hasn't risen, and it's pitch dark outside. As I look up I could see how beautiful the stars look sparking in the dark night sky for a moment. As we walk past grass-mud hootches, I can see the little candle lights flickering in the night because the hootches don't have doors or the windows don't have glass. I can see people moving about inside the hootches, every now and then I hear voices and little babies crying. Each time a voice moves across the night air, I jerk. It startles me, and I feel my body tense. I get the jitters and I feel that any one of those civilians will be the one that puts a bullet in me. I have to control my thoughts and emotions. "Think of something, Joe. It's ok, Joe, I can keep moving. I have to keep putting one step in front of the other," I tell myself and I'm praying at the same time.

It's weird being out here in the wide open like this. My fears are building as we keep walking to our night location. Are these civilians really innocent? Or are they VC and NVA, just pretending to be civilians, tonight? If we get ambushed, innocent people are going to get killed. I don't know, anymore, who's "friendly" and who the "enemy" is. We've walked past two small villages, they're only about one-half mile apart from one another. It's damn stressful doing this shit when you're only 19, and you don't yet understand what life is all about. This is the shits!

All the villages, here, are so close together! We've passed through four villages, now, and every time we pass through one, I feel like a bullet's going to slam into my head. Each village we enter makes my anxiety rise, that is, until I'm out of the village. Then we enter another village and my anxiety rises all over again. It's hell feeling my anxiety go up, then down, then up, then down then up, up and down like an endless roller coaster, except that this is no fun ride that stops at the bottom, and everybody piles off. This is a roller coaster of life and death and one that we can't get off until we're on that "freedom bird" flying us home to the "good old USA."

We stop. We're at our night ambush location, now. We're setting up our ambush in the garden, between these two villages. No one's tried to shoot us yet. Maybe that's because we haven't walked on the paths, but we haven't walked on the perimeters of the villages, either. We've been walking through the villages, between hootches. Anyone trying to shoot at us could easily have missed and wound up shooting into a hootch. Maybe that's why we haven't been ambushed but now it's time to set up our ambush location, soon things will change. The ambush location is between the paths leading out of the village to the left of us, and into the village on the right side of us. I can't tell if the path is a road or a trail. The terrain in Vietnam changes so fast, especially after the rains. Something that looks like a little-used trail to us at night, can be a heavily-used road for ox and carts, during the day. It's 2100hrs (9:00 p.m.) now. We've put our Claymore mines out. Our LT said that we can open up on anyone coming down the road, and shoot to kill. Since the only people out at night are the enemy.

It's been another long night, and the Moon is out, now. I can't believe that we're setting up a night ambush in the middle of these villages. It's weird. This damn heat, and the stress I'm under are making me sweat a lot. It's seems like we've walked a long way. My muscles ache from the patrolling, the sweating, and the constant tension that I feel. The noises, here, are so different from the usual noises we hear in the jungle: I hear people talking, somebody's got a radio on and it's playing Vietnamese music. Babies are crying someplace. In the darkness, far off in the distance, chickens, ducks, and dogs are making noises but it's hard to tell how far away since sounds carry for long distances in the night air. It's like an orchestra of human and animal activity being carried in towards us, in the dark of the night.

It's midnight, and all is quiet so far. Suddenly, off in the distance, about 10 to 20 miles away, I see the sky light up out in the jungle. Light spreads and looks like a halo across the horizon, lasting 10 to 20 seconds. It's so bright it lights up the jungle in our area, I can see shadows and outlines around us. It was eerie. After another 10 to 20 seconds, I hear bombs exploding, and the ground shakes under me. The shaking seems like it goes on a very long minute, and in my mind it seems like Mother Earth is crying out to me in her pain from the explosions.

From this distance the explosions sound like a deep rumbling roar. It's a B-52 strike. The bright flashes of light on the horizon are "arc-lights," from the B-52 bomb strikes. I don't know it then but later I learn that B-52s carry a payload of 54,000 to 74,000 pounds of bombs. It turns the night sky into daylight for miles around, I know immediately that a Company of men are going to have to go check that area out, tomorrow. My Company has done it, before. I'm sure we'll have to do it again but tomorrow, I just hope it's not us.

Boy, that air-strike sure brings me back to reality! I just remembered I'm still at war . . . to kill, or be killed.

It's 0425hrs (4:25 a.m.) now. It's been a long night, lying here. The Moon is still out. I'm thinking of home, again, in between the aches and pains, and suffering. My mind is working 100 miles an hour trying to keep "me" together in this hellhole. It's so hard pushing myself, keeping my shit together. We're doing "two men on" and "two men off" – two men on guard and two men asleep. We don't have any thermometers but it has to be close to 100 degrees all night, tonight. I've been lying still all night, but sweat's been pouring off me, rolling down my forehead, dripping into my eyes, the salt from my sweat keeps burning my eyes. Like always, I don't want to take a chance moving my arm to rub the salt out of my eyes. Moving might give away our position. All I can do is blink my eyes. All these damned mosquitoes buzzing around and biting me. All I can do is let them bite me. If I swat them away, I'll give away my location. I haven't moved in hours. I'm so stiff. I've been sweating so much my jungle fatigues are sopping wet, my armpits are wet, my back is wet, my shirt is wet, even my socks are wet. Everything is wet! Any salt in my body is now on my fatigues. I'm losing so much water and so much salt. My muscles ache, and I'm getting a charley-horse on my calf! Boy, I've tried everything to get rid of the charley-horse, wiggling my toes, tightening and untightening my calf, pointing my toes to stretch my calf. But it's still hurting! It hurts so bad, my eyes are tearing up! I want to move so bad, but moving would break the Grunts' code of honor to take the pain never make noise, and don't move don't *do anything* that could give away our position, so we can all survive this night! I've got to take the pain. I don't want to give away my location! This cramp is a sure sign that my body's been pushed to its limits. I didn't know my body could react with cramps this excruciating. Time after time, since I've been in-country, my body's experienced agonizing conditions that I never dreamt I could endure. I'm hungry, exhausted, and hurting all at the same time. I do what I can to relieve the aches and pains my body's experiencing in this environment. This sure isn't like the war movies I saw back home. I never knew I could suffer through so much in one night. And at the same time, knowing it'll start all over again, tomorrow. And each day, hoping I live to see the next sunrise before I get killed. Then daytime comes, and I'm hoping I live to see the Moon come up. It never ends, the pain, the suffering, the loneliness, the panic of being terrified. It's all so constantly on my mind I try to think of pleasant things out here, but something always slams me right back to the reality of this hellhole.

I can see the dark outlines of bamboo trees around us, and over by the two villages that we're in between. The ground stinks from manure. The villagers use it to grow their crops. They spread it on the ground as fertilizer. Aside from human and animal shit, who knows what else is in the manure! We never have time to pick up even a little bit about the culture, we're always on the move from one place to another. But no one needs to learn about manure, it stinks! And it burns my damn nose! But I'm stuck here all night long, and my only option is to lie here, suck it up, and take it! Everything about these damn night ambushes and patrols is one big question mark you never know what type of environment you'll encounter, tonight it's shit!

We're still lying in the field between the two villages. I'm lost in my own thoughts, and trying to get some sleep. I just close my eyes, when one of the guys next to me taps me on the shoulder and points toward the road. I look out toward the road. Since it's still dark, it takes me a few seconds to focus my eyes on what he was pointing at. I see movement in front of me, about 50 yards down the road. I see part of the outlines of several people on the road, walking. I don't have a complete view of what's on the road, the darkness, shadows, and vegetation make it hard to get a clear view of the road, so I can't tell how many people there are. It looks like they're walking with their bicycles next to them. They're speaking in low voices and I can barely hear them. But one of the bicycle wheels must have needed oil because it squeaked every time the wheel turned. The people, whoever they were – probably didn't know they'd just walked into the middle of our ambush or maybe they did know, I can't tell. I wait for one of our guys to set off his Claymore mine. But I don't want the "walkers" getting out of the kill zone. So I squeeze the handle to my Claymore mine several times. The Claymore explodes. I duck my head as the concussion from the back blast rushes past me, two more Claymores go off, from other locations, and then a fourth one explodes!

The explosions wake up the villages all around the immediate area. Dogs start barking, and a baby starts crying inside one of the hootches, from all directions, chickens, ducks, and other animals start squawking in their pens. In between all the noise, I hear startled adults and children wake up, some screaming hysterically or yelling in fear. Wondering if they were going to be killed next. The area wasn't a complete free fire zone due to all the civilians, so we're not allowed any artillery or mortar fire support. We can't have illumination rounds either, the flares will start fires on these grass roof huts. We don't want to give away our positions by firing our weapons, either. Our muzzle flashes will expose our locations. All we can do now is wait . . . and wait . . . and wait to see what's happening next. We don't know if someone's going to take any action against us. We don't know if the villages are VC. We don't know if another group will "walk" down the road. We don't know if we just killed a group of innocent civilians. We don't know anything yet. The only thing we know is that the "walkers" were out long after curfew and moving about before daylight.

I'm shaking because I just killed the "walkers." Did I do the right thing? Should I have waited for an order? Was I supposed to wait? Was I supposed to wait for a signal from the LT? Shit, what did I just do? Did I have the legal right to set off the Claymore, or did I just fuck up? Am I going to get court-martialed? Shit! This was a free fire zone, right? That's what they told us, isn't it? They said "no one is supposed to be on the road after dusk, till dawn." The villagers know that, don't they? Only the enemy would be out on the road during curfew . . . wouldn't they? What if it was just kids out enjoying a night, and they forgot about the curfew? Shit, I've broken my own curfews when I was in high school! Boy! The unknowns can really get to you out here, especially the waiting. I just don't know what's going to happen next. I just don't know how I take this shit day after day and night after night.

It's about 0500hrs (5:00 a.m.) now. The Moon's gone, and it's still pitch dark. Now it's 0530hrs (5:30 a.m.), and the Sun is finally starting to rise. The light in the sky is getting brighter. I'm starting to feel a little relief from being scared all night. It won't be long till curfew ends at 0700hrs (7:00 a.m.).

I'm waiting for the Sun to come up all the way. Time feels like it's really dragging, and I'm still waiting for the "unknown" to transpire in this hellhole. I can't believe the thoughts that are running through my head. I don't know if the people in the village will take any action against us or my CO. All I can do is wait and wait.

My thoughts are running 100 miles an hour, and I'm nervous about what I did earlier tonight. I'm hoping to see the sunrise to come up all the way. There's just enough Sun, now, that I can see the silhouettes of the bodies in the road. It's 0610hrs (6:10 a.m.), the Sun is up, and it's completely daylight. I feel some relief that it's not dark anymore, the dark brings its own fears to my mind. With daylight, here, I don't feel as vulnerable as I do in the dark, the daylight feels less terrifying, less confining, to me. When the Sun is low and daylight is gone, and darkness creeps along the horizon, my mind pictures that Death is coming. In my mind's eye, the darkness is like Death . . . a Death that reaches for me, and chases me, it wants to grab me and suffocate me. In the dark, I have nowhere to run from the arms of Death which constantly reach for me, in my own mind. The daylight frees me from my imagination, and gives me the strength to push on.

THE WALKERS IN A NIGHT AMBUSH
July 1968

It's time to check out the area. A few of us rise from our positions, and cautiously walk toward the road. Boy we're stiff and our bodies ache with every step. Our weapons are pointed out, ready to fire. I can see that we killed six VC. The bodies, and three bicycles, lie where they fell. As we approach, I count three young men, two young girls, one young boy. And a *baby*! There's blood covering the ground, and the bicycles are splattered with it. Oh my gosh, these Claymore mines can really do the job! The Claymores shredded their little bodies, making a mess of them. They were kids like me – much too young! Each of them had weapons, even the young boy. The young boy looked no older than twelve, and like us – the girls were in their late teens! Two of the men were in their early twenties, and the third one must have been in his thirties. The baby looked no older than a one-year-old!

My heart is straining at the sight of the infant. I'm horrified. But I make every attempt to show no emotion, I have a job to do. Why the hell did they have a baby with them! I will never know the answer to that question. Maybe they thought we'd never place an ambush out here in a populated area. My mind is racing with thoughts, I know the explosions happened in a free fire zone *after* curfew, I still cannot completely justify what happened, in my mind. I'm confused and conflicted. It all takes a toll on my own mind, and I realize that this event has the power to break me mentally. The military trains you to use your weapons, and to do it efficiently, but there's no training for this type of situation. This is *bullshit*! I just don't know anymore. Things have been bad over here, and getting worse, now, I have to live with this shit! Now, I have to try dealing with it on my own! We're all in shock at what we just did! We can only look at one another with sad, faraway looks, and shake our heads in disbelief. We don't say a word to one another. Our eyes say it. We don't dare speak, or our emotions right now will tumble out and overflow. We're men and soldiers. We're not supposed to cry. We have the job of soldiering to do. But even continuing to look at one another and seeing the quiet, tearful looks we see in each other's eyes might cause our emotional dams to break. The pain of what we've done and seen, is threatening to break our will. I think to myself, "What in the hell are we doing here?"

War is not supposed to happen this way. These kinds of moral dilemmas don't happen in the war movies I've seen. I fired off the first Claymore, and set off a chain reaction of Claymore explosions by the other guys. The LT didn't tell me to fire my Claymore. I did it because I was told that the curfew is in effect and the area is a free fire zone. Even though I had mixed emotions about firing, I still fired first, so I'm the one responsible for the deaths of those six people and the infant. None of the other guys in my Unit wanted to be the first to fire. By the time I fired, the VC men and women were almost out of the kill zone. Before I fired, I couldn't help thinking, "I've broken curfew before, at home, but my punishment wasn't getting fired on. These people could be innocent folks out too late from just spending time with one another. This is confusing. They could be me, at home, out late on a date."

No one tells you that this type of thing will happen or might happen! I finally decided to fire my Claymore, because the group was getting out of the kill zone. If the group was VC, then we just let them get away, and then they could kill us, instead. I was thinking, "Kill or be killed." Four months ago, I was a happy, 19-year-old Native-American teenager, with no real interest in the outside world. I was doing what most teenagers do, all over the USA, going to the movies, hanging out with friends, seeing my girlfriend. But then, I was drafted into this hellhole. I never wanted to be here. One day, a notice came that changed my life. I was drafted. I was forced to be here.

Now, I'm a killer. How am I supposed to live with that? All my life, I was taught that the Bible says, "Thou shall not kill." I had my Native faith, but I was raised Catholic, too. Now I've just broken one of the biggest commandments of the Bible. How am I going to answer to the Creator for that? How am I going to live with that? Why in the hell would our military commanders put us in a populated area and say, "It's night-time, it's a free fire zone, if anyone violates curfew, kill them." Oh my gosh, what are we doing here!? Now, I can say I know what war is like. But at the same time, there's no way to explain war. There's no way to explain its consequences, and there's no way to explain the wrong or rightness of war. Each war is different, and each soldier has to deal with it in his own way.

The group of men and women, lying dead on the road, had a lot of money, paperwork, and maps on them and weapons on them. Our leadership has told us that in the northern rural hamlets, the VC collect and/or confiscate money from the inhabitants, to buy supplies used by the VC. I guess these six people were confiscating money from the folks in the local villages. Why else would they have all that money on them, let alone the paperwork and maps, and weapons? It all proves that these three men and two women and a kid were VC. A day and a half ago our guys were dying left and right. Why? These dead kids lying on this road are as young as we are or younger. This seems like relative against relative, here, this doesn't seem like something we can win. It feels like a no-win situation. We fight so hard to take an area and then we give it right back to them. Why are we here? I just don't get it.

It's been half a century, since I saw the bodies of those kids and the baby lying in the road. We loaded their little mangled bloody bodies onto a chopper to take them back to our main base camp, to identify who they were. Even now, I can't get close to kids or babies. I'm scared to hold them. I couldn't even hold my own two children when they were babies and kids. Something happened to me on that sad day, decades ago. I can't explain it. Life is what it is and you have to make the best of things, regardless. Life's not fair . . . especially in war.

Our LT got on the radio to report the events of last night. Our Company had three Platoons spread throughout different ambush locations and each had to report intelligence back to the CO. Our LT forwarded information about the road ambush: body count, bodies, weapons, bicycles, paperwork, and money. The CO ordered a chopper out to our location to pick up and transport everything back to MI (Military Intelligence). MI needed to take a look at all the stuff, try to identify the bodies. And determine where they were from. As always, we secured the area for the chopper. Just as the sound of the chopper engines came into range, our LT told us to get ready to load the bodies plus any other items from the bloody scene onto the chopper. My LT didn't say anything to me about the ambush, I guess I made the right decision, after all, to fire off my Claymore last night.

It's 0700hrs (7:00 a.m.), the curfew has lifted. Me and the rest of my Platoon are resting along the road, waiting for orders from the LT, and watching the scenes of village life around us. People are coming out of their huts, and starting their daily routine. From the activity around us, I would never guess that an ambush took place or that six people and a baby had just been blown to bits. The only evidence is the blood on the road, and it doesn't take long before the dust and dirt covers up the blood.

The ox-carts, bicycles, and foot traffic moving up and down the dirt road soon remove any signs of the deaths. Watching this makes me feel disconnected and dizzy. Me and my Platoon are resting, but our mental radar is on full alert for any threats to us. But around us, life goes on as if there's no war, no blood, people are moving back and forth on the road. Villagers are rising and dressing, preparing breakfast, starting work. But for us, there's danger, exhaustion and frustration, death, and blood. I wish that what I did last night would disappear from my thoughts, as easy as the dirt and dust makes the blood disappear from the surface of the road. I don't like being around all these villagers. You don't know who the enemy might be. I'm very nervous, the other guys, too. Knowing that the enemy can be kids, now, makes us even more anxious, I'll be glad when we're back in the jungle. So we don't have to deal with this kind of bullshit from all these civilians. I can't believe it, I want to go back into the jungle just to get away from this shit! I want to get away from killing kids, and from worrying about kids killing me! It's finally time to move out to our LZ. We have to walk about a mile down the road and we've got to patrol every damn step of the way through a crowd of civilians who may or may not plan to kill us!

People in black pajamas are walking, or riding their bicycles along the same road that we're patrolling. Their conical straw hats look like someone took a circular flat straw plate, cut it along the radius and made a 35-degree cone with it, they're strapped to villagers' chins with silk or linen strips of cloth. The hat, a *non la*, does a great job of keeping the Sun off the upper back, face, and shoulders. Air can flow from the pointed cone on top of the hat and keeps the head cool, almost everyone wears one. Some of the villagers have big baskets tied onto their bicycles, they are either pedaling or pushing the bicycles depending on the size of the baskets.

Every now and then we stop one of the bicyclists or the people walking: we check for their Vietnamese ID (*Can Cuoc*), and the paperwork that gives them permission to travel through different provinces. And we check the baskets for any weapons or explosives. The baskets have food, or personal belongings, or pots and pans used for cooking, and lots of other items. The travelers usually carry pots and pans to cook their food while they travel, you can tell which pots and pans they use for their own cooking, since those pots and pans are well used, with burn marks, dents, and cheaply made tin or aluminum. I try to pick up one of the baskets, and it must weigh about 50 to 100 pounds, or more. Boy, it's heavy. Even some of the guys from our Platoon try picking it up just to see how heavy it is. For a moment, when we're experimenting with the baskets like this, it doesn't feel like we are in a war. With all these people around us laughing and smiling. Little kids laughing, selling us sodas again and speaking English, that adds to the feeling of being civilians hanging out in the countryside.

But what makes us nervous are the villagers, adults and kids, who don't smile, frown, or seem intimidated by us. Or the ones who scurry away from us, or who seem to carry some hidden anger towards us. We stop these individuals and investigate a little deeper into their behavior towards us. But normally, all these individuals do is clam up, answer with a single "Yes" or "No," or as few words as possible, and with very little emotion. Not quite poker-faced, but with more dread or fear hidden behind their responses. It's hard to tell if some of these people have experienced a lost loved one due to the war, because of

American soldiers. Or maybe they lost some precious income or objects just because some American soldier had taken objects of value from the villager, as souvenirs. Some American soldiers could be real jackasses about the way they treated the villagers, especially, in war. Some American soldiers just couldn't see the villagers as people, and tended to look down on all of them.

I saw the villagers as just human beings in a difficult situation. When I saw these people with their primitive tools and baskets, I knew these things were more valuable than money. Back home when we Native Americans made a basket or our tools it took a lot of time to make one. Money wasn't that important to us. But our handmade tools and baskets were. I didn't have the hate towards them that some of my fellow soldiers had. I felt sad for those villagers, I know how it is to be hated, because of my Native American culture. I experienced racism and bigotry because of it. While I was growing up in California, being Native American wasn't considered cool. Lots of Americans had negative stereotypes about us, and many beautiful aspects of our culture were taken from us. Even these days, stereotypes haven't changed that much, and Native peoples and their cultures are still ignored and abused in this country. But as a human being I try to live with it the best way I know how. But I still love our land in the country that was once ours, the good old USA.

Our Platoon is still moving down the road. Our Platoon and the rest of our Company's Platoons are supposed to gather at the rice paddies, about a mile or so down the road. That's where we'll get ready for our Eagle Flight out. It's a big rice field big enough for all the choppers needed to pick up our whole Company. It's going to be another hot day to deal with. We've been told that after our pick-up, we'll be flying up North, into the jungle, for another mission.

The choppers pick us up, and we head to Dau Tieng Base Camp, instead of another mission out in the jungle. Dau Tieng is one of our bigger base camps, about 40 miles Northwest of Cu Chi Base Camp. We go into Dau Tieng for a Stand-Down. Boy we sure need it! We've been through a lot so far being out in the jungle. I think a lot of us are stressed out by what we've been through so far. I still don't feel right about what I did that night, I keep trying to justify it in my head. I hope I can keep my shit together out here. I've never been through so much pain and suffering and seen so much death all at once. The more I'm out here the harder it is to keep on going and living this way, I just hope I can keep it together.

We've finally made it to the pick-up zone in this big rice paddy. We've secured the area around the rice paddy. We're waiting on the outside perimeter of the rice paddy, watching the pick-up zone from the jungle line. We're waiting for the choppers to come in and the other Platoons to come into the LZ. When the choppers finally come in, one of us will pop yellow smoke. The yellow smoke grenade tells us that the choppers are close and on their way, that all the Platoons are in the LZ, that we all need to get ready to board the Eagle Flights. I hear a "pop" and I look over at the direction the sound is coming from, and I see yellow smoke rising from a smoke grenade. I feel nervous and my emotions are getting excited again. Then I notice, our Platoon is getting ready to move out into the LZ in their groups. That's when we'll run and spread out into the middle of the rice paddy, in staggered groups of seven, moving into our rehearsed positions like always to board the choppers when they land. One of the guys pops a purple smoke grenade to show the choppers the landing location, and show them that it's clear to land, and that we will be boarding, shortly. When the purple smoke grenade goes off, most of us get anxious. That's because we know that Charlie is probably out there hiding in the jungle, waiting for the opportunity to fire on us, once those choppers start landing. We're vulnerable once we move into the open, and into position for the choppers, we know the choppers are coming in. We can hear them, now. Most of us are kneeling down, with the butts of our weapons on the ground. We're nervous and anxious, and we keep scanning the jungle line for any sign of enemy action. Our heads turn left, then right, and our eyes dart about looking for any sign that we're about to start getting fired on. Then we swivel our heads behind us to check our rear, then back to our fronts again. And then we quickly scan the sky, anxiously looking for the choppers. It only takes about a minute or two for the choppers to come into sight and land, but it feels like an eternity, an eternity with sweat pouring down our faces and onto our collars and from our hands. From the anxiety of watching for any enemy movement.

From the air, the chopper pilots see the formations we're in on the ground, and move in to land next to each group of Grunts. It's a well-rehearsed tactic, one we've done many times. The choppers fly in staggered formation, in the middle of a rice paddy staggered according to the groups of the Grunts waiting on the ground. Then we each quickly get up and sprint to our designated chopper which is the closet chopper to our individual groups and get on board. The choppers lift up, into the air, and I can see the top of the jungle as we leave and every now and then a village that was cut out of the jungle, the jungle is like an ocean of different shades of deep green, and thick with foliage. Looking down and seeing the rough and dangerous jungle, I feel relieved we're leaving this area. Even glancing at the jungle from this height, I feel like I'm in awe because of the thick canopy, and relieved to be free of the confining environment, below. Then I see the Saigon River and part of a burnt-out village near the river and that stupid ARVN compound where we were a few days ago. Then all of a sudden tears start coming down my face, all I can think of is those young kids and how bad they looked. Then I tell myself inside of me, suck it up.

Then I feel a cool wind blowing on my face and the vibrations of the chopper. It feels good to be in the air, again, and away from both the war and the jungle for a moment. It feels safe being up in the air, I can finally relax for a few minutes. All the stress and emotion is gone for a little while. Boy, how precious these moments are. But as soon as I think I'm relaxing, I get scared again wondering where we're going. What kind of place will we be landing in? We've been flying for only ten minutes. I look out the side of the helicopter, towards the direction we're flying. In the distance, I see streams of smoke rising out of the jungle. One column is in front of us, a second column is to the side of us, and a third column is just behind us, the columns of smoke are telltale signs of several battles taking place. Watching the smoke, I can feel myself getting anxious and sweaty, again. We're headed to another Hot LZ! As I watch the smoke, expecting that we're going to land up ahead, our helicopter makes a 90-degree hard left bank away from the smoke, and flies towards a large base camp in the distance.

I feel relieved to see the base camp. As we get closer to it, I see a dirt runway, instead of tarmac. Where are we headed, now? My mind flashes through several possible scenarios as we approach the airstrip. Are we going to switch helicopters and head up North? Is another chopper group taking over? Are we still headed towards those columns of smoke I saw earlier? I'm so exhausted, I almost don't care anymore. We've been on the go, now, for a couple of months, moving directly from one location to another, and then to another and another . . . and another. I see trucks near the runway. "What are those for?" I think to myself. We approach the landing strip and finally come in for a landing. I can hear the engines whining at a higher pitch as we slow down for the landing. The closer we get to Mother Earth, to the ground, the more the chopper blades kick up the wind, sending the runway dirt flying all around us. I hear the blades chopping the air, making a "whop-whop" sound in the moments just before we touch down. We get off the choppers and line up in Company formation behind our LT. He tells us to line up in groups of 20 guys by the trucks, so we can load up. We still have no idea what we're doing here at the base camp, and most of what we're doing right now, is "monkey-see, monkey-do." We run towards the trucks and line up.

I feel the heat rising from the ground, and the sweat starts pouring down my face. I glance at the other Grunts standing in line with me, and I can see sweat pouring off their faces, too. I look over at the truck driver, he looks so clean and neat. His shoes and fatigues look brand new, his fatigues are ironed and starched. He has Division patches, name tag, and rank on his uniform, he's also clean shaven. I think about myself and the other Grunts standing in line. We're filthy. Our fatigues are faded and sweat-stained. Our boots are covered with dirt and dried mud, and the leather is shredded and torn. Our faces are covered in dirt and sweat, we've been in the field for months. Seeing the contrast between the driver and me, makes me feel out of place, in a war, where we are all supposed to be at war. Where do we fit in, in their social structure?

The LT gives the order to load up on the trucks, so we load up. The trucks are "deuce-and-a-halves," the military's standard troop transport. It has "cattle" seats (benches) along both sides of the bed and a "cattle" railing around the bed. In Vietnam, most of the deuces never had canvas covers over the truck beds, out in the field. A Grunt couldn't see through a canvas cover, and there was no time to be walking in and out of a canvas-covered truck. Supplies and ammo just get tossed right over the railings. The deuce-and-a-half is so high off the ground that you had to climb into the truck by putting the tailgate down, first. Then you grab the railing and step onto the tailgate handle. Then climb up the tailgate into the truck. The first man into the truck usually helps the others into the truck by grabbing their hand and pulling them up, and also usually grabs their equipment. A man with all his gear could get easily bogged down trying to climb up, he was just as likely to plop off the tailgate without someone helping him. And as tired as we were, climbing up the tailgates, and into the deuces took a lot of effort on our part. But once we got in, we collapsed onto the benches and on the floor of the bed of the truck. Sitting there, on the bench, with the breeze in my face, I thought I was in heaven.

The drivers drove us to a compound about two and a half miles on the other side of the base where we can stay for the night. You could feel the hot air blowing on our faces and it was a bumpy ride on the dirt road as we went to the compound. The compound looked deserted like a ghost town and dirty. But at least we have a roof over our heads for now. We were far off in the compound, to keep us away from the rest of the base camp personnel. They didn't like us to mingle with the guys "in the rear with the gear." And to see how much better living conditions they had and how they had it easier than us! Now that we were at the compound we can refresh and resupply and rest for a while. This is what they call a Stand-Down, when they bring us to a main base camp so we can all rest at the same time for awhile and clean our weapons and be safe in a safe area. Maybe a day or two we might be here. We don't have to do patrol or night ambush. We sure need to get some rest and have time for ourselves.

They bring us ice cold soda and cold beer and fresh hot food to eat. And they bring us clean clothes to the compound so we can change. This time they are brand new clothes and boots. Out in the field they always gave us hand-me-down clothes. We all look at each other, we can't believe they're issuing us brand-new clothes this time. There must be something wrong. Also they escort us to the PX, to get haircuts at the barber shop next to the PX. Then we go some place to take a shower and shave. Boy we sure needed this! We looked real ragged coming in and we were real burnt-out being on so many missions. We were told we have two days of rest here. And then we'd be off again back in the jungle. To me it wasn't long enough! I guess they didn't want us to get used to the good life around here, it wasn't like being out in the bush.

We found out we won't be going down South anymore around all those civilians around Saigon. We'd be going up North from now on into the jungle. No more Eagle Flights or hedge-hopping three or four times a day along all those canals and rice paddies. Crossing those canals and open rice paddies from day to day, what a mind trip that was. Being in the middle of the canal and sometimes up to your chest in water and sometimes over your head. Then in the rice paddy out in the open where the enemy can easily put a bullet in your head before you could get to the other side. What a way to die. Boy that was the shits to do day after day after day. I'd never been under so much pressure and stress, being out in the open like that.

It's been a long time since I was back in the rear with the gear all the way back to my first day in Vietnam when I came in-country. That's when I was in a big fire support base camp. I never felt so alone back there in Cu Chi base camp. These guys have it made around here in Dau Tieng. It was like being Stateside. They had a PX store, theater, and mess hall with fresh food, TV, radio, beds, and a roof over their heads. They even had fans to keep them cool and showers every day! Boy, we're lucky to get fresh water. Now I know why they kept us away from the rest of the compound.

They didn't want us to feel bad because they had all the comforts of home. Or maybe they felt bad that they had it made and we didn't. All I know it wasn't fair to keep us out there so long. Day after day and night after night for three to four months at a time. Then just to give us a few days to rest and to freshen up. Unless you got wounded, then they had to bring you in early. Or if the Company got hit real hard they would bring the whole Company in at once, to get us some new replacements to fill in the KIA (Killed in Action) and WIA (Wounded in Action). But we never were full strength, we never had enough men, a Platoon was supposed to have 40 men, but we never had more than 20 or 25 men. All I knew we had it bad and we were at the bottom of the barrel. Like it or not we did all we could to survive out there.

It was nice being back in a big base camp in Dau Tieng to freshen up and not to have to worry about being on patrol, or sweep, or a night ambush and to be on guard 24/7. But then in no time they told us it's time to move out again. To get ready for the trucks to take us to the dirt landing strip, where the choppers are going to pick us up again.

Boy where did the time go! The rest of the guys and me weren't ready to go back out in the jungle. I guess they didn't want us to get too comfortable being here. So here we go again on another Eagle Flight in the land of OZ, on a mission where the little people are trying to kill us in the land of OZ. It was kind of funny. We all looked so young in our brand-new fatigues and all cleaned up, we looked like a bunch of cherry boys. But our eyes had that thousand-yard stare and that scared look of war and battle fatigue. It made us feel like old men inside ourselves. Our faces showed we were hardened soldiers that had been in a lot of battles.

Boy here come the trucks. I got scared again and I felt sick again in my stomach. I didn't really want to go. But we all got our equipment and our gear on and our clean weapons ready. We were all ready to go, with mixed feelings again. It's always the same when we go on a new mission, we were all scared and nervous to go. We loaded up on the trucks when they came and went through the compound to go to the airstrip on the other side of the base camp. As we were looking out from the back of the truck you can see the other GIs, all clean with their patches on. They were smiling and walking around doing their thing and so carefree in what they were doing. Here we were, stressed, scared, tense, and nervous. Trying to keep it together and to get ready to face death again. What a life for a Grunt! "The will of a Grunt is the will to live."

It feels like I've been here for years! You just don't realize how long a day is until you've been in war and in battle. I just hope I can keep on going through this shit. It's a rough ride going to the other side of the base camp on this dirt road to the airstrip where the choppers are coming in to pick us up for another mission. The truck driver said it's time to unload the truck and wished us good luck where we were going. So we get off the trucks and then the trucks leave, kicking up a lot of dust. Now we are sitting by the airstrip, it's an eerie feeling waiting for the choppers to come in. We are leaning against the wall of sand bags, about four feet high, that protects the choppers from incoming rounds from the enemy. We are trying to stay out of the Sun by staying in the shadow from the walls of sand bags. It's another hot day.

Your mind is running away with all kind of thoughts, just sitting here. You're hoping and praying that you can get through this new mission. You never know what kind of mission it's going to be, things are always changing from one moment to the next. All you can do is hope for the best and try to stay alive out here. What a life for us Grunts to be out here waiting for death and the unknown to happen.

I was in deep thought and before I knew it someone shouts out, "Here they come!" You just can't imagine the feeling that goes through your body when you see and hear the choppers coming. It feels like death is coming. I can hear them and I can see them now. Like little black dots far off in the blue sky with some clouds. What a sight to see all these choppers coming in closer and closer and all at once. We put on our equipment and get up on our knees and get ready to run to the choppers. As soon as they touch the ground for us to get on board they blew all kinds of dust in our faces, like always. It's hard to see, I can taste the dust in my mouth. We start running to the choppers in groups of seven per chopper. As I'm running I'm thinking how scared I am and hoping I make it home from this mission! I make it to the chopper and hop on board, I'm the last one to get on the chopper. All the choppers start lifting up about the same time with their noses pointing down and lifting up into the air and away we go to our new mission to the unknown again. It's always the unknowns that really get to you. You just can't imagine how it feels in that type of environment. How your mind puts all kinds of bad thoughts in your head. Trying to fight all the fear that's running through your body and your head. Trying to live like that from day to day. Hoping and praying that you come home in one piece and not in a body bag.

Well here I am sitting on the floor-plate of the chopper trying to calm myself as we go to our next mission again. Like always, being up here I can finally relax for a moment from the war. I feel so safe, but uncertain about our mission. Smelling the sweet fresh air calms me for a moment and so do the beautiful puffy white clouds in the sky. I try to see an image in the clouds and think of something pleasant, Mom and me used to lay down on the ground and look up into the sky and look at the clouds and see if we could see images and she'd tell stories about the images. What good times they were. What the hell? I feel my stomach go up. The chopper starts to descend. Here we go again to our new LZ, the unknown. The LZ looks like the Moon with all its craters. But these craters are bomb craters, it looks like a new B-52 strike that happened the day before. This is going to be one hell of a mission, to check this area out. Going in and around and out of those bomb craters looking for any enemy and setting up a night ambush in this area is going to be a living hell. That's all we need, more shit to be in. That's the life of a Grunt – "being in the shit."

MY FIRST NIGHT ON LISTENING POST
August 1968

We've been out in the bush for about four months so far already. I just got though marking my short-timer calendar again on my helmet for another day in Vietnam. I've been here in Vietnam 112 days so far. I still have 253 days left to do, it seems to be a lifetime away before I can ETS (Expiration of Term of Service) out of here. I just can't believe I don't know what day or month it is today. I only know the number of days I have been here and the days I have left because of my short-timer calendar. You just can't believe how long the days and nights seem to be out here doing the same thing day after day. Doing our patrols and sweeps and night ambushes in the rice paddies and jungle. I can't believe how long I've been here and scared to death. It's so stressful, walking point on patrol, and boring at the same time. I know walking point most of the time, it's always the point man who gets killed first, when VC and NVA open up on us. "Boy walking point can really get to you!" You're out in front of the whole Platoon about 50 to 100 yards if you're out in the open. But in the jungle you're only 25 feet from the Platoon. Then you're thinking it's going to be your last step on Mother Earth. Doing the same thing every day and every night. It's on your mind every second that you can die.

We've been losing a lot of guys out here. Because of those booby traps. After seeing a few guys with one leg or both legs blown away it gets to you. You get so mad at the enemy that they don't fight fair. You feel so vulnerable and hopeless out here. There are no front lines out here. It's 24/7 that you're on guard and so scared to death. You're just hoping and hoping and praying you don't end up like they did with their legs blown off or killed, you just can't believe all the things that run through your mind when you're out here on your own. How much pressure and stress there is on your mind trying to get to your destination. Hoping you don't walk into an enemy ambush and get the whole Platoon wiped out. Everybody depends on you to alert them that the enemy is out there or any booby traps. You're always straining your eyes and ears for any type of warning you're so tense, you're trying to stay tuned into everything that is going on around you. You always jerk and tense up at any sudden noise or any sudden movement in the area. You're so tense and scared you sometime piss in your pants because you are forcing yourself to move one step at a time and each step could be your last. But you know it has to be done to complete the mission and to save your friends in this hellhole.

We got the word that we will be moving up North to a new fire support base camp away from the Saigon area that they were building in the middle of the jungle. The new base camp is being set up in the area of the Iron Triangle and Ho Bo Woods near the Saigon River up Northwest from the city of Saigon.

We just had mail call. The chopper that resupplies us brought our mail today. It's been a few weeks since we had mail call. I can always count on my Mom to write to me over here. In one of my letters she wished me a happy birthday. I didn't even know my birthday passed a few weeks ago. It made me think about home and what I'm missing at home. Being out here is just another day. But it was always nice to get mail from my Mom. I could count on my Mom to write to me. Most of my friends stopped writing to me. I guess they are too busy being kids and having fun. At the end the only one that will be writing to me will be my Mom.

Here I am up North and it's been three weeks already doing our night ambushes and sweeps in the jungle to protect the building of our new base camp. There has been a lot of enemy activity around here. We already had a few firefights and sprung a few night ambushes. We've been working about two miles or so around our new base camp that's being built, that's called Mahone I. We haven't seen it yet, we hear the Engineers working in the far distance about a few miles away. We've been protecting the Engineers from being attacked by the enemy near our new base camp. Like always they're clearing about 200 yards or more of jungle away for a clear fire zone around the base camp and the road leading to it. That way the guys can see the enemy coming before they can attack the base camp, and the enemy wouldn't have any cover to hide behind as they run towards the base camp.

They said that we'd be going in for a few days so we could get a little rest and some hot chow and maybe a change of jungle fatigues and maybe a shower? We sure needed a change of clothes. We were tired and beat and bushed, from being out in the jungle for the past four months. It's been a long three weeks so far protecting the guys working on the new base camp. Boy!!! These past four months seem like I've been here for four years so far. These old guys also known as short-timers that have a few months or weeks left in-country, you can tell they're so scared and nervous, you can see it in their faces, in their eyes and in their body movements, by the shakes they have. I didn't like seeing that. It made me feel uncomfortable seeing them with the shakes. You didn't know when they were going to break or lose it out here. I won't understand it until I become a short-timer. Boy that seems a lifetime away. We've been in a few firefights and sprung a few ambushes so far and lost a few new guys and one of our old guys. You never know when your number is up. There's been a lot of movement around this area by all the new fresh tracks on the ground and all the new bunkers we've been finding in the area, even the new base camp has been hit a few times already.

I just can't believe how hot it is. It feels like at least 100 degrees out here, but at night it drops down to 60 degrees and when there's a cool breeze you're freezing your ass off all night, especially as thin as our jungle fatigues are. You can't move around to keep warm, that makes it worse. You have to stay still in one spot and take the cold and pain and take it and take it. Because you don't want to give away your location or position at night to the enemy. That's why it makes the nights seem so long and boring just waiting and waiting there. Being still and waiting for the enemy to come to you so you can spring your ambush.

I just can't believe how your brain acts out here. How you think of all kinds of things to try and take your mind off of what's happening around you right now at that moment. So you don't have to feel the pain in your body and being scared at the same time. It was so hot and humid it made you sweat so much, then some nights it got so hot, about 80 to 90 degrees. You would get dehydrated just by being out there in the heat. It was like being in a sweat lodge or sauna bath. I can remember one night as hot as it was I had a vision that I would get wounded and I felt like I was in a sweat lodge at the time. I can't believe how bad things get from one moment to the next. You never know how things are going to be out here.

We're now sweeping to our new base camp in the jungle. We came to a clearing in the jungle, about 400 yards wide. We can tell the clearing was freshly cut by the Engineers because of all the new vegetation and trees that were cut down. Boy! I can see the sky and I can really see how tall the trees are now. As I look up about 50 or 150 feet into the air I can see the tops of the trees on the other side of the clearing in the jungle.

As we moved into the middle of the clearing in the jungle there was a dirt road. The jungle was cleared about 200 yards on both sides of the road. You can tell it was a new dirt road that had just been cut through the jungle and that it had been used a lot. Because of how thick the dust was on the road. When I step on the road the red dust covers the top of my boots, it was because of all the convoys going up and down the road to our new base camp. That's why they cut away part of the jungle so the enemy won't have good cover when they try to ambush our convoys.

We went down the road that leads us to our new base camp about a half a mile or so away. We spread out and staggered ourselves on both sides of the road in two columns about 20 feet apart. Our RTO and our CO were in the middle of the column. You could see the antennas of the RTO in the air about four or six feet long, they moved back and forth as they walked while we swept down the road. I just can't believe how hot it is. I can feel the heat rising off my clothes and the sweat running down my face and my back. As we walk along the road our boots sunk into the thick dust and kicked up a lot of red dust in the air. It got all over our clothes and our faces and in our mouth and hands, you could see the red dust sticking to the sweat on our clothes, hands, and our faces as we walk.

Now I can see a bigger clearing in the middle of the jungle. It was our new base camp, called Mahone I. I just couldn't believe how small it looked, seeing it for the first time! All the jungle around it made it look smaller. The base camp was made into a circle, the bunkers were in a circle like covered wagons. It was out in the middle of nowhere in the jungle.

As we were walking on the road downhill I could hear the radio making that static sound. Then the RTO started talking on the radio to tell the base that friendlies were coming in from the road to get the all-clear to come in. The ground was dry as a bone. We had dust all over the whole Company by now. We got the all-clear to come in! We looked beat and tired and ragged as we started walking in a single line down the hill, we got ready to zigzag past the barbed wire and concertina wire, that went around the whole base camp to protect it from the enemy getting inside the base camp.

I could see rows of concertina wire and barbed wire that went around the camp and about ten to 20 bunkers spaced out around the base camp behind the wire. Then behind the bunkers were the four 155 artillery Howitzers in their pits, and between each artillery piece were the 81 mortar tubes in their pits. The pits were made with green sand bags, they were stacked three feet high to make a wall around each artillery piece and mortar tube. They protected the guys from incoming rounds. Also stacked by each weapon were ammo boxes and the rounds laid out ready to fire. The guns were pointing out in four different directions, West, South, East, and North. That reminded me of the medicine wheel with the four directions in that order! That made me think of my culture and who I am for a moment. What a relief that was for a moment to think of my Native culture. Now I miss home again.

Then you can see about where the CP was, with all the radio antennas sticking up in the air, about in the middle of the base camp. Then you can see Old Glory flying. What a beautiful sight it was! Waving back and forth in the hot wind. To see the different colors, red, white, and blue, in the middle of all this green camouflage and the green jungle behind it. It wasn't much of a base camp, but it was a whole lot more protection and safer than what we were used to out in the open jungle.

They were still digging more new bunkers inside the perimeter and putting more concertina wire and barbed wire in rolls outside around the perimeter. The wires stretched out about 30 or 50 yards in front of the bunkers in rows and rows.

We made it inside the base camp and we unloaded our equipment. Then we were told that we had to put more trip flairs and Claymore mines and set them up around the new perimeter and help fill sandbags for the new bunkers. It seemed like our jobs are never done. Even as tired as we were we still did what we had to do to stay alive out here in this damn jungle.

We put the trip flares on the concertina wire and on the ground. Then we put more Claymore mines on the ground with sandbags behind them so we wouldn't get the back blast when we set them off. Also we had to put up cyclone fences with engineer stakes in the ground in front of the bunkers. To stop RPGs (Rocket-propelled Grenades) from penetrating into the bunkers.

Boy we were tired already and beat but we still had a lot of work to do before we could get some rest. But it was a lot safer place to be in than what we were used to. Being out in the open and in the bush was not easy. Then I could see two Engineer guys on top of one of the Rome plows, one was driving and the other was riding shotgun and he was looking for any snipers in the area. There were tractors (I think they were D-6 or D-9 tractors) cutting through the jungle, the tractors were OD green and covered with red dirt and the front blades looked real used and beat so that you could see the bare metal on the blade that was shining in the sun. As we were working on our defenses on the perimeter they were still clearing away the jungle so we could have a clear range of fire in our kill zone.

There were a lot of GI (Government Issue) workers around the base camp. Some with their T-shirts off and some with them on and the same thing with their helmets. They had drinking water from the water bags hanging on engineer stakes or out of their canteens. Some guys were filling sandbags and some were hammering engineer stakes in the ground. Also hanging barbed wire and concertina wire on iron stakes around the perimeter. They were working on the bunkers and digging holes out in the open for our latrines. To make a temporary latrine we dug a hole in the ground about two feet deep with two sandbags on each side of the hole for you to sit on so you can make number two. We also used empty canister round casings that we put in the ground for urinals out in the open. That was temporary until they built an outhouse. The Artillery and Mortar guys were cleaning their weapons and getting their artillery and mortar rounds ready for a fire mission in the pits. Then you hear the rounds going off from the mortar tubes like dud pop sounds. We were busy little bees and kicking up a lot of dust working around the base camp.

I thought I was going to rest inside the base camp and pull bunker guard on the perimeter tonight so I can get a good night's rest. Instead they told me I'd be going out on LP. I really didn't understand what he meant. This was the first time I'd been in a small base camp (not like the big base camp at Cu Chi), since I've been here in Vietnam I'd been in the jungle or the rice paddies.

This was all new to me, they told me I'd be going out tonight outside the wire. That meant I had to be outside the perimeter tonight. It was a four-man team with a radio that would go out to listen for the enemy and alert our little base camp before they can attack. That meant we would be the ones out there in harm's way. That's all I needed, some more shit to do. We would be about 200 to 300 yards outside the perimeter of the base camp next to the jungle. Talk about tightening your ass up, this will do it.

It was only 200 yards outside the wire. But it seemed to be a lifetime away when you do this type of job. I just didn't know how I handled the pressure being out there. They told us there would be four posts in four different locations outside the wire, one at the North, South, East, and West side of our little base camp. We'd use the military alphabet for our call sign for each post – Listening Post-1 (Lima Papa-One), Listening Post-2 (Lima Papa-Two), Listening Post-3 (Lima Papa-Three), and Listening Post-4 (Lima Papa-Four). HQ will be monitoring our radios throughout the night to hear our call sign for any movement out there tonight.

They'll be calling us on our call sign all through the night. All we do is squeeze the handle that made a squelch sound on their radio. This way the enemy can't hear us talking and it also lets HQ know that we're awake and alert during the night. And lets them know we're doing our job at the same time.

So here we go, our four-man team gets ready to move outside the perimeter. We just finished eating our C-rations and I just put my P-38 can opener back on my dog tags. Then I got all my equipment and my ammo and weapon ready to go out tonight. I made sure that I still had my toilet paper, mosquito repellent, and my extra grenade pins on my helmet. And my small survival compass I got off a dead NVA a few months ago. I made sure it was still tied onto my buttonhole on my shirt pocket, I use one of my old shoelaces to tie it on. Then I remembered what my Mom told me, always put a small rock or a button in your mouth to keep it from being dry. Boy, it sure does work out here in this damn heat.

My LT told me I'd be carrying the radio tonight with one of the teams and that I'd be in charge of one of the teams and he told me to go to the CP for my assignment. Boy that's all I needed, to be responsible for these FNGs and to be in charge of the radio. That's all I needed, more pressure and stress. I still feel like a new guy. Now we were at the CP waiting for our information. They told us what we'd be doing out there. Then they told us to saddle up! I told the guys to lock and load when we get to the wire. We started walking toward the barbed wire. As we walked past some the guys in the base camp they had that look, better you than them to be out there. It made me feel real uncomfortable to see that look, it made me feel like I'm going to get killed tonight. We enter the wire and we lock and load our weapons as we zigzag past the barbed wire and concertina wire. I felt so insecure leaving our little base camp and scared as all hell. I really didn't need this shit. We finally zigzag past all the barbed wire and concertina wire.

We go out the South side of the perimeter. Team One waited for it to get dark before they could go straight out about 300 yards or so. Then Team Two and Three went right and my team, Team Four, went left a quarter of the way around the base camp. Then we waited to go straight out East about 300 yards or so. All the teams waited for it to get dark so we can have some kind of cover from the dark night to walk out in the jungle.

There was a cool breeze that night. It seemed like a long way to our night location for me and the new guys. I can't believe I'm in charge of these guys and to myself I really didn't want to be in charge because I still feel like a new guy! I was told to do it, like it or not I follow orders. I didn't let anybody know I didn't like doing this shit. I hated doing it. I put on an act like it didn't bother me to take responsibility, I knew when I made a decision it would be a life and death decision. In fact it was trial and error but when I made my decision I had to live with that the best way I knew how within myself.

It was already getting dark and the Sun is almost down. Time seems just to drag on when you're waiting to go out into the land of OZ. It's dark now and it's time to start walking to our night location. I could see the Evening Star behind me to the West. Boy it's so hard to make the first move, to move out. Every step seems to be your last step on Mother Earth, you just don't know when you're going to die out here.

You hear the guys talking and playing music on their radios in the distance in our base camp. It's weird listening to that as we are walking out to our LP. The things that run through your mind at that moment, you have all kinds of mixed feelings in your head. The things you think of, are you going to be alive tomorrow or will you be dead? Then you think about home because of the music that was playing. By the time we got to our location moving East and zigzagging, it was real quiet back at the base camp now. A half hour has gone by.

Our location is 300 yards or so out. I remember seeing a fallen dead tree I saw early in the day. It's almost 300 yards or more out, that way we'll have some kind of good cover beside the dark night. We'd be behind the trees for cover and we could put our Claymore mines out and we didn't have to worry about the back flash from the explosions when we set them off. It was weird being out here, it seems to be a long walk to that fallen tree especially at night. We finally make it to our night location. It starts to get colder because it's dark now and it's so quiet. A half hour goes by as I was looking into the sky. I can see flashes of light, lighting up the dark sky in the far distance every now and then. Then you hear the explosion ten seconds later. I know by counting the seconds between the flash of light and the explosion it was ten miles away. You know there is some type of battle going on and people are getting killed and it could happen to us at any moment.

I never felt so alone and scared and nervous back then. I just can't believe what I was doing! I'm sweating to beat all hell. The things that go through your head, I was scared and nervous. I didn't want the responsibility of taking care of these new guys. I really didn't know what the hell I was doing out here anyway. I felt like the rest of the guys were hoping for the best. I didn't need this shit. I hope I do the right thing out here.

If somebody tells you they know what they're doing out here! It's a bunch of bullshit. Because things change so fast out here. Things are never the same and all you can do is hope for the best and that you make the right decision at the right time at the right moment. Out here you don't get a second chance. You do what you have to do, "or die plain and simple."

Once we settle in I reported to our CP-One. The call sign is Charlie Papa-One. I call in, "Charlie Papa-One this is Lima Papa-Four at its location and we'll be settling in for tonight in our night location. Over." This will be the last time I talk on the radio until daybreak. From now on we just squeeze the handset. We'd be on our own until daylight.

What a night this is going to be for me and the rest of the guys. Being here in the unknown of the night. Waiting for something to happen. It was about 1800hrs (6:00 p.m.) in the evening. We were in the winter months and the Sun was down already.

I told the guys we'd be doing two-man team on, and two-man team off, in two-hour shifts throughout the night. Which means two men stay awake, one man monitors the radio, and one stays alert. The other team of two sleeps.

We didn't really start our shifts until 2100hrs (9:00 p.m.). It was hard to go to sleep right away when you're scared shitless. They started calling us on the half hour after I reported in that we were at our night location. You can barely hear the call sign on the radio handset. "Lima Papa-Four are you awake and alert, this is Charlie Papa-One radio check. Over." Then you squeeze the button on the side of the handset to make that squelch sound. We squeezed the handset three times to let them know we were wide awake and alert and that we were settled in for tonight. Then we started to squelch back and forth for the night. Each night location was on its own frequency to our CP.

I hold the handset close to my ear. As we are lying out here in the dark I'm looking at the stars. They are so beautiful in the black sky and they look so close that you could touch them. I feel like I am up in the mountains again when I went deer hunting and fishing with my Mom and Dad and brother back home. Boy what happy times it was back then. I am really feeling homesick now, being out here alone. Even with the guys next to me I feel so alone a lot of times. I guess a lot of times we are in our own thoughts in our own little world. Living our lives in our own ways in our head. Trying to get away from this bullshit, being in hell as I was staring out into the darkness in "no man's land."

Then I heard our call sign on the handset, it startled me, it brought me right back to reality in this hellhole. I squeeze the handle three times to let them know Lima Papa-Four was wide awake and alert. For a moment I was back home feeling good about myself. The Moon is starting to come out and the stars look so far away. You can see a lot better out there in the jungle now. It's about 2200hrs (10:00 p.m.), things are real quiet out here in the jungle in front of us.

But far away you can hear explosions going off in the distance. You know somebody is in some kind of shit and are going through hell trying to stay alive. You know it can happen to you at any moment. It gets on your nerves every time you do this shit, hearing gunfire and explosions in the distance. I really don't feel safe out here. If the enemy tries to hit our base we'll be the first to get killed.

We all knew it! That we'd be right in the middle of it. We'd be right in the middle of the battle. Right in the middle of the firefight and we'd be getting it from both ends. I just hope our guys know where we're at and don't shoot at us. I knew we had to do this to alert the guys and give the guys in the base camp a better chance to get ready to fight. It looks like we are here to sacrifice our lives to save their lives which I didn't like doing at all, it had to be done like it or not.

All the training in the world can't put the fear of God in you like this place every day and night. It was time for the first shift to go to sleep. It was a long day for us too. It's going to be a longer night tonight. The nights always seem to be longer than the days when you're facing death, the unknown, in the darkness. The unknown can really get to you, it's one hell of a feeling. Lying there still, sweating your ass off waiting for the enemy to do something. Just waiting and waiting and waiting for something to happen is really the shits.

Now it was me and the other guy's turn to go to sleep, but I couldn't really sleep. I could still barely hear the squelch on the radio handset, which kept me up. Then you hear the bombs exploding off in the distance again so you really didn't sleep. You just try to get as much rest as you can in this type of environment.

It started to rain. Here we go again! It's going to be another cold miserable night, just trying keep yourself warm and your shit together. Boy this time it was a cold, cold rain, you're lying there shaking like a leaf trying keep your senses intact.

We had no poncho or poncho liners, we just had the clothes on our backs. Your bones and hands hurt because of the cold. You can't get out of the rain, you can't walk around to keep warm, you have to stay in place like it or not. You have to suck it up and take it. It was a long, long night for us sleeping off and on and being cold and wet in the rain, it was a miserable night. They woke me up and I woke up the other guy, it was our turn again. It was the last shift before sunrise and it had stopped raining. I could hardly move, I was stiff as a board. I didn't want to move but I had to even though it hurt. I look up and there were no more clouds in the sky. I could see the Morning Star just before sunrise, it looked so bright in the clear night sky.

I knew I was facing East towards the sunrise. We Natives know our sense of direction by the stars and the sunrise and sunset. We do our blessing by facing East first to the sunrise and then facing each direction moving clockwise to the four directions by our Medicine Wheel, as we do our prayers and blessing and burn our sage, tobacco or sweet grass, and we also give them as gifts. The smoke will carry our prayers to our ancestors and to the Spirit World and the Creator.

The Sun is almost up now coming from the East. I could see the Morning Star from the East in front of me. It will fade away in the sunlight as the Sun comes up before you know it, then the night will be gone. Then we will be going back West to our base camp as soon as we get the ok from our CP.

It's about 0530hrs (5:30 a.m.) now and the Sun is all the way up. The Morning Star disappears in the sunrise. I can see the steam coming off our fatigues and helmets as the Sun is shining on us. It feels good to feel the heat on your wet clothes and our bodies from the Sun.

I call to get the ok from the CP to let us know if we have the all clear sign to come in. That way they can alert the perimeter and let them know that they have friendlies coming in from the East. The other LPs will be doing the same thing, calling in to get the all clear sign to come into our little base camp.

We were lucky this time that they didn't attack us last night. We would have been dead meat if they did. The CP gives us the all clear sign for all of us to come into our base camp, they have alerted the base that friendlies are coming in.

Boy what a long night it was. Now we are walking back the way we came, you can hear the guys talking and the music playing on their radios. I guess everybody is awake now. We finally got to our perimeter where we can enter the barbed wire and zigzag past through the concertina wire and be back into our base camp. As we came in we could see a Platoon was getting ready to leave the base camp to go on a patrol in the area to find the little people, the NVA or VC. Boy I'm glad it's not me going out there today, I guess we all have that same thought! It's better them than you to go out in the land of OZ. Especially when you know how bad things can get out there. I guess we have the same look in our eyes like the guys had that night when we left for LP.

Now all I wanted to do is eat some C-rations for breakfast and try to get dry and get some good sleep and rest and relax in the Sun. My bones hurt and my legs and arms are cramping from not moving around all night in the cold. Boy I just didn't know I could handle so much pain and suffering at night and there is more of that to come. Because I still have a lot more time to do in-country.

We stayed one more night at our little fire support base camp. Then we were back out doing our sweeps and night ambushes far out in the jungle. We try to give them as much protection as we can from the enemy that were attacking our little base camp.

It's the life of a Grunt always suffering in the elements and in harm's way to protect others, it's even a lot harder when you lose somebody in a war, "Especially when it's a buddy."

Living the Pain of War

Losing a Buddy and Getting Wounded

September 1968-December 1968

RUBBER PLANTATION
September 1968

Here I am again on another mission taking a break. I just got through drinking some warm water out of my canteen. I just marked another day off my short-timer calendar on my helmet again. It's been five months and I've been here 149 days. Our new mission is that we'll be going into a rubber plantation that was run by the French. This will be the first time for me to see real rubber trees. I just can't believe there are so many different types of plants around here I have never seen before. They said we'll be setting up a night ambush on a trail that leads to the old burnt-out French fort in the rubber plantation. It's far inside the rubber plantation and it's time for me to walk point again. Because of this new LT. He hasn't learned the golden rule of old guys not walking point. It's time to move out. Like they say it's my turn like it or not.

It should be dark by the time we get into the rubber plantation. It's bad enough moving around in the daytime. It's worse at night and walking alone between these rubber trees, I just don't know. As I'm walking you can see where they cut into the bark of the tree, to milk the rubber from the trunk of the rubber trees. It looks like it's been a long time, since they worked around here. Because the bark is growing over the cuts on the trees. All these ants are crawling up and down on the bark of the trees. You can see their nests hanging from the branches, where the leaves were all bunched up. There would be hundreds of red ants in a nest, if you knocked one of them down and it landed on you, they would bite the hell out of you. The rubber trees are tall, as I look up and all around me the leaves are falling down from them every now and then. The trees are in rows as far as you can see. Boy! Walking on these dead leaves from the trees is something else! They make so much noise walking on them. I tried walking heel first, then I tried walking flat foot, no matter what I do the leaves still made noise as I walk.

I just wish I was home away from all this shit. I miss my Mom and Dad. I want to try to think of it as a bad dream. Here I go again thinking to myself again, trying to calm myself down. But every time I smell something, or hear things or see things or feel strange things it brings reality right back to this awful place.

I hope there are no booby traps out there especially along the trail. I know I won't be able see them with all these dead leaves covering the ground. We've been losing a lot of guys because of these booby traps. You're damned when you walk on the trail and you're damned when you don't. Every step could be your last step on Mother Earth. I've been lucky so far.

I can remember a week ago I was walking point and the fourth guy behind me stepped on a booby trap and it went off and blew his foot right off. I couldn't believe it, I just walked through there. It could have been me that lost my foot! I didn't see anything unusual on the ground. You just don't know what life has in store for you. It scared the hell out of me knowing it could have been me. Things happen so fast around here from one moment to the next, you just don't know who's going to be next to step on one, or is it going to be you.

Well we are almost to our night location, the Sun is going down real fast and it's starting to get dark. Boy you just can't believe how scared you get when it gets dark. All kinds of thoughts go through your mind at that moment. It's dark now and the Moon is starting to come out. Now I'm walking real slow, taking my time more, one step at a time hoping for the best. That's all I can do for now just take it easy as much as I can and keep moving. I can't believe how I feel. I feel enclosed like the trees are moving in on me as it starts to get darker. It was real quiet in our area and that made me feel more enclosed. You can hear explosions real far off in the distance going off. It's real spooky walking around in the dark now, to feel this way is something else. Then you have all these different thoughts going through your mind. I just have to put one foot in front of the other. I'm so nervous to take each step one at a time. Thinking every step would be a booby trap! I'm just going through the motions taking each step. I just have to sweat it out until we get to our night ambush and hope we don't run into the enemy. I hope we can set up our ambush site before the Moon comes out all the way tonight. I look back every now and then to my Sergeant, he pointed to me to keep going straight.

This trail looks like it's been used a lot. I've been walking along the trail about ten feet away from it. We are well inside the rubber plantation now. The Sergeant finally snaps his fingers to let me know. We finally made it to our night location where a small canal crosses the trail. It's like I said we didn't talk much when we were on patrol. We did a lot of different things to communicate to each other, not to make so much noise. Now we are ready to put our ambush site up along the trail by the canal. We didn't talk much at all, all we did is give a lot of hand signals and pointing. It was kind of weird how we did things. It was like we could read each other's minds, just by our expressions and hand signals. We put our Claymore mines out like we always do. We did a two men stay awake and two sleep every two hours, like always, we paired off in twos. Boy this is going to be another long night just waiting for the enemy to come down that trail, to kill them.

As I look up I can see the Moon is out and shining between the tree branches now. I can feel the hot air on my face. The Moon is moving across the trees and the moonlight is so bright now. You can see the shadows of the trees, it looks like things are moving out there. Then you hear the bombs exploding and gunfire off in the far, far distance a few miles away again. It's a weird feeling looking out in that direction seeing the flashes of light over the trees and in the sky that lit up the night and hearing the explosions a few seconds later.

You know somebody is in the shit. You know the VC and NVA are moving around out there. You know it could be us at any moment. Waiting there can really get to you and it's so hard to keep your shit together. Knowing you're going to have to kill somebody or somebody is going to kill you. How time drags on and drags on during the night and hoping and waiting for the Sun to come up. Things feel like they are closing in on you as time goes on. I don't know how many times I prayed to the Creator to see the Sun come up and to make it another night in this damn place.

It's no game being out here! It's for real! Kill or be killed. At 19 it's hard to think that way but you had to. Even as innocent as we were you had to. There was no way of getting out of it! You're stuck here and sweating it out to make it through another night. You're hot and nervous, scared about the unknown and how spooky it gets as time goes on. You know the enemy is out there moving around trying to resupply their units or trying to set up their own ambush for us too.

Then it's my turn to get some sleep. It's 0100hrs (1:00 a.m.), talk about being tired, I am! It was a long day for me and I'm ready to get some sleep. I try to but I can't really sleep I just doze off and on. I can't believe how tired I am but I just can't sleep. I guess I was out for a few minutes into a deep sleep. Then all of a sudden an explosion! One of the Claymore mines went off then another and then another.

Then all kinds of different sounds of automatic weapons started firing, I was startled from my sleep. I tried to see what the hell was going on. I couldn't get my eyes to focus. I started rubbing my eyes with my hands, they had sweat on them. The sweat from my hands burned my eyes a little bit more. I was scared as all hell. I started shaking and I tried to focus my eyes and things were happening so fast I was confused on what was going on.

All I knew I was trying to get my weapon ready to fire. By the time I came to my senses everything was over. It happened so fast, then everybody stopped firing. It was over in just a few seconds. Boy I wanted to ask what the hell happened? But we had to be quiet in case any enemy were still alive out there. Boy I'm wide awake now. I was scared to beat all hell, I was shaking like a leaf. I was still in shock. I was still trying to come to my senses after being startled that way.

Then you hear incoming illumination rounds going over our heads, then you hear a pop. They're flare rounds lighting up the area. The flares came down with little parachutes hanging down from them. But the metal plates that came from the flare rounds, they make a funny sound like wings fluttering when they come down out of the canister and fall to the ground. When they hit the ground it makes a dud sound.

But if one those plates hit you it would kill you. I used to curl up and try to crawl into my helmet and hope for the best, that it won't hit me. When the flares are coming down between the trees, the bright lights from the flares are moving back and forth, hanging down from the little parachutes. They cast the tree shadows onto the ground and all around us, the shadows were moving back and forth. It looked like things were moving out there. That made it scary as all hell and spooky at the same time. You didn't know if the enemy was moving around out there or it was just the shadows moving.

Then you feel the hot breeze coming between the trees. Then leaves are falling down every so often. It feels so peaceful now and spooky at the same time. Then you hear another round come in and you hear it pop. Then you see the flare light up the whole place around us again. The leaves are wet and damp from the humidity. The leaves are shiny because of the light from the flares reflecting off the wet leaves. Then you hear the flare fizzling as it's coming down. It brings you right back into reality. It's a scary moment for me in fact for all of us, we hate this shit! Every time we do this shit at night, you just can't get used to this shit. You just can't believe how stressful this is! Not knowing if you will be alive to see the Sun come up and to feel the Sun's warm rays again on your body. It seems like you just live to see the next day, from night to day and day to night.

It's going to be another long boring and scary night just waiting for daylight. I think we have three and a half hours before daylight. I hope they don't come back. Knowing we just killed some of them, you feel haunted. What is waiting out there? I don't need this shit anymore. Boy I started to get soaked and wet, especially when you're sweating to beat all hell and the dew from the leaves is now dropping on you. It felt like it was raining, but there were no clouds in the night sky as I looked up. You couldn't move around to get comfortable. You had to say still in place and take the pain from your body. That is something else we had to do a lot of, is take the pain even when it gets so severe.

Now I'm looking up again between the trees and can see the stars. Anything I can do to take my mind off the pain. The stars look so beautiful it takes me back home again when I used to go deer hunting. The stars look the same just before sunrise. It's sure a lot different now. Now I know how a deer feels like when it's being hunted and now I'm the hunted and not the hunter. It's starting to get daylight. The sunlight is coming in between the trees, it feels warm. You can see the steam coming off the tree bark and leaves on the ground and off our clothes. It's time to check out the trail to see how many enemy we killed. Boy my bones hurt from not moving around and I'm stiff as all hell. I didn't know I could take so much pain in one night. I guess when your life depends on it, I guess you can take anything especially out here. But we have a job to do, like it or not it had to be done over here.

This time it was NVA not VC, there were eight of them and they had a lot of equipment on them. We did good last night. I just hope we don't run into their Company. I don't like this, it means that we're going to have to find them. It doesn't look good. I've been here five months and the shit I've been through doesn't get any easier. It's been enough for me so far. I don't need this shit anymore. I just don't know if I can take it anymore. Then I look at the Claymore bag that I carry. It's what I use as an ammo bag where I carry 30 magazines for my M-16. It had a bullet hole in it. It went through two magazines! I had it next to my head that night. I was lucky last night, I could have been killed in my sleep.

The LT said, police the area and pick up all their equipment and that we're moving out of the rubber plantation to a clearing so a chopper can come in. So we can get rid of the equipment and belongings we captured and we can get resupplied again. It was a long walk out to the clearing. Repeating the same stress that it took coming in. We finally made it to the clearing and we spread out to secure the area for the helicopter to come in. We got the equipment the NVA had on them ready to be picked up.

We could hear the chopper coming in, then one of the guys popped yellow smoke for the chopper to come in and land. So we could load the equipment we captured and we can pull our supplies off the chopper at the same time. The chopper landed then took off making that same old sound when it left. Boy every time a chopper came in I wanted to get on it and get the hell out of here and go home! It made me feel homesick when a single chopper came in. But when a group of choppers come in I feel like hell because I know we are going on another mission again.

So we got our supplies and we rested for a while. Now we're getting ready for another mission to go on. I can see the LT talking on the radio getting orders for our next mission. It was a long night last night and I was lucky again and made it. I just hope my luck doesn't run out. I keep thinking how close that bullet was to my head last night. I could have died in my sleep! Now I'm hoping for the best on our next mission and trying to stay alive and to keep it together out here. Every day is a challenge from one day to the next and the unknown can really get to you mentally. Really this whole damn war can. We're going back to another big base camp called Dau Tieng back to the rear with the gear for another mission.

WHEN YOU LOSE A FRIEND IS ONE THING
BUT A BUDDY IS SOMETHING ELSE
October 1968

I've been in the bush about six months now, 169 days. I just marked off my short-timer calendar again on my helmet. I just can't believe what I've been through so far. At times I wanted to end my life. Because of all the misery, pain, and suffering I'd been going through. Also all the death and mutilated bodies I'd been seeing in this awful war I've been in so far. I just don't know when my life is going to end in this awful place. I just hate being here in Vietnam. I didn't know to become a Warrior that you would go through so much pain and suffering, how you get to understand what time is really like. How a second can make you or break you or kill you from one moment to the next in war. When you're in civilian life you don't think about time that much and how really important it is. Because you're not in a life and death situation all the time. Well here I am out in the middle of nowhere thinking to myself again. Trying to keep myself together in my own way in this hellhole.

When you're in a war you don't know who's going to be your friend or your buddy out here, it just happens. You can't pick them, you just come together. Once you learn their ways and have the same things in common then you end up liking each other. I guess you will become friends for a while. Then as time goes on, you end up being buddies because you got to know each other a little bit better than being a friend. You get to know their every move without thinking. You're like one person.

I had this one friend, he was a tall big lanky white kid with blond hair. He came from a poor family, the way he talked about home. The way he talked about home didn't sound bad to me. I didn't need the things he was talking about. I had a simple life growing up, as long as I had love and food on the table and a roof over my head I was rich. That was the way of life for me as a Native American. We started hanging around together a lot. He carried the M-60 machine gun, his name was Milky. We'd been together on line for about 162 days already, since I met him about a week after getting in-country. He was nice guy to talk to. Somebody to "break bread (have a meal) with." We talked a lot about home, it was funny back then we didn't talk much about how scared we were. We talked a lot about what we were going to do when we got home. How nice we would look in our dress uniforms and how the girls would like us and things like that. We didn't know at the time that we would be hated when we came home and all the other things that were going on in the States. I just don't understand why they picked on us when we came home! They sent us there. I didn't want to be here, I didn't join to be here, I was drafted. I had to come here or go to jail. My whole life was turned upside down and would never be the same when I got home.

We also talked about what kind of job we might be doing when we got home or what kind of car we might buy when we made it home. Then we talked about our Moms, how they cooked our meals and what kind of meals they made and all the different types of foods they prepare. How it tastes and how it smells so good when it comes out of the oven and how our home life was back there. We also shared our goody packs we got from home.

I just can't believe the little things that we missed from home. Boy being out here in the jungle it sure made you miss home a lot, and all the little things you were used to. It wasn't a little thing anymore, it sure meant a lot to us now. When you had to do without.

Then our letters that we got from home. How important it was to receive a letter even though it took a few weeks to get to us. How it brightens your whole day up to receive ten to 15 letters all at once. Telling us what they were doing back home and how my Mom and Dad still going hunting and fishing and things like that.

Boy you just can't imagine the stupid things we talked about, just to keep your mind intact for the "Real World" back in the States. Being out here seeing war at first hand can make you or break you. I just don't know how I handle all the trauma and emotion and suffering and still keep my sanity intact.

We always talk about going back to the "Real World." We try to bring the "Real World" to us in Vietnam with anything that can remind us of home. Like when your Mom sends you some homemade cookies, newspapers, or magazines. Or every time you got a letter or pictures from home. It reminds me of things back home and it made you feel better and more homesick at the same time. You're damned when you do get things from home and you're damned if you don't get things from home. But it helped me get pleasant thoughts later when I needed it in the time of battle.

So you learn a lot about life and how precious time is, to be in a real war. Then you learn a lot about one another, in that hellhole. The next thing you know he is your buddy, he's not just a friend anymore. You become a lot closer to each other. You would die for each other in this hellhole. People don't understand what it means to be close like that in that type of environment when your life is on the line every second of the day and night.

When we are willing to fight for each other's life and die for each other, it meant a lot to us as being Grunts to have that type of bond. There's a type of love there that only young men in the Infantry understand during war time.

There's a bond that only happens once in your lifetime, in battle. When you lose a friend is one thing. But losing a buddy, it's even harder. Don't get me wrong it's hard for either one. But a buddy is just a little bit closer than a friend. He becomes a part of you.

A buddy knows your every move you're going to make, you both feel like one person, you're part of him. You had to be, doing that type of job as a Grunt. You had to have somebody close to you like that, it's the only way you stay alive in that place and keep your sanity intact.

But when you lose a buddy in combat it's really hard to understand the consequences until it happens. When something like that happens to your buddy it can really change things in your life and the way you think. Things will not be the same anymore, it's like part of your life is gone. You feel so lost within yourself. Knowing he will not be there by your side when you need him. Then you get mad because he's gone, then you feel sorry for him and for yourself. Then you just get all mixed up in your head. All you can do is try to deal with it the best way you know how. Because we never had any kind of training for how to cope with this kind of bullshit. You're on your own and all you can do is hope for the best and try to do the right thing at that time and moment.

Things just seemed to happen in this type of environment. It was really hard to take it back then! It can really fuck your head up. Once you lose a buddy you won't do it again. You won't have another buddy, you just have friends and the friends you make will not be close friends anymore, just friends. Because it's too hard on you when it happens to your buddy or a close friend, when you lose them. Their names end up being put on a tombstone or on a wall of stone.

There was one night we were going on a night ambush. We had to walk through this village to get to our night location, our ambush site.

But this time I didn't have to walk point on this patrol. I had enough time on line now, it's been six months already, it felt like six years. My LT said you've had enough time walking point and you made E-4 Specialist today. It didn't seem that long that I'd been walking point. I guess I'd just been going through the motions day after day and night after night.

Boy was I happy and at the same time I felt sorry and sad for the next guy who was going to take my place. I hope he is strong enough to take it and strong enough to deal with it day after day and night after night like I did. It's not going to be easy for him in fact it's not easy for any of us when we have to do it. I just hope he makes the right decisions being point man out there tonight.

Milky, my buddy, carried the M-60 machine gun, that made him our "60 Man." He was a big tall lanky white kid. He never had to walk point because he carried the M-60 which we called the Pig. It weighed about 45 pounds loaded. The Door Gunners in the choppers used them – but they didn't have to carry them! It was Milky's main job to carry the M-60. You had to be strong to carry the M-60 and 500 rounds of ammo on you! What a load he had. I was small and thin so they liked sending me down those holes in the ground they call tunnels. That was another job I hated to do. What a pair we were. We'd been together for about five or six months now, we'd been through a lot together and seen a lot of shit together and had a lot of close calls in a firefight.

We always carry an ace of spades on our helmet. It was our calling card of death. We were at the point that we didn't care anymore about life and death. I think we were burnt out. There was so much death around us. Our emotions were numb and our hearts were hard, we were just going through the motions. I told him I didn't have to walk point tonight and I made E-4 Specialist.

He said that's good that I made Specialist and it must be your lucky night tonight. I smiled back at him but I thought to myself why did he say that? "It must be my lucky night!" What is so lucky about going out on a night ambush? Where is he coming from? I thought to myself. Like I said your buddy can feel things that you can't or the other way around. We were like two peas in a pod. So we got our ammo and filled our canteens with water which was hot and got our C-rations and the rest of our equipment ready for tonight's ambush. It had been a long hot day, at least 115 degrees. We just came in a few hours ago, sweeping around our base camp. We were beat and tired of being out in the bush for the past three weeks. At least we might get a few hours rest before we go out tonight.

We ate one of our dinners from our little box of C-rations, and like always

I gave away my cigarettes because I didn't smoke. Then we talked a little bit about home again. I just had enough time to write home. I wrote a letter home to my Mom on part of a C-ration box. We used the cartons from the C-ration boxes as writing paper, I didn't have any writing paper at the time. We'd been out the past few months. We didn't need any stamps. All we had to do is write 'FREE' where the stamp went on the letter which was nice that the Government gave us free postage.

I just told Mom everything was ok! That not much was happening around here so far and so on. I really didn't tell my Mom what I was really going through out here. I didn't want to worry her. I would write about how things looked like around here. How beautiful the land looks and the people and how they dress and look. Then all the different animals and insects and how they look. I really didn't write to her about what I was doing. That way I wouldn't have to lie to her.

Now that we are back in our little base camp for a while I can mail my letters home! I don't have to carry them around till I come back to our little base camp a few weeks or months from now. My Mom wrote to me every day, she didn't miss one day writing to me over here. But we didn't get mail all the time. Sometimes we go without mail two to three weeks at a time and sometime months. Most of the time we got our letters in bundles when we came back to our little support base camp where they kept it for us.

But when we got our mail it was something else! You just can't believe how important it was to us and how it made us feel so happy. I always counted on my Mom's letters that way I knew about how many days we'd been out in the bush. A lot of time we would lose track of the days. My Mom also numbered her letters to let me know how many days I had left in Vietnam. I also had my short-timer calendar on my helmet that I drew up and marked the days off as time moved on.

The LT said get ready to move out. Then he said after our night ambush, we'll be sweeping the area around the village in the daytime. After that we'll be going on an Eagle Flight to another location out in the jungle. Me and Milky hated going out on a night ambushes, in fact we all did.

We all had that scary look on our faces and in our eyes. We all had that thousand-yard stare. Every time we go out it was the same look of being scared to death. Something different always happens out there at night. You just have to deal with it the best way you know how at that moment. There was 25 of us guys going out tonight and sometimes only 20. We were never at full strength in our Platoon of 40 guys. Guys come and go so fast around here, we've been through three LTs and two COs so far. We'll be moving to our night location from our little fire support base camp Mahone II in the Iron Triangle near the Saigon River.

We would be going past our old base camp Mahone I, where we almost got overrun by the NVA several times. Being in that was something else! It was a living hell trying to stay alive. We had to move away from Mahone I in the valley and make a new base camp on top of the hill which is now Mahone II. Which was a better area, we could see more area around us and cover more range of fire on the enemy.

We knew there'd been a lot of movement out there lately. We knew we will be facing death again. I told Milky I will be watching his back tonight instead of him watching mine all the time. He said that was cool! Our LT said lock and load, let's move out. As we move out you can hear our radio transmitting. Letting HQ know we are moving out to our night location and checking the radio at the same time and to turn down the volume. We move zigzag past the concertina wire and barbed wire of the base. The ground was hard and dusty as we move out. As soon as we pass the barbed wire we started spacing ourselves a few yards apart from one another and walking in a column.

The Sun is almost down, as we're walking out you can see the guys' silhouettes and the outline of the jungle in front of you as we moved out in the dark night. We could hear the music playing on the radio and guys talking as we're leaving the base camp. The Moon hasn't come up yet. Now that the Sun was all the way down it was real dark, it was still hot and I was still sweating to beat all hell. I had that button in my mouth, so my mouth would not be dry. I'm scared as all hell doing this shit, going on these night ambushes. All you can see is barely the guys in front of you as we were walking down this little hill going away from the village.

The things that go through your mind, it's like a roller coaster rushing up and down. It got real quiet back in our fire support base camp. Then the RTO made his last radio check to hear that we had cleared the wire and are on our way to our night location. Then we heard the squelching sound on the radio as we were walking down the hill, it was kind of spooky. You just can't believe how weird it was, the things that run through your mind as you're walking and how each one of us felt alone inside ourself. Each one of us sees things different in our minds as we walk down the hill looking for the enemy. Then you get the shakes as we move to our night location, sweating to beat all hell. The unknown can really get to you. As you move one step at a time closer to the unknown.

It's crazy how your mind and ears play tricks on you. You think you see something or hear something out there. What a trip it takes you on! It's really weird to be out there like that. Knowing the enemy is out there to kill you. It was so dark, as we were walking away from the village, about 300 yards and now we doubled back towards the village. That way the enemy didn't know which way we were going. It was dark enough for us to double back to the village now.

We had to go through the village to get to our night location. I was thinking to myself this was not a good idea to do that! This was a new LT, I was just a Spec 4, anyway they must have had a good reason to do that. All I know I was scared and I didn't like what we were doing. It wasn't right and I didn't feel right about what we were doing.

As we were walking I noticed that we were walking through our old base camp. I knew we had a half a mile or less to the village and it was up on a hill. I tap Milky on the shoulder and whisper, half a mile to the village and he whispers ok. We knew the VC had control of it at night. We get a lot of incoming rounds from there during the day and night. It was supposed to be a friendly village.

That's why we're putting our ambush on the other side of the village to stop the VC from coming in the village and collecting taxes and harassing the South Vietnamese people and making young Vietnamese join their forces.

The Moon is starting to come out, we're almost to the village. It was hard to see anything, we're on the road now. I thought to myself, what the hell are we doing on the road?

I tap Milky on the shoulder and whisper, this is bad being on the road. Milky said I know what you mean! I thought to myself, where in the hell is the point man taking us? I knew we were supposed to stay away from any roads and trails at night, they can ambush us easy. Then we heard loud talking up front where the point man was at.

Then all the sudden gunfire erupted we all hit the ground, we started firing our weapons. Milky was hit with the first blast, he wasn't moving so I grabbed the M-60 and started firing to put more firepower out there and I moved to the side of the road. I was shaking, breathing so hard and my heart was pounding so fast. We started firing more in all different directions. To make sure the enemy wouldn't get the upper hand on us.

I was scared! And shaking and sweating to beat all hell. Then I heard Milky calling for his Mother. I can't believe what I did next. I went back into the kill zone. Still carrying the M-60 with me and I dragged Milky back to the side of the road so we won't be in the kill zone. I was scared shitless and I was shaking I couldn't believe what just happened, that Milky got hit. I knew we were in a kill zone. I've seen what happened when you are in the kill zone. I saw it happen too many times. Then the rest of the guys stopped firing! The shooting, it happens so fast.

I called for Doc our Medic to give First Aid to Milky, the word was passed down to our Medic. Milky was bleeding a lot. He told me it feels like it is burning and it hurts real bad inside. I put a First Aid bandage on his chest to try to stop the bleeding. My hands were shaking when I was putting the bandage on, I had his blood on my hands, it felt warm. I was still scared and shaking and I told Milky real quiet, it's going to be ok, not to worry, things are going to be ok. The Doc is coming. He'll be here to take care of you soon.

Even as dark as it was I could see his eyes and that look he had on his face. It looked like death was coming. I kept saying it's going to be ok, it's going to be ok. Hold on, this is your ticket to go home. You'll be back home with Mom before you know it. Just hang in there. I didn't know I had the strength to drag such a big guy and carry an M-60 that far off the road with him. I can't believe I did that. All I know I wasn't thinking of myself. All that came in my mind was to put firepower out there and to get Milky off the road and out of the kill zone. I didn't even think what could have happened to me in that moment. I knew time counts out here! I did what I had to do at that moment. The medic and another guy came up and dragged him back to the back of the column to a safer place to give him more First Aid.

Then the LT told me to move up front because now I'd be carrying the M-60. So I grabbed the four ammo belts of 100 rounds each for the Pig that Milky was carrying on him. I became the third man from the point man now. That meant another new guy is going to be walking point and someone else behind him. I bet he felt like me, I really didn't want to do this shit anymore, but it was our job now like it or not. I just follow orders and hoped for the best, I guess the new guy feels the same. But I didn't want to leave Milky. But I knew I had a job to do. So I moved up to the front to where our new point man was and the other guy was. We walked past the dead point man and another one of our guys lay dead on the road. I didn't know they got killed until I moved up front. All I know they made a mistake and they paid for it with their own lives. Or whoever told him to walk the road. Or whatever, it cost them their lives and guys got wounded and killed in our Platoon.

We had some of the guys drag the bodies to the back of the column. So we can move up forward to the village. The Moon was out and you could see better now and the enemy could too. Now we had to move up the road on the hill like it or not. The enemy knows we are out here by the village now. We moved up one step at a time shaking like a leaf and sweating to beat all hell. We came across four VC dead on the road before we got to the village.

I didn't like this! I didn't like taking over the Pig, the M-60. I knew it belonged to my buddy and it made me get mad for what had happened to him. I wanted answers. I had all kind of mixed feelings going on. About what just happened and what was going on. I knew I had to get my shit together or I wouldn't make it home alive. It's so hard to calm your emotions, you had to suck it up and move on. It takes a lot to do that. I just don't know how I did that, I just don't know. All I could do is put one foot in front of the other shaking like a leaf as we moved up.

We started moving up into the village. I knew we had to secure the area in the village so we can get a Dust-Off in, a Medevac chopper. I'd been through this before, this time it was a whole lot different. It was my buddy. I would have done anything for him to save his life.

It happened so fast. All I knew, he was dying. I knew we had to get the chopper in as fast as we could. Time counts in this type of situation. I know the Medic was taking care of him and doing as best as he could. I wanted to know how serious his wound was, I know it was bad but how bad?

Because we were up front securing the area I didn't know what was going on with him in the back. I wanted to talk to him and to see how he was doing. I knew he was in the back and they were getting him ready for the Dust-Off. But I didn't know how bad he was hurting, I just knew he was hurting.

I knew we had to secure the area so they could bring the Dust-Off in. I didn't know at the time a few more guys got wounded and killed in the back of the column. Things were happening so fast. I just can't believe how things happened so different just a few feet away from you. Just inches and things can change. I could have been killed or wounded like Milky.

We finally secured the area. We finally can take care of the guys that got wounded and get them the hell out of here and to the hospital. Our LT set everything up to bring the Medevac helicopter in.

We needed to use a Star-Cluster (colored flare) and a strobe light to guide the Medevac helicopter in. It was early at night, around 2100hrs (9:00 p.m.). Boy I just hope things go right when this chopper comes in. The Moon is bright and the VC like shooting down our Dust-Off choppers. We can hear the chopper off in the distance coming in. You can tell it was flying in low by the sound it made going over the jungle canopy. That way the VC didn't have a good shot at the chopper when it's flying low to come into our LZ.

My eyes are wide open trying to look for any movement out there around the village. I could hear the chopper coming in closer to the pickup area in the rice paddy. Then I heard a pop, it was a Star-Cluster, a green one. It lit up the sky, with three little flare balls that shot up into the sky and spread out and fell back to the ground. It only lasted for a few seconds. Our LT is showing our Dust-Off chopper where we are, to come in. Then one of our guys was out in the rice paddy where the LZ will be. He turned on the strobe light and held it inside his helmet as he heard the chopper coming in close. He held his helmet over his head so the VC can't see the light flashing on him, because then the light goes up – not out. They had the wounded there by him, ready to put them on the chopper. Now the chopper is starting to descend into the LZ. It made a hard right bank into the LZ by the sound of the blade cutting through the air.

I wanted to be down there to help put Milky and the other guys on the chopper and see if I can talk to Milky before he left, one more time. Then all of a sudden there was movement. We're seeing VC getting ready to shoot the chopper down. They came out of the ground near the village. We opened up on them. They disappear and the chopper veers off. My LT wanted to know what the hell was going on? We told him we had movement, he said you better be right.

All I know, we had to start all over again to bring the chopper in. We knew the guys in the chopper must be more scared shitless now like we were. Now they know this could be a Hot LZ and they might get shot down, anything can happen. This will tighten up anybody's ass now.

So we started all over again using the strobe light to bring them in. We were all scared shitless more now. At any moment things can go wrong again. We had no choice but to do it again. We needed to get our wounded out. Time really counts in this type of situation. This time they loaded our guys up that were wounded. I still can remember hearing the echo of the chopper blades chopping the air as the helicopter lifted up and flew low over to the tree line and up and away in the dark. It was a weird feeling hearing the echo of the blades cutting through the air, going off in the dark like that. The sound faded away in the still of the night in the jungle. Then there was silence on the ground, it was weird, it was a hollow feeling.

I felt so much sadness and pain and loneliness inside of me. I was cold and shaking and sweating at the same time. It had to be at least 100 degrees tonight. I had no control over how I felt. I tried to control my feelings and my tears, it took me a few minutes to get back in control of my emotions. How stressful and painful that was.

All I knew, my buddy was gone and I knew I won't see him again. Guys with that kind of wound don't come back out in the field. All I can do is hope that Milky made it home alive. I felt like part of me left me now, and I feel so alone in this damn place. But the pain didn't leave me! My emotions drained out completely. All I know, I have to get my shit back together again to keep myself alive out here. Now I have nobody to really talk to about my personal things in life or somebody to look up to for support. We both supported each other in this hellhole. I know every second counts in this type of situation, I hope it wasn't too bad for him. I hope he made it home alive. Not to know, it messes with your mind. Life is not fair out here in a war zone in the middle of Vietnam.

But we moved out again back towards the village. It seemed like a long walk up there. We found two other VC dead by a hootch in a spider hole in the direction we were firing at. Our LT said we did well in protecting our LZ. But we still had to go to our night location just on the other side of the village. I still had Milky's blood on my hands and on my fatigues. I ended up carrying his M-60 that night. That made me think more about him. I couldn't stop thinking about him, the blood on my hands kept me in touch with him and his M-60 all night. I wanted to say more to him before he left.

I can still hear him calling for his Mom. The way he said it and the way it sounded was nothing but pain in his voice. I don't care how big you are and how strong you are, you will call out for your Mom or somebody you love so dear to you.

I found out most guys call out for their Mom when they got hurt. I guess because we were still kids. Even though we are men out here. I guess the kid came out of us when we felt pain. We're a lot closer to our Moms than our Dads. That's the way it was for us men out here.

I still don't know if he made it home safe or if he died in Vietnam. Things like that will haunt you for the rest of your life. Not knowing what happened to guys like that, if they made it home or not. All I know, when Milky left the field like that, I didn't care about anything anymore. I lost part of my feelings. I thought I already knew how much it hurt to lose somebody and see death. But to lose a buddy, somebody so close to you, who was like a part of you. I couldn't believe how much *worse* it was now. Nobody can understand that feeling until it happens to them.

We finally made it to our night location, it's about 2300hrs (11:00 p.m.) now. I just can't believe how hot it is out here tonight. We had to bring our dead with us, the chopper had no room for the dead. We didn't want to take a chance of a chopper getting shot down for the dead.

We set up our night ambush and waited to spring. I can't believe how tired I am but I couldn't sleep at all. I was thinking of Milky too much and what happened, how did he get hit? And the other guys too and not me. I guess Milky took it for me. If I was in front of him I would have taken it for him. I could have been the one that got wounded or killed that night. Like he said before we left that night. It was my lucky night. He had to have felt something for me, that's how close we were back then. Like two peas in a pod. I just can't believe the things we had to go through in this war and to live that way, it was so hard and sad.

I didn't understand what happened with the point man. Why he was talking to somebody out there in front of him? He should have fired first then asked questions later. The only thing out there at night is the enemy, it cost him his life and the guy next to him. I didn't know that three other guys got wounded in the back of the column and two got killed outright. Things were happening so fast you just don't know what the outcome will be. The new guy walking point was here only a week in-country. I guess he didn't listen to what the Sergeant said! The Sergeant told him, "Shoot first ask questions later." I guess he didn't have it in him to shoot somebody yet. Like they say don't think, react, to kill or be killed.

It's going to be a long night again and it was a hot night it had to be at least 90 degrees now. I was so uncomfortable and sweating and I felt so drained out and also I had too much on my mind. Time wasn't moving fast enough for me out here tonight. Time seemed to really drag on at night. So far there's been no movement in our ambush site. Thank God and the Creator for that. Now the Sun is starting to come up, I guess we will be sweeping the area, to see if there are any more VC in or around our area.

Then our LT said that we'd be going back to Mahone II. The chopper came into what was to be an LZ, we secured the area for the chopper to pick up our dead and the equipment the wounded left behind, and we won't be going on an Eagle Flight out into the jungle. We went back to Mahone II. As we went back through the village and down the road we picked up the dead VC we killed. Then we took them back to our little base camp. Then we put them on a chopper to see if the Intelligence people can identify who they were or if they were from the village.

I found out the LT had to make a report on what happened that night. All I knew, we got another LT. They come and go and we're the ones that are stuck out here. If somebody makes a mistake it costs people's lives out here.

I wish I could remember Milky's last name. The guys that got wounded last night, they already took all their personal stuff and shipped it out. Boy that was fast HQ already knew who got wounded and died last night. After Milky was gone, I couldn't have a buddy anymore. I just didn't need that kind of pain again. I didn't know it would be so hard on you. That kind of pain doesn't go away, it will haunt you from now on till the day you die. It was a lot to learn when you're just a kid! Especially when you don't know what life is all about yet? You're still growing up, but you grow up so fast in that type of environment. The kid in you wants you to be a kid and you can't.

So you end up with all kinds of mixed feelings. So that's why you had to learn to deal with it on your own even if you didn't know how. Because everybody else is trying to learn to deal with it too at the same time on their own. I found out really nobody can tell you how it feels and how to act because everybody feels things different and takes it in different. That type of pain is so different when you're so young. It's so hard to understand it when you're at that age.

So don't ask me how I did it? I don't know I just did what I had to do. I guess there is no right or wrong when you're trying to stay alive. That's part of life we don't understand until you're in it and if you do understand it, you'll be the first to do so. Survival is a whole different way of living. The rules are not fair in death and life situations, the decisions you're going to make are hard. And when you do you have to learn to deal with it. You learn it the best way you know how. If you're strong you can handle it and if you're weak you're going to lose it. It's going to make you or break you out here.

To go through this when you're only a kid, you don't even know what life is about and you have to make those kinds of a man's decision, it's real hard on you. I don't know how many times I tried to get answers. In those kinds of situations, there are so many answers. And so many answers are not right. I guess not knowing will haunt you. Or maybe knowing will haunt you more till the day you die. You just don't know what life has in store for you. You just don't know what's going to happen to you out here.

You just don't know when you're going to lose it or it's going to break you. I do know one thing for sure that you'll never be the same in life. When I came over here to Vietnam I was so young and innocent and full of life. But when I left Vietnam I felt like an old man and beat, tired and alone and all confused over what I did and what I saw.

What is right today can be wrong tomorrow and what is wrong today can be right tomorrow. So who wins? Really there are no answers. So you live with it the best way you know how. "Only you can live with it and only you can deal with it." Nobody can do it for you, life is not fair to any of us. We just take it one day at a time and hope for the best and that's the way it is for me. You can plan it, but it doesn't mean it's going to happen. Life is from day to day, that's the way it is, you live it the best way you know how and hope for the best. Now I know what my Dad meant. When he said to me before I left for Vietnam that I'd be more of a man in my Native ways and stronger when I came home one way or the other. He also said I will have to live with my decisions and to learn how to deal with it on my own. Nobody can do it for you. Life is a gamble, you never know what life has in store for you. I didn't really know what my Dad meant back then? I do now. It's all up to me to deal with it in the best way I can. My Dad knew a lot about life and he knew he couldn't teach me everything about life. I had to learn life on my own, like I said, he was a smart man.

LIKE THEY SAY WAR IS HELL NO MATTER HOW YOU LOOK AT IT!!!!!!! How true that is. I know my whole life has changed because of this place. I hope I can get used to this place from day to day and make it home in one piece physically and mentally intact. Our new LT said it's time to move out. Boy! Here we go again on another mission in "no man's land," the land of OZ to fight the little people again.

INTO THE LAND OF OZ
November 1968

Here we go again! We just came in for the day into this big base camp they call Dau Tieng. It was just for a few hours to clean up and to eat at this deserted compound they brought us to inside this base camp. There was dust everywhere. At least we had a roof over our heads and it was going to be our rest area for now. At least it was some kind of comfort even if we had to lie down on the wooden floor. We didn't have to worry about the ants biting us or anything else. It seemed to be a safe area for now, we didn't have to worry about anything right now.

After we rested for a while and ate it was time to saddle up again. They took us straight back through the base camp to the airstrip by truck. We got off the trucks on the runway in Dau Tieng Base Camp and got ready for the choppers to come in. As we were waiting I had time enough to mark my calendar again. It's seven months, I have 192 days in-country and that means I have 173 days left. It didn't take long for the choppers to come in. It was another Eagle Flight, a group of ten choppers. We got in groups of seven men on the runway. We were spaced out away from each other to give enough room for all the choppers to come in at once and pick all groups up at the same time. You can hear the choppers coming in to pick us up, Alpha Company, 1st of the Wolfhounds.

What a sight to see and to hear. Every time the people in the basecamp see an Eagle Flight coming in it meant two things. That a Company is coming in that's been through a lot of hell! Or it's going out to face hell all over again. Because every time we see these base camps the guys look at us with that sad look, it's better them than me. We could feel it the way they look at us.

Anyway here we go again. We'll be going into the Iron Triangle, they said it was a real bad area to be in. We didn't like hearing that shit! It meant we'd be losing a lot of guys again and we'd be thinking it's not going to be me that's going to get killed. I can't believe how many guys are out here now. A lot of the old guys have been ETS'd out of country and getting wounded or killed.

Boy hearing the choppers coming in, it made you sick to your stomach when you know you're the one going out on another mission. Then your emotions start kicking in. You feel miserable, your muscles tighten up, and you get the shakes. You're so nervous as all hell and sweating at the same time, you know you're going to face death and go back into hell. Here I go again thinking to myself again and trying to get myself mentally prepared for this mission.

Here they come, you can see them, another Eagle Flight of ten choppers (or slicks – a slick is another way to say chopper, when they're in a group, I learned that after being in-country). They came in a long line offset from each other and four gunships all making that popping sound and blowing all kinds of dust all over everything and in our faces as they landed. The ten choppers landed in a staggered line. The same way the groups of men were. The gunships were still flying around us, giving us cover as we loaded up. We were all kneeling down as they landed, we all got up and ran to the choppers and loaded up with all our gear on. It was something else to see so many choppers and so many young men going to their death. We're going into the land of OZ where the little people are waiting to kill us.

I just don't know if I'm ready for this shit anymore. I guess I'll never be ready for this shit. A few minutes ago I was in a safe area for a few hours in the rear with the gear. It was great to be free from death and for a little bit from the fear of war. Having fun with the guys and writing letters home and kicking back for a few hours was great. To be eating in peace and not to worry about the enemy attacking us at any time or any moment. What a luxury that was to be safe for a few moments in a big base camp surrounded by friendly personnel.

Here we go right back into the unknown! An area where I can get killed at any moment. I just don't know anymore. We'll be landing in the land of OZ out in the open. Some damn rice paddy near this river in the middle of nowhere. Here we go again, it feels so safe to be up here flying in the air. With that cool air blowing on your face and you can smell that sweet air again. It feels so nice to be up here and away from everything down there. The only time I can really relax is up here where I know it's safe to be. To be so close to the Creator and to see Mother Earth in its beauty from above the jungle, and to feel like an eagle flying in the air, and being free as a bird.

Before I knew it! I felt my stomach go up and then down, the chopper started dropping down toward the red smoke, as I was looking out toward the ground, where our LZ was. I could see the artillery just finish prepping the area. Now I can see our gunships going in to work the area over too. Boy it looks like they destroyed part of Mother Earth, there are all kinds of bomb craters, everything is blown apart down there. It looks like they've been working this place over for a while. I guess there's been a lot of enemy activity in this area. It sure doesn't look good for us. Like I said I don't need this shit anymore! A few minutes ago we Grunts were breaking bread together and feeling good about ourselves in a safe area, now we are hoping to stay alive.

Here we go again, the whole Eagle Flight is going in at once. As we get close to the ground, you start feeling the hot wind blowing against your face, it's not cool any more. Then that bad smell of death is in the air going up into your nose and before you know it the sweat starts coming down your face and in your eyes. Then inside your mouth it starts feeling dry as a bone. Then you get nervous as all hell and you start shaking to beat all hell. "Okay Mom I got that button out of my pocket and put it in my mouth again, to keep my mouth from being dry."

I'm looking down at the ground, I can't believe we are going down there. We all have that scared look on our faces, that thousand-yard stare. Our eyes are wide open, you can see the dark shadows around our eyes and the whites of our eyes every time we do this shit! I just don't know how we do this every time being so nervous and scared to death.

I just can't get used to this bullshit! Hearing the radio transmitting and all that chatter on the radio. I can hear the fear in their voices. Then hearing the blades on the choppers cutting the air and making that popping sound and all the other different sounds that are going on as we go in. Then both Door Gunners start opening up with their machine guns. Then the other gunships flying along with us give us cover with their mini-guns and machine guns firing. I can't believe how this really tightens your ass up.

And before I knew it we touched the ground and landed. I didn't want to get off the chopper in the back of my mind. But we all started jumping off the chopper and hitting the ground. Dust and pieces of grass were flying everywhere in the air and on us. It was getting in my eyes and mouth and in my clothes and it was hard to see. I was sweating to beat all hell and the dust was sticking on my skin and clothes because of the sweat. The guns firing were real loud as I landed on the ground with both feet and then I hit the ground in a prone position. Then I'm waiting there on the ground and I was looking all around. As the choppers lifted off and flew away, they were still shooting out of them around the area. The sound of the choppers and the gunfire faded away as they flew away.

But I moved and jumped into a bomb crater that was close to me. I wanted to have some kind of cover in case the enemy opens up on us. Before I knew it! It got real quiet. But I was hugging the ground. My heart was running a hundred miles an hour and I was breathing hard and still shaking and I was scared to beat all hell.

Next thing I hear, the LT says move out and move up to the tree line next to the river bank. I didn't want to move out of the bomb crater, I felt so safe. But I had to follow orders like it or not. Then I heard the gunships flying over us and around us again. Giving us cover as they fire their guns into the tree line as we move to the tree line near the river bank.

Boy running out in an open rice paddy again firing my weapon and trying to get to the tree line along the river bank was the shits. Boy! All the things you think when you're running one step at a time toward that tree line. It's like a broken record! You think about stepping on that booby trap. Is it going to be this step or is it the next one? Then you think of a bullet going through your head. Then you think about your Mom and Dad and the things you used to do back home. How your whole life flashes right by you. How every step might be your last step on Mother Earth. I just can't believe how hard it was to push yourself to do that when you're just a kid. Knowing that you can step on a booby trap at any moment or be killed by the enemy at any moment, or there could be bamboo stakes sticking out on the bank of the tree line. That alone puts a lot of fear in you, knowing that.

Then the enemy can open up on you before you get there. It's also a lot of stress on you just knowing the enemy could be there waiting to kill you, waiting to put a bullet in your head. It's hot and I'm already sweating and dirty again. It looks like we've never been cleaned up. I'm right back where we started in this hellhole. Here we go again on another search and destroy mission in the middle of nowhere. I didn't know this was the Saigon River again. I didn't know it went this far up North. There are no villages and if there were they'd all been destroyed and there were no civilians around in the area.

This makes it a lot easier to shoot now knowing it's only the enemy out here and it's a free fire zone. Now we can have all the support and firepower we need out here. The closer you come to the tree line the more pressure and fear run through your body. How your whole body tightens up and shakes at the same time. Thinking and thinking! An enemy can put a bullet in your head out here before you can get to the tree line or river bank. We made it to the river bank near the tree line. There were bamboo stakes along the river bank camouflaged by grass, if we landed on them, they would have gone right through our bodies, so we made our way around them. Boy what a relief it was! We made it without being shot or landing on the bamboo stakes. I am hoping our support fire scared them away. Now we'll be searching for the enemy and enemy supplies and destroying their bunkers. We found ten bunkers along the river bank and some enemy supplies that were hidden in some of the bunkers and in the river. At the same time we found eighteen NVA bodies in and out of the bunker all messed up, by our artillery and gunships. They did a good job this time they were right on target. Boy if they were alive it would be one hell of a fight to clear them out of there. A lot of us wouldn't have made it out of the rice paddy to the river bank where the tree line was. Today the support unit saved our ass! Now it's time for us to move down the river to look for more enemy. Then we'll be setting up an ambush tonight waiting to ambush the enemy coming down the river on their sampans. Or they'll be walking along the river banks near the tree line.

I guess we'll be doing this for a while sweeping by day as we patrol and setting up our night ambushes. Our mission is always changing, nothing's ever the same out here. Every time we come to an inlet, we search the area or put up a night ambush. I didn't know there were so many inlets in this river.

It seems like we've been out here too long, time really seems to drag out here. We've sprung four ambushes in a week and a half already. We killed about fourteen enemy. There's been a lot of movement around here at night. Boy the daytime seems a lot safer than the nights. The fear of night and the unknown can really get to you out here. But there is so much fear of the unknown out here all you can do is hope for the best and do a lot of praying. Boy! I didn't like all these little creatures (poison spiders, poison snakes, red ants, black ants, lizards, land and water leeches, etc.) that come around you at night. The nights have been real hot so far, it's been about 100 degrees at night. It seems to bring out a lot more of them little creatures. I guess it's more because of the heat and humidity. We ended up with a lot of bug bites. Your face or hands and legs swell up and you end up being put on a Dust-Off helicopter the next day back to the main base camp. We had some of the guys end up losing a leg or a hand because of that. I just can't believe a little bug can take you out of the war! Some of the guys didn't take their malaria pills and ended up with malaria. I guess it's better than getting killed or blown apart.

We had one more night left before we moved more inland. It's already been three weeks so far out here. But we sprang one more night ambush before we moved inland. There were three sampans moving down the river this time. We thought they might be going into the inlet, but they stayed in the main part of the river. But from our side of the bank they were an easy target. So we set off our Claymore mines and opened up with our weapons, it was about 0500hrs (5:00 a.m.). We were lucky they were on our side of the river, they were like sitting ducks. Our LT called in for some flare rounds to light up the area for us. Like always it made it spooky at night.

You can hear the flare sizzling as it's coming down. Then you see the light from the flare reflecting off the river water, as it was coming down and hanging from its little parachute. The guy next to me, I can see the shadow of his face and the white of his eyes. His eyes look so big at night. Then that scared look we all have on our faces and the sweat coming down our faces. All we can do is look at each other and say nothing and hope for the best. Just sweating it out as we wait for daylight and the Sun to come up. And hoping no more enemy will come down the river or behind us.

I was looking out now to the East, I could see part of the sky was dark and the stars fading in the sunlight. Before I knew it, it was daylight and the Sun was almost out. It was time to search the immediate area. It was hard to get up on your feet, I was stiff and my bones hurt from not moving around all night. We couldn't find anything, so we moved downriver because of the slow current. We knew the sampans would float downriver.

We found one sampan stuck in some branches near the bank and two bodies inside, it also had five sacks of rice, 100 pounds each. The sampan was about 100 yards downriver a little way from our ambush site. Every time when we do this shit I just wonder when this is going to happen to us again. The odds are not in our favor, we haven't been hit lately, it's a matter of time till we will.

I guess they are waiting for us to make a mistake and for the right time to do their ambush. This is a hell of a way to make a living out here in Vietnam trying to kill each other. This is one hell of a life to live day after day and night after night, kill or be killed.

Boy am I getting real tired of this shit night after night and day after day. The days seem real short and the nights seem so long. I just can't believe living out in the open for months at a time and going without food and water for days at a time, I wonder how I did it. From day to day and from night to night. I guess when you have to, you have to.

We move down the river to see if we can find the other two sampans or did they get away. They seem to be like ghosts when we can't find them. You would think! But a lot of the time they would carry their dead off and leave no evidence. But you knew we killed more of them. We move down the river about a half-mile or so. We find the other two sampans stuck along the river bank with supplies in them. There are two more VC dead inside each sampan.

There was no way they could have made it alive as close as they were in our kill zone. For a while I thought they were ghosts and disappeared in thin air. There they are in the sampans with all kinds of holes in them. These Claymore mines can really do the job. The other sampans have medical supplies and ammo boxes and weapons in them. We destroy the rice by throwing it in the river and we destroy the sampans by blowing them up in place.

Our LT calls in a chopper to pick up the rest of the captured supplies we have. We secure the area for the chopper to come in. Here comes the chopper! As it comes in we can see the Door Gunners' and the Pilots' faces. They look so tense and nervous the same way we did, it wasn't a good feeling. We all know they are a big target and the enemy will do anything to destroy one. They start yelling at us to hurry up and take our supplies off the chopper. We unload our water and cases of C-rations and ammo that they brought to us that the CO ordered for us. We really needed it, we were out of water and C-rations. Then we load up all the captured supplies as fast as we can on the chopper. What a relief that was to get that chopper out of the area! It only took a few minutes to unload and load it with the captured VC supplies. Now we can start moving inland into the jungle to do our sweeps and night ambushes. This shit never ends out here day after day and night after night, it's that broken record again! We just keep repeating this bullshit. That's the life of a Grunt and Infantryman. Every day and night is a living hell for us. The suffering never ends for us, the pain, tension, nervousness, survival guilt, being scared, and all the trauma that goes on around you and especially out here. So all you can do is try to deal with it. One day at a time and even one second at a time and hope for the best and try to keep your sanity.

We finally move inland doing our sweeps and patrolling in the jungle. There's been a lot of activity going on from the enemy. We knew it was a bad area because it was hard to see them in the jungle. We had to cut our way through a lot of vegetation to find them. Talk about how hard that was! We finally ran into their ambush a few times. What a nightmare it was. I've been lucky so far and made it through all that. We've been losing a lot of guys lately. The enemy just comes out of nowhere. Also we've been running into a lot of booby traps and punji pits. The punji pits were made with a lot of sharp bamboo sticks and put inside a hole in the ground with the points pointing up and camouflaged with leaves covering the hole. If you fell in a big punji pit you were a goner. There were other types of punji pit holes that were just big enough for your foot to fit in. Also, we've been finding a lot of tunnels and spiders holes. Damn! It's just as bad as it is being down South out in the rice paddies. You're damned if you do and you're damned if you don't. I feel like my time is running out for me. All I can do is hope for the best one day at a time. But I finally got wounded in an ambush out in the middle of the jungle, my luck ran out in the land of OZ. A day I will never forget.

WORKING WITH THE NAVY ON THE PBRS
AND JUST OUT OF THE HOSPITAL
December 1968

I just got out of the hospital and I'm going back to my Company. It's my eighth month with 225 days in-country. I got wounded a month ago on November 17, 1968, back in my seventh month in-country. Back on that day I'd just marked another day on my helmet, early in the morning before we moved out. I'd been in-country 195 days already back when it happened. It was just before Thanksgiving in an ambush early in the morning in the jungle of Vietnam. I lost my helmet with my short-timer calendar when I got wounded. Afterwards, I made Sergeant and I was issued everything new to go back out in the field to where Alpha Company is. Clothes, boots, weapon, ammo, grenades, canteens and web-gear and so on. I look like a FNG (Fucking New Guy) from Stateside. Now I am leaving the hospital after my checkup. I'm the only one going back to my Unit. I'm flying in on a Chinook helicopter that's going to resupply Alpha Company.

The Crew Chief was watching the supplies through the cargo hole in the middle of the floor-plate. The supplies were in a cargo net connected to the cable hanging on a cargo hook down under the Chinook helicopter in the cargo hole. The sound of the helicopter and vibrations put me in deep thought. I was thinking of home and how scared I was going back to the war again. My mind was running away again with all kinds of crazy thoughts, I was looking at all the different things inside the helicopter and the porthole window. Then the Crew Chief startled me by hollering at me to come over and look down the cargo hole. I got up and move over to where he was, I looked down through the cargo hole, I could see we were coming to a river. Also I could see the cargo net with our supplies hanging from cargo straps that hooked to a cable from the helicopter.

Then the Crew Chief points down to the river. It looks like a big snake with all kinds of curves stretching out for miles. Then he says that is where your Company's at. Then I can see the PBR-Boats (Patrol Boat, River) on the river between the cargo net and the helicopter and the other boats look like little toy boats. As we come closer I can see it's my Company and the guys are on top of the boats. Some of the boats are next to the banks already. There are more boats that are moving into the banks at the same time to let the rest of the Company off. They're securing the rest of the area for the drop-off point for their resupply that we're bringing in. They drop the cargo net with the supplies near the bank of the river were the boats are. Then the helicopter moves over. The Crew Chief was by the cargo ramp then he pushed the bottom to drop the cargo ramp down in the back of the helicopter. Then the Crew Chief said for me to jump off the ramp while it was hovering over the rice paddy to let me off. I jump into the rice paddy right back in the shit, again it never ends.

When I finally get to my Company on the ground, I don't see anybody I knew in my Squad or the Platoon. I don't know half the Company, most of the old guys I knew are gone. And there is a new LT in charge now of the Platoon. I didn't know we lost so many guys that day. All I knew, I couldn't move, I was going in and out of consciousness and I was lucky to have survived and to be here now.

Now I'm with all these FNGs or should I say kids because they all look like fresh meat. I don't like this shit at all. I feel all alone again in this damn place. I'm just tired of being alone and making new friends and before you know it, they are gone. I can't believe how they knocked the shit out of us that day.

Just before I got wounded back in November, HQ said we had to move out as fast as we could. Out of the area in the jungle where we were at. Because they were going to have a B-52 strike in the area, sometime early in the morning that day. We were moving as fast as we could in the jungle, so fast that we walked right into an NVA ambush the first thing that morning.

They said they spotted an NVA Battalion in the area. I guess that's why we sprung at least three ambushes in two days, before we ran into them. There'd been a lot of movement in the area. We knew it! It was just a matter of time, we would get hit hard. We got hit a few times by them running into us during the day time. Or the other way around, who knows!

We lost a few guys and a few got wounded, so we called in a Dust-Off to take them out of the jungle. It was just a matter of time for us to run into their ambush. I knew my luck was running out since I'd been walking point most of the time and seeing all these new fresh tracks on the ground. The ones we'd been killing had new weapons and equipment on them and new uniforms on them.

We were all scared shitless. We felt surrounded by the enemy. Just by the way we felt and the way things were looking around the area, it was just a matter of time before we got ambushed. It was a scary feeling like everything was closing in on us. It was early in the morning, about 0700hrs (7:00 a.m.). But earlier that morning about 0500hrs (5:00a.m.) we sprung another ambush. We killed about five enemy. One of our guys got killed and two wounded. So we called in a Dust-Off as soon as it got daylight about 0600hrs (6:00 a.m.). We also loaded up the enemy equipment that we captured, and our KIA (Killed in Action) and our two WIA (Wounded in Action) on the Dust-Off chopper.

Our CO was told that we had to move out because we are having B-52 strikes in that area and that it's coming in our area at 0900hrs (9:00 a.m.). We had to go to an LZ about a mile and half away, to a pick-up zone. That gave us two hours to get there. It was time to saddle up and to move out to be at our LZ in time for the choppers to pick us up. I'd been walking point the past few days. But this time they told me another guy was taking my place. Boy was I glad of that. I'd been so scared and tired of being up front the past few days. I think it was getting to me. I guess my LT saw it in me. We started to move out. I was about the third man from the point man and the scout dog handler. These guys were up front ahead of me. We were cutting through the jungle for about a half-hour or so already. We only moved half a mile. But we were moving too fast I thought to myself. Before I knew it we were on a trail and I thought to myself what the hell are we doing on the trail now. I started to tell the guy in front of me to tell the guys up front of us to get off the trail. But before I knew it, there was an explosion.

All I could remember! The next thing I knew I was flying in the air and my skin on my face was pushed back. My face and eyes had that burning sensation, I felt like a rag doll. I could see the sky and the ground then the sky and the ground again. Then I felt it when I hit the ground. I must have gotten knocked out when I landed so hard. I couldn't move after I hit the ground. It felt so hard when I landed. I think I hit my head first on the ground. I was going in and out of consciousness everything was spinning around. All I knew! That I could see that I was in an old bomb crater facing up looking toward the sky. I had ringing in my ears and my head still felt like it was spinning around. I didn't even know I got hit in the arm and leg and stomach. I guess I was numb. I don't know how long I was out. I lost track of time. I opened my eyes up again and I was looking up and then I saw an F-4 jet it was painted in camouflage OD green and OD brown in color, and it was dropping its bombs and napalm. I could see the Pilot in the cockpit. I could hear the roar of the engines as the jet went by. I could see a ball of flame and smoke rise above the jungle and I felt the concussions from the bombs and napalm when they exploded and the ground shook. Then I could feel the heat from the napalm and it sucked up the oxygen from the air where I was at. I could hardly breathe. I could smell death in the air. I was scared shitless! I couldn't move and I didn't know why. All the noises and sounds sounded like they were far away. But I knew I was real close to the action when I felt the heat from the napalm and blast from the bombs that shook the ground.

I wonder if they knew where I was at and that I was still alive up there. I must have been real close to the enemy. But I could barely hear the explosions that were going off and the shooting that was happening around me. My ears were ringing so loud and I could smell death. I just couldn't move! I must have lost consciousness again. All I know! I think I had an out-of-body experience. I could see a bright light it felt so good to see it, it felt warm on me and inside of me, as I was looking up in the air at that bright light. I could feel my body move towards the bright light, my body felt so light in the air. As my body was moving towards the light like an eagle flying in the air, I looked down where I was. I could see there was a body on top of me inside the bomb crater. The next thing I knew when I opened my eyes it was dark. I still couldn't move, I wondered is that why I couldn't move? I couldn't move my head, I felt paralyzed, all I could do was move my eyes.

Then the next thing I remembered Doc was putting bandages on me and a tag that he wrote on. The next thing I noticed I was being loaded on a Dust-Off with the dead and it was nighttime. I noticed one of the dead was my LT. I must have been the last of the wounded to leave. Because usually our dead were the last to be put on the chopper. I must have been in the kill zone that day. I guess that's why they couldn't get to me right away to put me on a Dust-Off early in the day. It took all day and part of the night to reach me. I guess I was lucky that I got blown into that bomb crater. I really think the bomb crater saved my life because it gave me a lot of protection and cover from the enemy gunfire and the explosions that were going off near me and around me in the jungle. I found out when I was in the hospital, they told me that a little part of my flesh from my ear was eaten off by all those ants that were on the jungle floor and I had all kinds of ant bites all over my body. I didn't even know that was happening to me at the time. I was in and out of consciousness at the time, I couldn't feel any anything because my body was numb. My whole body was numb.

But when I started coming to my senses I started feeling again. I started feeling all kinds of pain throughout my whole body. I never felt so much as we were flying back to the field hospital unit. I never felt so vulnerable and scared, alone in being in that kind of predicament when you face death at firsthand. I remember seeing the ants eating on our dead before and on the enemy but I didn't think they would eat you when you were still alive! As a kid you didn't think of that kind of thing and you didn't know that kind of stuff would happen. The more I am out here the more I learn about life and how hard it is to survive out here in the jungles of Vietnam. People just don't know how bad things get in war until you have to live it and see it firsthand.

Now, here I'm back with my Company and scared shitless of being back. Here it is, sometime in December, a few weeks before Christmas in my eighth month with 214 days in-country. I guess I might as well draw me a new short-timer calendar again on my helmet. I really didn't want to come back here. Knowing now that things can really happen to you like getting killed or wounded. When it happens to you reality really sets in. Most of the time you always think it's going to be the other guy. But I can't think that way anymore. Reality really hit me right in the face.

I'm so scared to be back and to be in charge of these new kids, it puts a whole lot more pressure on me. I don't need this shit. I've had enough of trying to deal with me coming back out here and staying alive. Boy I just don't know how Sergeant Bones put up with this bullshit day after day. I have about four more months left to do. I just don't know if I can take it anymore! All I do is go through the motions, one step at a time and hoping for the best. Now that I've been so close to my own death I feel even more vulnerable being out here. I'm so scared to death of dying and being with these new guys doesn't make it any easier for me. Life is not fair. It's all about luck out here it isn't how much you know. It's about being in the right place at the right time when things start happening. But there is one thing that really helped me get through this! It's remembering what my Dad and Mom taught me and their words of wisdom and believing in the Creator.

Here we go again on a new mission working with the Navy on the PBRs and on a different type of operation. I don't like this, I never was trained for this type of mission working with the Navy. It looks like we'll be working up and down the river sweeping the river banks.

We'll be sitting on top of these PBRs going up and down the rivers trying to draw enemy fire and hoping for the best to stay alive. Things are not getting any easier out here. Sitting on these boats I feel like a sitting target or sitting duck.

If the enemy opens up on us we have no place to hide. If we get hit and fall off the boats we are sure to drown with all the heavy equipment we have on us. This is one hell of a way to live from day to day. I'm still a kid, I just can't believe all the responsibilities I have now. I never felt so much pressure being a Squad Leader of these kids.

No matter what we did we were dead meat. I just hate this shit, day after day. I can't believe the stress we were put through so young! Knowing death is just around the corner. Now that I'd been wounded and I'm so young and coming back out here can really get to you. I just don't know how I did it. Talking about the things that go through your mind is something else. You just can't imagine the things you think of! When you're only eighteen and 19 or twenty and how scared you get and how upset your stomach gets and how stressful it gets out there. "Only if you'd been here" could you understand how it was. Now I have nobody to talk to. All my friends and my buddy Milky are gone. Now I wonder about how bad the other guys got wounded or who got killed in my Platoon. I didn't know then that this will hunt me till the day I die, not knowing who died and who made it. This has really changed the way I think about life.

Well here we go again. We got our supplies and ate our C-rations and got ready to move out on the boats. Most of the boats are ready to move in against the bank so we can get on them. We all load on the boats to move out and down the river. We'll be sweeping down the river banks and inlets in the daytime and putting night ambushes along the banks at night. Our eyes were wide open sitting on top of those boats going down the river and how hot it was. The only thing that was good about being on the boats was that we didn't have to walk as much and even all that hot air felt cool when it came off the water. And the spray of water that blew on our faces every now and then. It felt good as we went down the river looking for the enemy. How the little things in life like cool hot air and the spray of water on your face is such a luxury to us now. As I look at all these young faces it makes me feel so sad for them! With their baby-faced look and their eyes that look so young. No dark shadows around them, they haven't got that hard look yet and the white guys' skin is milky white, not burnt like ours and they look so innocent and they still have a smile on their faces. It's just a matter of time, they're going to lose all that innocent way of life. I just wonder how many are going to make it through their first battle of hell.

We are going up and down the river now and into the canal inlets. Boy how scared you get and how vulnerable you feel out in the open water. Those inlets are something else to go in. The PBRs can't go down the inlets. So, in six-man teams, we have to use rubber rafts and paddle our way up and down in them, to look for enemies and enemy supplies. Talk about the hazards, it was crazy. We paddled 50 to 100 yards up into the canal inlets and prodded with poles in the water to see if we could find any enemy caches of supplies in the water.

You can hardly see because of all the vegetation in the area and on both sides of the canals. A lot of time you have to cut your way through the vegetation. Because it covered up the canal inlets. You can come up to a bunker and not even know it. Boy when that happens it scares the holy shit out of you. Then if they were there it would be too late to do anything about it. You were dead meat if the enemy was in there.

The leeches, snakes, spiders, ants, mosquitoes, and any other creatures will bite the hell out of you and the elephant grass is something else. It's about four feet tall or sometimes taller. The elephant grass is large with very tall stems with long flat leaves, they're like straps with sharp edges and hairs and flowering thorns on them. Boy walking through that would cut you to pieces a little bit at a time before you knew it! Talk about all the hazards we had to go through. That was something else back then.

Now they are going to drop us off before it gets dark again so we can set up another night ambush along the banks of the river or in the canal inlets. We have to walk a half a mile to get to another canal inlet. Boy talk about all the hazards we had to go through and cutting though all that vegetation and walking in all that mud and water, it was something else. Sometimes there were no banks to lay on. There was just water to sit in. Sometimes we had no choice, and talk about being in the water all night, it was something else. Because by the time we got there the tide was up, we had no banks to be on. We had to sit in a foot of water for hours and hours until the tide would go down or daylight comes.

It'll be dark and the boat will be long gone. The boats won't pick us up until tomorrow morning. Then they'll move us up and down the river to another location. As always we sweep the banks to check out the banks and canal inlets for any enemy bunkers and supplies and the enemy.

We did this for three to four weeks working with the Navy guys on the boats looking for the enemy and their supplies. I didn't know there were so many canal inlets to this damn river. We sprang a few ambushes and captured a lot of enemy supplies, that were hidden under the water or in the vegetation along inlets and river banks. We also destroyed a lot of empty bunkers and sampans also hidden in the vegetation.

They ambushed us a few times when we were moving down the river on those boats. It was in the middle of the afternoon and it was another hot day. Talk about all hell breaking loose. When VC opened up on us and all we could do was hold on for dear life and hope for the best. I was praying to the Creator and the Almighty Spirit to keep me safe. Boy talk about your ass tightening up and getting all panicked and stressed out, that will do it. Your heart is running a hundred miles an hour and you're hoping you don't get killed or fall into the river.

You have no control over what's happening on the boats. You just hang on and hope for the best. Then at the same time on the PBRs the Navy guys open up with their M-60 machine guns, 50-caliber machine guns, M-79 grenade launchers. The noise is so loud and all the hollering that was going on! You can hear the panic in their voices and you can feel it at the same time. What an awful feeling. As we break away from the kill zone where the VC ambushed us from, I'm hollering at my guys to hang on in a panicked voice too and hoping we get out of the kill zone in time.

The Navy drops us off up the river about 100 yards or so. So they can go back and destroy the enemy and we can stop them from running away from their ambush site. Now we're making a sweep back to where the VC ambushed us from. We lost three new guys and four got wounded from our Platoon and some of our Navy guys too and we lost one PBR which got hit by an RPG. Which we found out later in the day. We can hear the Navy boats working the area over. They called in the helicopter gunships. You can hear the rockets firing from the choppers making that funny whoosh, whoosh sound as the rockets came out of their rocket tubes. Then a few seconds later you hear the explosions going off. We're still moving up to where the enemy was at. We're in the tall elephant grass and in the mud and water up to our knees and sometimes up to our waist. We can hear the bullets going over our heads. I hope our LT moves us more inland so we can be on some dry land. I guess he wants to keep us close to the river so we can have support from the Navy boats and won't be in the line of fire.

We can't see in front of us. Boy I hope the Navy boats and gunships kill them all. This is going to be one hell of a firefight, if we hit the shit in this shit. There's nothing to hide behind, the only cover we have is the tall elephant grass. Boy when you think things are bad, things can get a whole lot worse at any time. Anything can happen at any moment and like I said, the things that go through your mind are something else.

We stopped! The LT told me to move my Squad up to the front. So we move up to replace the other Squad. Here I go again I don't need this shit. As we move up front passing all the other guys they look like they are scared to death and beat. We come up to the point man, he looks more beat! And sweating to beat all hell and his face is real red. He'd been cutting through all that elephant grass. He's about to pass out from heatstroke! I tell one of the guys to give him some water and pour some on his head for the heat, so it won't cook his brain, and call a Medic to take care of him. Now it's our turn to move forward! The firing has stopped. I don't feel right and I know my point man is scared as all hell. The helicopter flying over our heads is making that popping sound, you can hear the engine of the boats sitting idle. We can't see them with all the vegetation. I know we are getting close. We move up another 50 yards and come to a clearing about 50 yards long 10 yards wide where everything was blown apart.

We can see some of the bunkers were blown apart and the vegetation blown away. Then some dead fish and snakes in the water and on the ground. The terrain is uneven because of all the bomb craters and the trees that were blown apart and we have to climb over them. We could smell death in the air! We pass the word back about what is in front of us. We start searching out the bunkers. One at a time as we move down the river bank. Talk about being stressed and sweating your ass off to beat all hell, this will do it. We start finding bodies in the area.

We found 15 VC dead. There were three women and 12 men in all. We police around the area and pick up their equipment and destroy the rest of the bunkers in place. There were seven bunkers in all. Boy we were lucky we didn't get messed up more than what we did! What a day it was so far! These new guys in my Squad, they look so young and scared and beat, I guess I'm getting too old for this shit. Then I think to myself these guys are just as old as me or one year younger or older.

Anyway it was just another day trying to stay alive. I just don't know! If I like being the old guy out here now. And I don't mean by my age. I mean how much time I have in-country. Now I have the responsibility of keeping the new guys alive and the headache that goes with it. I guess this is how Sergeant Bones felt when he made Sergeant, hoping he had made the right decisions and praying to God. Hoping he could keep his shit together too.

I didn't know how stressful this would be, taking care of these kids over here. This is a bunch of bullshit to put on me so young! I just hope I don't lose it over here because of the responsibility I have now. All I know is that I have to adapt and hope for the best in what I'm doing. All I know now is I'm going to have to live with the decisions I make out here. I know a lot of these new guys will not like my decisions but I still had to make them do it. I know it has to be done so most of us can survive out here. I've been lucky so far and I hope my luck doesn't run out again, after being wounded I don't feel that lucky anymore. I feel so lost in my feelings, I feel numb in my decisions I have to make out here. There is nobody I can really talk to about how I feel and about how scared I am, and that my buddy Milky is gone, and I don't even know if he's alive or dead! All I know is that I have to be strong and have faith in my Native ways, and what my Mom and Dad have taught me about surviving the elements and how to control my fear of the unknown.

I guess somebody has to do it. Boy I wonder if I'd had the training to go to NCO (Non-commissioned Officer) school if it would've been easier for me to handle the responsibility that I was given to do. I guess I will never know! I even saw guys that had NCO school training lose it. I guess it depends on the person, on how they were raised. All the training in the world can't make you handle this kind of responsibility. You have to have it in you already and I guess I did. I guess my CO and LT saw it in me. That I had leadership in me.

It's time to move out again for another mission. We are leaving the Navy behind on their boats and moving back into the jungle again. I'm glad this mission is over with! It was another "on the job" (OJT) training. I hate adapting to all these different missions, it's really scary to learn as you go. I didn't know the service would do this to you, especially as young as we were.

The only thing I did know, I learned a lot about life and death experiences and how to deal with it in my own way real fast. Nobody can teach you about that kind of experience. You have to live it to understand it. I found out that life has so many different paths. Each path you have to live it to understand it. That's why nobody can teach it to you. Everybody sees life different in their own way. They can teach their opinions. It doesn't mean it's right. It's all up to how you deal with it. You have your own way to adjust to it as fast as you can. If you don't you're going to die! Now that I've been with the new guys for a few weeks already. They don't look so innocent anymore, it looks like they're starting to get hard. They're starting to understand what life and death are really about out here in "no man's land." It won't be long, all their innocence will be gone and that baby-faced look. This was part of my eighth month in December 1968.

WHEN THE ENEMY ATTACKED OUR LITTLE BASE CAMP
December, 1968

I can remember one of the times that our little base camp out in the middle of jungle was attacked. It was at night and all hell broke loose. It had only been five weeks so far since I was put in charge of a Squad of men. And my Squad had all these new guys in it. It was so hard to look at these guys with their baby-faced look and how scared they look.

I don't like it! The way they look up to me. I'm just as scared as they are and I can't show it now, because of the responsibility I have now. I can't be myself, I have to act different. I can't show my feelings anymore. It's a lonely job to be in charge of these new guys. The way you look at life now has to change. You can't be close to anybody because you won't be able to make the right decisions out there with an open mind. All I know, I have to do what I have to do to keep us all alive. Boy! I always wondered, if I had the training in leadership, could I have done better in my decisions?

We were back in our little base camp called Mahone II, we just came back from our patrols being out in the jungle. It was in the evening, almost 1800hrs (6:00 p.m.), we just had enough time to settle in for the night and to eat something. We were all tired from being out in the jungle doing our sweeps and night ambushes. We were assigned to our bunkers around the inside of our perimeter for the night. So we did our duty by guarding the perimeter around our base camp.

Then it was about 0400hrs (4:00 a.m.). I was dead asleep. But all of a sudden I was startled from my sleep. By the guys shouting incoming, incoming! I woke up and grabbed my weapon. As I was running around in the dark I was telling my guys to get into their bunkers.

We all ran into our assigned bunkers to take cover. I can hear the rounds coming out of the enemy mortar tubes as I run into our bunker. They are close to the base. Their mortar tubes must have been about 500 to 1,000 yards out, to hear them firing. Then you hear the mortar rounds exploding all around our base camp and some landing near our bunkers. The ground shakes and the dirt comes down from the ceiling from the sandbags as we are in the bunker.

I have to grab some of the new guys to get them up on their feet. They're hiding down in the corner of the bunker and not looking out of the bunker porthole. I can see how scared they look. Some are crying to themselves, I tell them to get their asses up and start looking out for the enemy. They will be coming.

We're looking out of the bunker where you can see the enemy starting to come. They're trying to get through the concertina wire and barbed wire. Our mortar tubes are firing flare rounds in the air and lighting up the whole base camp and perimeter. We open up on them and the whole base is firing their weapons, there were all kinds of different weapons firing. The firing, it's so loud, there's a lot of shouting going on. People saying ammo, ammo, Medic, Medic, they're coming in, they're coming in. It is scary as all hell. I have to go check on the other two bunkers that I'm assigned to, to make sure everything is ok with the new guys. To make sure they're doing their job right. And let them know I didn't forget about them and to give them confidence that I am still around.

I don't know for sure if the enemy got through the concertina wire and barbed wire, on the other side of our base camp. Until later that morning when our LT told us. But our guys did kill the enemy that got through the wire, and the ones that blew the ammo bunker.

I knew they hit our ammo supply and blew it up that night because of hearing all the explosions and smelling all that CS-gas (tear gas) in the air. We were downwind from the ammo bunker. The CS-gas blew right into our bunkers on our side of the base camp. We were in and around our bunker firing our weapons.

It's hard to catch your breath and it's hard to see the enemy. Because of all the tear gas grenades that blew up into the air. The gas is strong in the air, it's like a fog on our side of the base camp. It's a spooky feeling like death is right around the corner waiting for us. It really makes our eyes water and our noses run and we're choking at the same time. But we still open up with our weapons at the enemy and hold our position and do our job as best as we can under that kind of condition. We kill them before they can get to us. It seems like a long time but it was only a half hour or so into the battle. But to me! It seemed to be a lifetime.

Our 155-artillery and 81-mortar started firing their rounds towards the enemy and putting illumination rounds up into the sky. Then the flares lit up the whole base camp and around the whole area of our perimeter. Then it got quiet, the enemy stopped firing then we ceased firing.

Then every now and then you hear another illumination round go off. You hear that pop sound just before the flare lights up the area. It's just the same as always, when you hear that sizzling sound as it comes down real slow in a little parachute. The flare's hanging down from the parachute rocking back and forth. The light from the flare is doing the same thing, moving back and forth, as it lights up the whole area.

Here goes that feeling again! It looks spooky out here the way the flare lights make all kinds of different shadows on the ground as they move back and forth. It makes it look like things were moving around out there. It's going to be another long night again for me and the guys and the four guys I sent out on LP. I just start staring out into the dark and waiting for the enemy to strike us again. It seems to be a lot safer to be in the base camp than out in the field on a night ambush or patrol, where we don't have any protection just the cover of night, on a night ambush, and no cover out in the open rice paddy or on a patrol.

It's almost daylight, I hope the guys I put on LP are ok. We get the word that we'll be going outside the barbed wire from our little base camp. To check out the surrounding area around our perimeter and to make sure it's safe for a Dust-Off to pick up our wounded. The Sun is up now and it's time for our Platoon to move out and check out the area now.

I can't believe it! The whole base is watching us going out there. They're waiting for something to happen to us. They can see how scared we look going out there. I guess it's the first time they're actually going to see how an Infantry Unit works. When we're going to face death. I bet they're saying to themselves, it's better them than me to be out there in harm's way! Boy I don't need this shit. All we can do is follow orders like it or not. As we start to move outside the wire we can see some enemy dead around the base and inside the barbed wire and hanging there on the wire. It's going to be a long day again.

As we move around the base, we check out the dead bodies on the ground and the ones hanging on the barbed wire and outside the wire. Making sure they're dead and not playing dead. As we go by the bodies, we pick up their weapons. We find three that were wounded, we took care of them and gave them First Aid. Then we have to kill one that went for his weapon. We had some of our guys take the enemy back inside our base camp and get them ready to be picked up by our Dust-Off chopper.

The next thing, we hear a chopper coming into our area. We thought it was our Dust-Off coming in to pick up our wounded and the wounded enemy. It's a chopper playing music! I can't believe the music they're playing! That look I see on my guys' faces, they're in shock like me. That chopper is playing Christmas music and has a Santa Claus in it, saying Merry Christmas and ho-ho- ho!

He's also throwing out candy canes at us. They land by my feet and on top of the enemy bodies that were blown apart on the ground. I thought to myself what the hell was going on is this Christmas Day? I didn't even know it was Christmas Day! I guess I just forgot about it. I'm too busy trying to stay alive. Because every day out here, is always the same thing, trying to stay alive. You can easily lose track of the time out here.

Boy! I can hear the LT calling on the radio! We hear him yell into the headset, what the fucking hell is going on? You better get that damn fucking chopper out of here right now. I need a fucking Dust-Off chopper right now. All I know, I feel like shit and I guess the rest of the guys in the Platoon feel like I did. I don't know what happened to me that day but it changed the way I think of Christmas.

All I know, I wasn't having fun out there and it wasn't a joyful day for us. There were people dying out here and we were trying to save lives and secure the area for a Dust-Off for our wounded.

I was wondering where in the hell the Dust-Off chopper was. We all knew time counts out here for our wounded every second and every minute. It's a life and death matter. Did they send us the wrong chopper? All I know somebody messed up and we had to pay for it with our feelings or somebody's life. Whoever did it should have his ass in the wringer. I just don't know if I can take this bullshit anymore. Do the higher ranks know what the hell we're doing out here, do they care about us?

As time goes on it's getting worse out here. Do people know what they're doing anymore? It's getting real crazy out here or should I say do the guys in the rear with the gear know what they're doing anymore? All I know something happened to me that day. I just hate to see a candy cane and I don't like Christmas anymore. When I came home I would feel so sad every time Christmas came around, I just hate it! I'd be right back in Vietnam that awful day. People couldn't understand the way I acted and the way I looked when Christmas comes around. Especially when my parents saw the way I looked at Christmas time, they tried to talk to me about it, I would get upset real fast at them. To them it seemed to be for no reason but they didn't understand why I looked that way. I couldn't talk to them about it, there were a lot of things I couldn't say about what happened in Vietnam.

After that we secure the area, the Dust-Off finally comes and picks up our wounded and the wounded enemy. Then we have to pick up all the enemy dead bodies and pieces around the perimeter and put them in a dump truck. So they can haul them away from here to a dump site. So they can bury them. The bodies started to smell because of the heat as we were picking them up. You don't see this kind of bullshit in the damn movies. It's another hot dirty job that day at least a 100 degrees or more out here. As I was picking them up I would find a candy cane every now and then. That was messed up! I would smash the candy cane into the ground. It made me get mad, how they could do that to us. That was supposed to be a special day for us.

That was another dirty job we had to do that day. December 25, 1968 meant that I'd been in-country 242 days now. After that we don't even have time for a Christmas dinner. We had to go right back out into the jungle to find where the enemy was firing their mortar tubes from, and we started doing our patrols and night ambushes around our base camp and tried to keep it safe from the enemy. It's the life of a Grunt it never ends when you're out in the battlefield and death is everywhere at any moment. There's so much pressure and stress on you when you're facing death every second of every day and night. Well it was one hell of a Christmas for me! It's something I have to live with now, I just hope it doesn't get to me as time goes on. The only good thing about it was, only one of my guys on LP got wounded and got a Dust-Off and the other three are back in the Platoon.

While we were on patrol, here this kid on his bicycle comes out of nowhere selling sodas for a dollar, these sodas were ice cold, I wonder where did they get their block of ice from? We could not get ice in our little fire support base camp.

Here I am smiling for my Mom, you can see my ace of spades card (our calling card) on my helmet, you can see how tired and sweaty I am. This is my brown towel that I would use to wipe the sweat off. You can also see the rice paper in the background on the roof and the side of the hootch where the bamboo structure holds the rice paper, which the Vietnamese made.

Here we are again, it has been 45 days without being able to come into our main base camp in Dau Tieng, this means no showers or clean clothes. We are just beat, tired, and smelly. We have been on so many different missions in November, we just got dropped off at the flight line where we are getting ready for another Eagle Flight. Not all the guys made it, in this particular mission, this is when I got wounded, early in the morning on November 17, 1968. But I didn't get dusted off till late that night.

Here I am leaning against the quad 50-caliber machine gun on the PBR boat, getting ready to move down the Saigon River, into and around the river which is called "Snoopy Nose." This mission lasted about a month.

Here I am holding my M-15 rifle while patrolling on the river bank next to the Saigon River, looking for the enemy, after they opened up on us. Our protection was that thick jungle brush, before they sprayed Agent Orange on it.

My Mom (Josephine), me, and my Dad (Selzo), this is when I came home from Vietnam, my eyes show so much grief that I have aged. We couldn't even smile, even though we were all glad I was home, but so troubled in my mind. Yes I have all my medals, but I would give them all back to have my innocence again.

Going Home

January 1969 – Today

DEALING WITH THE NEW GUYS' VIEWS OF THE WAR
January 1969

I just don't know about these new guys coming in now. They're coming with all different kinds of views of the war. All I told them, keep their Stateside views to themselves. What's happening back in the States, leave it there! Over here things are a whole lot different. If you don't follow the rules here, you're going to die plain and simple. You don't get a second chance around here. Also I told them I didn't want to die over here in this forgotten land. Because of one of you "cherry boys" making a mistake because of your Stateside views. You can't protest the war over here when you're in it, that will cost somebody his life. Then I told them I will shoot them myself if they don't want to listen to me. I'm too short for this bullshit anyway.

This is my ninth month, 249 days in, I have 116 days left to go. I want to go home like the rest of the old guys that did make it! Not in a body bag, because of some FNG cherry boy making a mistake out here. I just couldn't believe all the shit that they were telling me that was happening back Stateside. That they hate us GIs for being over here. And all the riots and killings and people protesting against the war in Vietnam and what are we fighting for over here? I really didn't want to know what has been happening back in the States. Not that kind of bullshit. If they can't tell me anything good about the States, I didn't need to hear it. I have enough on my mind to deal with trying to keep everybody alive out here.

We got the word that we'll be moving inland. No more Navy boats going up and down the river. No more night ambushes and sweeps along the river. No more sitting like a sitting duck on those boats. That made me feel a little better now knowing we won't be on those boats.

Boy the more time you have on the line in-country the more pressure builds up on you. The shorter you get in time the more stressful it gets. Being a Sergeant now put a whole lot more pressure on me. And with these new guys coming with their different views of the war and their protests is something else to deal with. I didn't need this shit from them. I told them the only view you need to know is how to stay alive over here in this damn place. Because life can end real fast over here.

So I told the guys you better listen to me and to what I have to say. Like it or not you better listen. It's the only way you're going to make it out of here alive. If you don't you'll be going home in a body bag. Now that we're moving inland it should be a little easier moving around. But death is just around the corner or waiting for you at any moment. Those booby traps are something else, they're the unknown! You never know who's going to step on one, that's on your mind all the time.

Here we go on another patrol out in the jungle. I can't believe that walking in this shit, you can think of three or four things at the same time. You'll be thinking of home, what's going on around you, and about what just happened and what you're going to do next. All your five senses are working too, plus your combat "sixth sense," which means you know when danger's near, to help you survive. How your mind is running 100 miles an hour. How intense that is. I just can't believe that I could do that every day and night. Being in a war zone you do a lot of things that you never did before when you were in civilian life. I just can't wait to be a civilian again and be free from all this bullshit, and away from all this madness and fear around here.

Life is so different out here in the jungle! It's all about life and death, all the pain and suffering and the fear that you have to go through. Also about how your whole life will change in the matter of a second. You can lose your arms or legs, your eyes or even part of your face, just like that in second. Your whole life will change just by seeing all of the awful things that you never saw in your life before!

I hope these new guys get enough time on the line to learn how to deal with this stuff on their own. To give them time to know how to adjust out here. Before we get in some real bad shit. So they can make it home before they lose it or get killed out here.

Sometimes when I was thinking to myself how bad I feel inside, it was because I would be leaving these new guys in this hellhole. I guess I was feeling guilty, I knew if I stayed I could save some of them out here. Then I think about how much pressure I'd been through, can I keep on taking this shit day after day and night after night?

Just trying to stay alive and keeping them alive and if that wasn't enough, giving orders and making the list on who will be walking point or who's going on LP and keeping them motivated to do their job. That was the hard part to keep my guys motivated and doing their job out here. It's not like Stateside, if you make a mistake there you get your hand spanked, if you make a mistake out here in Vietnam you're going to die or be crippled for life.

I didn't have any type of training in leadership, it was another OJT for me. If it wasn't for my Dad and Mom showing me my Native ways and how to survive in the wilderness to be strong and how to use common sense, and show leadership, I wouldn't have made it back home in one piece. And being lucky. I've given a lot of thanks to my Mom and Dad for bringing me up the right way in life, I listened to what they told me and used it.

Your LT couldn't see what the hell was happening up front so you had to make the decision right there and then. You had no choice but to put your guys in harm's way and get them to move. A lot of times you had to put yourself in harm's way first to get your point across. Even when you didn't want to go. That was the hard part of leadership. A lot of times that's not true you had no choice but to move or get killed it was a matter of life or death.

It wasn't guts and glory like they say in the movies, it was a spur of the moment action. You don't know how people are going to react in that type of situation, especially some FNG who might have been going to war protests just six months ago. You had to do a lot of things you didn't want to do to keep yourself alive now that you're here in Vietnam. It was so stressful on you all the madness that was going on. But I knew one thing I did my best with the little training I had.

All I wanted is for everybody to make it home alive and go back to the States. But I knew in the back of my head that wouldn't happen. It was just of matter of time, I would lose somebody because of one of my orders. The odds were against me, I still had too much time left on the line! Three more months of leadership before I ETS out of Vietnam.

All I know the decisions I made, I had to live with them, even those when I had to put guys in harm's way. But when they got hurt or killed, some didn't even last a week or two in the battlefield and some got it on their first day on a Line Unit. That made it even harder to see their baby-faced look, they were still fresh meat from Stateside. They didn't have that hard look like we did and sunburn and dry skin and that thousand-yard stare and all beat to hell. But when you lose an old guy it was just as hard. But if he was close to you it was even harder on you. No matter what you do! It takes a toll on everybody every time this shit happens to you on a Line Unit.

During the last two and a half months I've been doing night ambushes and sweeps, dealing with the FNGs before I leave for home. I hope they learned what I taught them about military tactics and how to survive out in the bush.

I've been out in the field eleven and a half months, I marked my short-timer calendar on my helmet 351 days so far. I've been waiting to get my orders to go back home. We're supposed get our orders, two weeks prior before our ETS. So you can get your paperwork in order, before you can leave for the States.

Now another week goes by, I only have six days left on my short-timer calendar before my ETS – and they're still sending me out on patrol! I've been here in Vietnam 359 days so far. I'm scared as all hell! I'm wondering if they extended me and they haven't told me yet. Because we got a new LT and two new Sergeants a week ago and I'm the oldest guy out in the field now! My new LT and the two new Sergeants have been asking me a lot of questions about how it is out here and how bad it is and how we do certain things. All I could tell them, you can't always go by the book out here. I guess they still need me out here. I didn't need this kind of shit, all I wanted was to go home.

Even the guys in my Platoon wanted to know what was going on. I guess they could see I was nervous as all hell. I kept telling myself everything is going to be ok. I just had to keep my shit together out here. Our Company was finally told that we'd be moving back to our little fire support base camp.

As we were patrolling our way back to our little base camp I was getting ready to ask my CO, have I got my orders to go home yet? But as we were walking I could see our little base camp, it felt good to see it again. It was about noontime, it was hot, it had to be 110 degrees. We finally made it inside our base camp, I felt safe again.

That's when my CO finally told me to saddle up and move out to go home. I had a half hour before the convoy leaves the base camp! Boy I finally had a smile on my face and I was nervous as all hell. I am finally going home! All the guys were happy for me, I just had enough time to get my things. The only thing I had was my little ammo can that had everything I owned in it. That's what I was living out of for the whole year. It wasn't much but it was all I had. A few letters, my 104 Instamatic camera, two pencils, razorblades, toothpaste, toothbrush, writing paper, and some toilet paper and few personal things. Like I said it wasn't much but it meant the whole world to me, especially the transistor radio from my Mom, and my compass, my knife, my watch, and my pictures.

I was ready to get on the convoy going back to Dau Tieng that afternoon. I didn't have much time to say goodbye to everybody! Just a quick goodbye and off I went. On that dusty road back to Dau Tieng out in the jungle on Ambush Alley, hoping to make it home alive to the States. This was April 27, 1969, it was a Sunday afternoon. Vietnam is 17 hours ahead of the USA.

LEAVING THE BUSH TO GET PROCESSED OUT OF VIETNAM
And to the Good Old USA, April 1969

I was finally told to go back to Dau Tieng. I'm at the end of my twelve months and I'd been in-country 363 days, so far. Me and the guys thought Army Headquarters had extended me for another two or three months. I should have been off-line two weeks ago to get all my paperwork in order to go home!

I hope this doesn't make me late, for me to go home. So my CO told me to get on a convoy that was headed back to Dau Tieng. From there I would take the next steps to head home to the USA. I didn't like going back on the convoy. We had to go right through Ambush Alley in the middle of the Michelin Rubber Plantation and the jungle where the road went to Dau Tieng. I didn't need this shit anymore. I wish I could have gone back by chopper.

It was a long ride back! I rode shotgun on a truck on the way back, another OJT. I didn't need this shit I'd be glad when I get the hell out of here. The vehicles were spaced out about 50 to 100 yards apart as we moved down that dusty dirt road about 20 or 30 mph. I was eating dust and hoping that we won't get ambushed today. It was a bumpy ride. But it beat walking out in the jungle.

The 30-mile trip took about two or three hours. They had to clear the road of land mines while we were convoying back to Dau Tieng. Charlie would put land mines on and off the road and blockade it on a regular basis, and our Engineers would have to clear the land mines. Then we would either have to drive around the obstacles or move them out of the way. Our trucks had to stop every time we had to move an obstacle, we were sitting ducks every time we stopped. That would be the time they could ambush us! Every time we slowed down or stopped our asses would tighten up, hoping it's not an ambush ready to be sprung on us.

I didn't know we had new guys on the convoy who didn't know to keep their asses on the trucks. Charlie would set booby traps right off the side of the road. Some of the new guys got off to stretch their legs, and one of them set off a booby trap when he stepped on it. We heard the explosion, so we knew one of the guys had made a mistake by going off the road to either stretch his legs or use the bathroom. He lost his foot, a Dust-Off had to be called in to Medevac him out to the hospital, that took time because we had to secure the area.

But I finally made it to Dau Tieng Fire Support Base Camp where there was a dirt runway with corrugated steel panels for the planes and helicopters to land on at the airstrip. From there, I got on a helicopter to go to Cu Chi, my home base camp where the 25th Division Headquarters was, and to get my orders to go home. When I got to Cu Chi, I couldn't believe what I was seeing. It had been a long time since I'd been back, and the airstrip had more than doubled in size. The last time I saw it, the runway was just a little dirt track with corrugated steel panels like the one in Dau Tieng.

Now the runway was an actual tarmac runway, with a black-top pavement running from one end to the other. The roads were paved throughout the base and between most of the main buildings. It looked like a small town, I can't believe how much things changed around here.

I went to my small unit that was on base. I can't believe everything looks so nice around here and it's like being Stateside. They had fans, TVs, radios, and new furniture and all kinds of other things. Boy they sure had it made around here. I had to turn in all my equipment. But I kept my helmet (and the cloth cover) that had my short-timer calendar on it, and a few other things. I felt so naked without my weapon and equipment. The personnel LT told me to report to the Supply Sergeant to get some new clothes and boots and report back to him. I asked the Supply Sergeant if I could borrow some soap, "So I can take a shower, it's been a long time for me." He said, "I'll see if I can get it for you, I know how hard you guys had it out there in the bush." Then I ask him, "Can I keep my old jungle fatigues?" He said, "Yes that'd be ok."

I reported back to the LT, he looked at me in my new fatigues and said, "You can't go around looking like that, without all your patches sewn on your fatigues. The MPs will give you a citation for not having them on. So go buy your patches and have them sewn on." I thought to myself, "What kind of bullshit is this?" This isn't Stateside.

We had to take everything off (name, rank, insignia, everything!) when we were out in the bush. I told the LT I didn't have any money to buy my patches – I'd been out in the bush for the past four months and I hadn't got paid. And I hadn't been back here in Cu Chi for over nine months. He said, "Here, take this ration card, and get your patches put on." Then he asked me, "When did you come in?" I told him, "This morning." He said, "You should have been here two weeks ago, to transfer you out of here and for you to get your pay and paperwork in order. Now we have to do everything as fast as we can, if we can, in time to get your ass out so you won't miss your plane out of here. You have three days before your departure."

He told this Private to run me through the process, and to have me through by the end of the day, so they can fly me out "tomorrow morning to Long Binh, in Saigon" to finish my out-processing.

I *knew* they should have let me go back earlier to "the rear with the gear!"

I just knew it!!! I hate this damn place! I just hope I don't miss my flight! It was a long night being here, in Cu Chi. I'm thinking of the guys out in the bush, and how they're doing, and about me – how I'm getting home from this place. So far, it's been a long day, I'm tired and feel bad inside and I'm scared but I'm excited to be going home. But I'm still on the go, and it's not over yet.

I step outside the hootch, it's about 2200hrs (10:00 p.m.). I can see the flashes of light in the sky. I know it was a B-52 strike. I wait, I know what's coming next. A few seconds later, I hear the roar of bombs exploding in the distance, about 10 or 20 miles away and then the ground shakes a little bit, from the roars and flashes, I know the planes dropped from 70 to 100 bombs. That's a lot of bombs. Something big is happening, I don't know what it is, and I know somebody will be going out there to check it out tomorrow.

The NVA or VC will be moving out around tonight to get away from that area. They'll come crawling out of the tunnels and bunkers once the bombs stop. And our guys will be waiting to spring an ambush, there tonight because the NVA and the VC will be moving around. I think to myself, "I hope no bombs hang up in the bomb bays and land on 'friendlies.'" It has happened before in this damn place. I know my guys are thinking the same thing, I don't envy the terror and stress my guys are going through, waiting out there in that hellhole to do battle.

I feel bad that my guys are still out there but I'm glad I'm going home. I can't sleep, it's another long night. Just when I manage to drift off to sleep, it's time for me to wake up, it's 0600hrs (6:00 a.m.). I'm up. I'm finally dressed. I go and thank everybody for re-issuing me new jungles fatigues. I hadn't seen new clothes in what seemed like forever. Like all Grunts, you wear the same fatigues for months at a time. After a while, all that's left of those fatigues is a set of shredded rags. I wanted to keep my old fatigues and helmet cover with me when I got home and to see them again and to make sure it wasn't a bad dream I was in.

When I arrived on the chopper yesterday, I had on a pair of worn-out fatigues that I'd worn night and day, for months. They were filthy, stiff from sweat, dirt and blood, and the clothes and I stank from the battlefield. It was so wonderful to have new, clean clothes and a shower. I felt human again, it was important for me to take time to thank the supply guy and office personnel for taking care of me. I also thanked them for processing the paperwork which got me out of Cu Chi, and on a chopper, on time. They just don't know what it meant to me, all the help they gave me back then. I felt human again, being clean and shaved.

Now I'm on a chopper flying to Long Binh. My orders say I'm supposed to go to the 90th Replacement Center in Saigon, to get the rest of my papers done and get my travel pay. And my orders to my new duty station Stateside. The Sergeant got a jeep and took me to the chopper pad where the chopper was to pick me up. He said to me, are you sick you don't look good. I told him I couldn't sleep much last night, I guess I'm tired from being up most of the night. I could hear the chopper coming in. I asked the Sergeant, could he mail this package for me, it had my old fatigues and my helmet cover in it. He says he would. I say goodbye to the Sergeant and got on board the chopper.

The doors on the chopper were wide open as we were flying out of Cu Chi. The Door Gunners had their hands on the guns, but they weren't on alert. They were relaxed, laughing and talking over the "intercom" with the Pilots and the other Door Gunner and Co-pilot. They knew that we weren't flying into battle. In battle, the Gunners' faces would be tense and they would be scared, with that thousand-yard stare in their eyes. With the doors open, the wind whipped throughout the chopper, the smell of fresh air was sweet, it was like Heaven. On the ground Grunts only smell death. On the ground, combat Grunts only smell the "death of battle." Grunts know battle destroys everything in its path, trees, plants, animals, humans, everything, and leaves nothing but a terrible stench! It's a stench of human sweat and stress, the stink of the jungle and gunpowder, the smell of stagnant water, human waste, animal and human decay. All mixing together in the heat and humidity, after a while there are no good smells in combat.

The canvas seat was hard under my rear, and I enjoyed the cool air hitting my face. The air whipping around inside the chopper caused my fatigues to be flapping against my body. These were precious moments. The noise of the engines took away the noise of battle, it was a peaceful sound. The chopper vibrated in rhythm to the engine, the whop, whop, whop from the blades sounded like drums to me in the background. Every now and then, turbulence made the chopper bounce up and down, which even felt good to me.

I turned in my seat and looked out from the chopper. On the horizon, I saw columns of smoke rising from the jungle in five different locations, the columns got my attention and I began scanning the vicinity of the smoke. I looked down at the jungle and the patches of rice paddies down there on the land. Then from inside the chopper I saw giant fireballs shoot up into the sky from a couple of sites close to us, several miles away. Then I saw planes dropping napalm on the sites. I knew that at each of these places there was an air strike going on, somebody was "in the shit." It made me feel bad inside, again, I felt lost and alone again, I felt like I wanted to cry, and almost lost control of my emotions.

The Door Gunner and me made eye contact. We had the same expression in our eyes, we knew what was happening on the ground, we understood each other without saying one word. We were both relieved that we weren't "in the middle of it" but we both felt guilty about it. And our eyes said it all. He was heading to a safe place, and I was heading "Home" to a safe place. For a moment it seemed our emotions were about to break through that wall soldiers have to put up out here. It was painful! We broke eye contact. Even though he didn't have to, the Gunner turned to man his weapon I turned to look out the front and watch the pilots fly the chopper and listen to their chatter on the radio. Me and the Gunner just wanted to distract ourselves and distance ourselves from the pain that had come to the surface when we made eye contact. My awful memories of those faces of the young men in battle, and horrible feelings of pain and death will haunt me till the day I die.

LEAVING VIETNAM TO GO BACK TO THE WORLD
The Good Old USA, End of April 1969

We finally landed in Long Binh and I went to the 90th Replacement Center, where I finished processing my paperwork out of Vietnam. Now that I have all my papers in order, my travel pay, and military orders to my next duty station in the States. It's time to check in at the airport.

I couldn't believe what I was seeing, guys in their dress khakis, with all their ribbons on, duffle bags hanging on their shoulders, and their souvenirs from Vietnam in their hands! Such as umbrellas, walking sticks, little Vietnamese dolls, and shopping bags. It looked like they'd been on vacation! The only things I had were the clothes on my back and a small cardboard box, as big as my little ammo box that held .50 caliber rounds which was 6" wide x 7" high x 12" long, with all my personal possessions inside.

We had to go through a security checkpoint before we could go to the airport by bus. The guard asked me "Is this all?" I said, "Yes." He looked at me in a strange way that made me feel out of place, then he opened my box and threw my possessions on a table. He looked through my belongings and starting confiscating some of my stuff, saying, "You can't take this . . . and you can't take that." The SOB took my military watch, some of my pictures, and my survival knife and compass, the ones that I carried though my whole tour in

Vietnam! Boy, was I mad about that! But if he would have taken away my little transistor radio that my Mom and Dad sent me, I would have went off on him. I didn't have much in my box and he took the things that were most important to me! I still think he kept them because he wanted them for himself, all the other guys got to bring all that other junk home with them! I felt disrespected by what he'd done and by the way he'd handled my things, there was something mean about his attitude towards me.

He had a "guy in the rear with the gear" mentality. Guys in the rear were either envious of us Grunts, or afraid of us (and afraid of the way we looked, our attitude, and our thousand-yard stare). If they envied us, it was because to them, we were something they would never be, we were "men's men." We had proved we were battle-hardened soldiers we'd faced death and suffering on a daily basis and endured the trauma of war. If "guys in the rear" were afraid of us, it was for the same reasons as those who envied us, but most especially, they were afraid of what we were capable of doing.

Somewhere around 2000hrs (8:00 p.m.) to 2100hrs (9:00 p.m.) we were loaded onto a bus, and taken to the airport. I sat alone in the back of the bus, away from most of the guys, with someone's duffle bag next to me on the seat, it had a tag on it with its flight number on it and his name. The rest of the guys seemed to avoid me and didn't want to bother me. It seemed that they didn't want to be around a Grunt, who just came out of the bush and it irritated me. I didn't realize then that I was also ill with bleeding ulcers, I was transferred out of county so fast, there was no time to take a complete physical (the bleeding ulcers wouldn't be diagnosed for months). The ulcers had added to the hollow-faced look that combat soldiers get over time, and made me look even scarier. The airport was off base, because they had to drive through the outskirts of town to get to it, we were escorted by the MP's to the airport. The ride to the airport felt like any regular bus ride through any city, it felt nothing at all like the ride that brought me into Vietnam.

On my bus ride into Vietnam in 1968, the fighting on the outskirts of Saigon and the pot-shots at the buses, had forced us to duck down and keep our heads below the windows throughout the entire trip. This ride was different, no one was shooting at the buses, and we were allowed to sit up normally, like any city bus rider. The ride from the 90th Replacement Center to the airport, took us around the outskirts of Saigon.

The drive was smooth, the road was dark, and the Moon was out, I could see the outlines of grass hootches or huts along the road. Most of the hootches either had no door or just a curtain covering the doorway, and there was a light breeze blowing. Candle lights were flickering through the doorways of the hootches as we drove by, every now and then, I could see a couple of wires, with a light bulb attached to the end of them, hanging from the ceiling of an adobe-style building. Most of the buildings in the background into the city were two-story brick buildings.

There were no roads between the hootches. Just trails disappearing into the darkness, the smells of food cooking and human waste mixed in the breeze as we drove along the road. People were moving inside of the hootches and buildings, living their daily lives. Doing their nightly chores or relaxations.

The ride was slow, and there were some people walking around on the trails and alongside the road. It shocked me. It scared me to death, to see people moving around at night. I panicked, I wanted to grab a weapon and shoot them. I was sweating, my hands were shaking, and my heart was pounding at 100 miles an hour. I almost pissed my pants. I was supposed to be in a safe zone, but I felt like I was about to come under fire. Most of my time in Vietnam was spent in free fire zones where the locals were restricted from moving around at night. Free fire zones were official combat zones, people could be shot if they violated the curfew, usually 1900hrs (7:00 p.m.) through 0700hrs (7:00 a.m.).

Seeing the locals moving along the trails and roadside, set me on edge, I tried to hide below the window. The guy across the aisle asked, "What's wrong?" I said, "Aren't those VC? It's after hours to be out." He said, "The curfew starts at 2300hrs (11:00 p.m.), around here in the city."

I felt embarrassed by the way I'd acted. Most of the guys on the bus were talking and carrying on like everything was ok. I couldn't believe it! I didn't know what time it was, because the MP confiscated my watch! It was disorienting. My watch was gone. My survival knife, compass, and my weapon were gone. The four main things I needed for survival out in the bush, and they were gone! Taking those things was like taking away my identity, I felt lost and naked without them, with no control over my environment. My life felt turned upside down, and violated, by the way I was processed through the Replacement Center. And now, here on this bus, my life was being flipped upside down, again. But I knew it had to be close to 2100hrs (9:00 p.m.), since we had to be at the airport by 2100 (9:00 p.m.). I think it took us less than a half-hour to get there. But for me, the drive seemed to drag on for hours. I was on edge, I couldn't wait to get off the bus, and on the plane.

We finally arrived at the airport's main gate, the MP waved us through. We drove onto the tarmac and stopped next to a commercial plane. There were two metal stair-ramps, one at the front of the plane, and one at the back. Everyone grabbed their gear and started exiting the bus. I had no gear, just my cardboard box with my personal effects which I carried onto the plane. Everyone else had to place their duffle bags, luggage, and bulky objects on a luggage cart, which got driven to the back of the plane. Where it was loaded into the cargo hold by conveyor belt. Once the luggage cart was loaded, we boarded the plane.

A stewardess at the door directed us to towards the seats. Since we didn't have seat assignments, I headed to the back of the plane and took a seat by a window. Where I could sit by myself. I was still tense when I sat down. I was looking out the window, lost in my own thoughts, with all kinds of mixed feelings inside. I felt sick. I could hear the guys laughing and talking, like they'd never been in a war zone. I couldn't believe it, I guess they didn't see the ugliness of war like I had. I was still in shock. I felt out of place. I think I was still in pain having to leave my guys out in the bush! And here I was having to be around a bunch of happy people that made me feel out of place! Yes, I was happy about going home. But I guess I didn't show it. I think that's why nobody sat by me, at the time, on the plane. I must have had that look of being beat all to hell. I guess my eyes said it all! That thousand-yard stare, that "killer" look.

Well things had't changed for me. I came to Vietnam alone, and I'm leaving Vietnam alone, even with all these people on the plane I feel alone.

I felt out of place, everything felt so strange. I couldn't stop being scared of everything and being on guard all the time.

The stewardess finally closed the doors and the lights came on. From where I was sitting in the back of the plane, I could look forward down the rows of seats and see "Fasten Your Seat Belts" and "No Smoking" signs down the middle of the aisle, lit in red. All the passengers were GIs, we looked like a sea of green and khaki in our jungle fatigues and dress wintergreens. We were all headed somewhere Stateside eventually but for now, we were all headed to Travis Air Force Base, about 35 miles East of San Francisco.

Once the lights came on, all the guys quieted down. Soon we started moving down the tarmac. We stopped at the end of the runway. Where we sat for almost a half hour waiting to take off. For me, though, that half hour seemed like hours. Sitting there, on that runway, made me real uneasy. I had no weapon on me, I was confined, and I couldn't see or hear what was going on outside because of the dark. My fear had me agitated. I was sitting in a place where I was supposed to be safe but I was still on "24/7 On-Guard" from the bush. Once you've spent a year on "24/7 On-Guard," there's just no way stopping it just because you're on a plane that's taking you home. It was quiet on the plane. All us GIs were thinking pretty much the same thing, are we going to be able to leave Vietnam? Is something going on to stop our flight from taking off? What's happening out there? When the *hell* are we going to take off!?!

The plane started down the tarmac, and the pilot announced he was turning off the lights in the plane. I heard the roar of the engines as the pilot increased the plane's speed, I could hear and feel the rhythmic thumping of the tires as they rolled across the concrete slabs on the tarmac. The plane went airborne, the nose tilted upwards, I was jerked up and back into my seat. And I heard the landing gear folding up into the plane, then locking into place.

I looked out the window and it was pitch black. There were hardly any lights in all that darkness. All I could see were white flares glowing against the sky, in the distance. The lights from the flares were rocking back and forth as they fell towards the ground, I could see the jungle outlined in a kind of black-green, under those white flare lights. Green Star-Clusters (flares) shot up into the sky as I was watching, and burst into three green spheres of light that also fell towards the ground. I knew the Clusters meant a Company was marking its location for some type of action. Before I knew it, I saw the tell-tale signs of red tracer rounds falling downward from the sky and ricocheting up off the ground, this caught my attention since red tracer lines meant only one thing, gunships.

During the few moments that I'd been looking out the window, watching what was happening, gunships had been called in. And were firing towards the enemy. The tracer rounds coming with the Star-Clusters, told me that somebody was in "deep shit" again. I knew someone was in a heavy battle and needed all the gun support they could get, and were taking casualties. Shooting off Star-Clusters is usually a last resort. Done when you need to tell the gunships where they should not fire because there are friendlies in that area. It also means all hell is breaking loose on the guys on the ground, and help is needed now! It made me think again about my guys, the guys from my Company the ones that were still out there and if it was them "in the shit."

Suddenly, the sky turned jet white and I couldn't see anything. We were in the clouds, raindrops were sliding across and off the window. A few moments later, I could see the stars twinkling in the night sky. I was thinking to myself, "I just can't believe I'm leaving this place." I was still looking out the window when the pilot announced, "We are now out of Vietnam air space, and over the sea, and in a safe air zone now." I was in such deep thought thinking what was happening on the ground, thinking about my guys out there "in the shit" thinking about leaving this place. The pilot's announcement startled me out of my thoughts and jerked my attention to what was happening on the plane.

Most of the guys broke out into wild cheering, but not everybody did. A few were like me. Lost in our own thoughts. The guy across the aisle asked me, "What's wrong?" I replied, abruptly, "Nothing, I must have been in deep thought." I was sweating, I felt cold. I must have had a real sad, scared look on my face. I didn't say anything to anyone for the rest of the flight. I stayed in my own little cocoon, lost in my own thoughts, lost in the Land of OZ, for the rest of the flight. After about six hours, we stopped in Japan for a refueling layover, by the time we left Japan, the Sun was coming up and we still had thousands of miles left to travel. The flight home, Stateside, was a long, lonely ride of about 16 hours or more. To be in the Vietnam War for a year and one day was a hell of a lifetime experience for me.

FINALLY BACK IN THE GOOD OLD USA
April 1969

By the time we finally made it to Travis Air Force Base, it was 2300hrs (11:00 p.m.), one and a half days had passed since I'd gotten my orders from Cu Chi. I still felt dislocated. I felt like I was living an illusion. The whole experience from Vietnam (Cu Chi) to Travis Air Force Base, still left me feeling out of place.

At around midnight, after we landed and checked in at Travis Air Force Base, the Air Force transported us by Greyhound bus to the Oakland Army Depot Station. On the ride to the Depot Station, I sat in the back of the bus, I could hear the humming sound of the engine, and it relaxed me, and I thought, "Here I am, in the Real World – and no little people are trying to kill me."

Looking out of the bus window, I could see the Bay Bridge lights shining in a row from Oakland through Treasure Island, and on towards the city of San Francisco. When I looked towards San Francisco, I could see the city's lights in the distance. Fog was coming in from the Bay, it was hanging over part of the city. The lights from the buildings and streetlamps were shining off the fog in the sky. Making a sort of halo over the skyline, I thought to myself, "The Real World is so beautiful, tonight." I could smell the cool night air of *our* Pacific Ocean and the breeze that brought in the fog, had also brought in the smell of salty air and *my* San Francisco. It smelled sweet. And it looked so beautiful! It was nothing at all like what I'd been seeing for the past year, it felt great to see those sights again! It felt good. I'd forgotten what it felt like to feel good inside myself.

Buses have a way of making you go inside your head. Here I am feeling guilty, again. Here I am feeling relieved, again. Now here I am thinking, "I can't believe how scared I was on that plane, hoping nothing would go wrong on the way home. I didn't want to die on that damn plane, after surviving in that hellhole of Vietnam for a whole year! Boy, it was a long flight to be on. Boy, seeing all those city lights and the Bay Bridge lights made me feel safer, and at home." But now I feel guilty for being home. I'm thinking of the guys that I left behind and most of them FNGs, and the new LT. I know within a month some of them will be dead.

We pulled into Oakland, and finally to Oakland Army Depot. We drove through the gate and into the Depot, and stopped in front of a warehouse. The bus driver told us, "It's time to get off the bus." A Staff Sergeant was outside waiting for us. He told us to move inside the warehouse, to the staging area. The warehouse was a large building split into five sections, the PX, supply, mess hall, personnel, and staging area. Once we were in the staging area, the Sergeant told us, line up and have your orders ready, so they could look at our orders, to process us again. This time the Sergeant didn't holler at us, you could tell that he'd been in Vietnam by his patches. Then the Sergeant looked at me, saw I only had my little cardboard box tucked under my arm, and no duffle bag or suitcase, and said, "Sergeant Maes report to the Supply Sergeant, first, and get your clothes reissued for your next duty station and also you get a free steak dinner for making it home."

The Sergeant then told the rest of the guys (that didn't need to get resupplied with "Stateside" clothing) to go get their steak, before leaving the Depot. They already had their clothes issued to them in Vietnam, before they left to come home. Before I went to the Supply Sergeant I called home, "collect," to my parents, I wanted to let them know I was Home, and in Oakland. Getting ready to be processed out of Oakland Depot for my next duty station, and that I had two weeks leave. My Dad and brother weren't home, they were out but my Mom was, and she was excited when she heard my voice. She got even more excited when I told her I was Home, and in Oakland and that I'd be home in a few hours! Boy, it was real nice to hear her voice.

I headed over to the Supply Sergeant, he took one look at me and said, "You can't go out looking like that in your combat fatigues! You have to put your wintergreens on, and have all your patches and ribbons put on before you leave here."

Boy, here I go again the same bullshit in the way you have to dress. Now, I know I'm back in the Army with this Stateside bullshit, again. Now, I have to change my way of thinking, I'm going to have to play Army, again. Because I still have six months left to do in this so-called Army. I didn't even know that three hours passed since I got here and when I called home.

It was about 2:30 a.m., and I was in the PX getting my patches and ribbons for my new uniform, along with some of the guys that needed them too (the PX was open 24/7 because of all the troops processing in and out of the Depot at all hours of the day and night). Then one of the guys that worked here came to me, and asked me, "Are you Sergeant Maes?" I said, "Yes." He said, "Somebody is looking for you outside the warehouse on the ramp."

I went outside on the ramp. I still had on my jungle fatigues and jungle bush hat, the floppy hat with the brim all around. And I was still suntanned chocolate brown from the Sun in Vietnam. When I got on the airplane in Saigon, I was leaving the summer in Vietnam behind me, where 100-120 degrees in the shade was the average temperature. Under those hot conditions everyone turned dark. Especially us Grunts who spent all of our time out in the bush in the Sun.

I looked around and saw dozens of GIs out there. Some were smoking out on the blacktop next to the ramp, some GIs were walking around the cargo doors. Or through them to enter the next section for some sort of processing. I saw a guy in civilian clothes looking at all the GIs in dress uniforms who were out there walking around on the ground and up on the ramp, like he was looking for someone. I was looking for a Sergeant because I thought I was being given some type of duty, so I didn't pay much attention to him. The civilian's back was towards me, but when I started walking along the ramp, he turned in my direction and started walking. It was still dark outside, the lights were dim so it was hard to see who the guy was.

It wasn't until we were about five steps away from each other that I realized it was my brother. I expected him to say, "Hi!" But he walked right past me. I said. "Selzo it's me!" He turned around and stared at me. His face said it all. His eyes had a sad, horrified look in them when he finally recognized me. He said, "Is that really you Joe? You look like skin and bones, and sunburned!" Then he got concerned and said, "How are you? Are you ok?" I said, "I'm ok, where's Mom and Dad?" "They're in the car. I'll bring them here." I said, "No! I'll go where they're at."

I thought to myself, "I must really look bad! Is that why everybody stared, and stayed away from me on the plane? I guess! I look sick to everybody." When I finally got home to Mom and Dad's house, I weighed myself, I found out I only weighed 96 pounds when I stepped on that tarmac at Travis.

I said to my brother, "Let Mom and Dad know I have to go back inside the warehouse, right away to finish what I'm doing, to get the hell out of here." But when I went to the car to say Hi to my Mom and Dad real quick, my Mom started crying and said, "What did they do to you?" I told her everything was ok. "I'll be right back when I finished maybe another hour or so." I felt bad inside, for my Mom. I didn't know it was going to make her sad to see me the way I was. It was almost 4:00 a.m., already. I guess if I would've gotten off the line two weeks earlier, they could have put some weight on me, and I would have learned how to relax before I came home!

I went back into the warehouse so they could sew on my patches and tailor my pants and coat. While the tailors did that stuff, I went to the mess hall. To eat my steak dinner and drink some milk. The steak wasn't that good, but the milk was! About the time the tailors finished with my clothes, I started feeling sick. I went into the latrine and threw up all the food I just finished eating a while earlier, I guess the food was too rich for me, or the milk. It was almost 5:00 a.m., and the Sun had not come out, yet.

I finished all my out-processing, I only had to get my uniforms. I went back to where the tailors were working. No more jungle fatigues, bush hat, and jungle boots, I walked out in my new dress wintergreens. It looked big for me. The tailor left all my uniforms a little big for me. He was gentle with me. He said, "Maybe you can gain some weight by eating some home-cooked meals, before you get to your new duty station." I put my new duffel bag full of new cloths, and boots, on my shoulder, it was heavy, but I didn't care. I felt weak. I guess I was tired from being up for two and a half days without much sleep. As I walked out of the warehouse, I felt the cool breeze on my face and that sweet smell in the air. It was still kind of dark, and it was about 6:00 a.m. Then I walked across the ramp, down the stairs, and across the blacktop towards where my Dad's car was parked. As I walked it felt different, not like in a war zone, it scared me as I was walking alone without a weapon. I made it to the car.

My family was asleep in the car, and the windows were foggy. So I tapped on the window real lightly and woke them up. It was a cold morning. They were glad to see me and ready to take me home.

I got in the car. My Dad was driving. My Mom sat in the back seat with me, and my brother sat in the front. I didn't say much I just said yes and no to questions. I was tired, they were tired, too. I closed my eyes. After a while I opened my eyes and started talking to my Mom asking how things had been at home, and what was going on. At some point, my brother asked me what happened over there, and how did I get wounded. I told him, "We don't need to talk about that, at all." All I wanted to know was what'd been going on around home, and our home town, and how they'd all been doing since I'd been gone.

Before we got home, I got sick again, my Dad had to pull over so I could get out of the car. My Mom asked me, again, "What's wrong with you?" I said, "Maybe it's the food I ate. Maybe it was too rich for me. I guess I'm not used to this Stateside food, yet." Then she said, "Are you sure?" I said, "Yes, Mom." I can't believe I'm home, and going down that same old highway going East! The Sun is coming up, and it's starting to hit us on our faces. The Sun felt warm on my face, and looking out at the landscape it looked so beautiful. But I still didn't feel right being home.

The sounds are not the same here, so many different sounds, it feels so different now. I'm scared of being home and I don't know why. What was happening to me? Can I handle this kind of isolation? I really can't talk to anyone that doesn't know what I'd been through. All I can do is live with it the best way I know how. I hope I am right in what things I do in life. I just hope I can keep my shit together. Right now I don't really know how to act in civilian life, I feel so out of place.

We finally made it home. My Mom said she's going to make me some soup for breakfast. She said it might help to make me feel a little better. I just ate a little. It was too salty. It felt strange to sit at the table and have a roof over my head, I felt closed in. I knew my Mom made good soup, it had to be me. It must be me, and my stomach, and my nerves and all the stress I'd been through. I'm still not used to this rich food.

The next few weeks I couldn't sleep at night. I was having bad dreams. I was still scared to sleep at night, and scared of all the different sounds in the daytime and nighttime

All my six senses are still kicking in, and are very sensitive. I can't stay in the house. Being inside makes me feel like things are closing in on me, I feel trapped. It scares me. All I do is go outside to the back yard, while everybody's asleep and look at the stars and think about the guys back in Vietnam, and wonder what they're doing. And I keep hoping they make it home.

I only slept a few hours at a time in the daytime, like I'd been doing when I was overseas in Vietnam. I think I was still stressed out about what I'd been through, I was but I didn't know that at that time. I didn't feel right being home. It must be survivor's guilt, I just don't know what's happening to me. I guess I was not ready to come home yet, I felt like killing myself. Committing suicide. All kinds of thoughts are going through my mind, I just don't know what I am doing here.

My Mom and Dad knew there was something wrong, they didn't

understand what was happening to me. They couldn't do anything about it. Their faces showed concern all the time, and they were watching my behavior. They knew I had changed a lot and that I was not the same happy-go-lucky young kid that I was before I left for Vietnam. All they knew was that I was alive. And safe and at home now. I was glad to be home, and back in the USA. But at the same time I felt guilty for being here and putting my parents through so much pain. But I didn't know all this at that time. What does a twenty-year-old kid know about war's impact on a guy's state of mind? I'm just a twenty-year-old kid and I'm still trying to learn how to grow up. But I had six more months left in the Army. I wasn't looking forward to that, boy that was something else to do! So I left to go to Fort Hood Texas, my next duty station. Where I would find out I'd be training troops to go overseas and to Vietnam. That was last thing I wanted to do. It was another job I hated to do, it was another OJT. I had to play Army and play these war games with these young kids. I didn't need this kind of bullshit. I felt like I was sending them to their death! I knew all the training in the world can't prepare them for a real war. All I wanted, is to get the hell out of the Army and be left alone. I didn't want them to tell me what to do anymore. All I wanted is to be home and try and get my life together and get a good job. I thought the Army would train me for a job so when I got home I could be ready to go to work and be a civilian. Then when I became a civilian, and they found out I was a Vietnam Vet, it was hard for me to find a job. They would tell me that I was a fool for going to Vietnam, and they didn't want anything to do with me. I always had to do everything on my own the hard way. Nothing has changed and like I've been saying, life is not fair. But I made the best of what I had and tried to live life to its fullest.

This is my story of my experience of war that I went through and saw and felt. Every Vet should tell his or her story because once he or she's gone their war experience is gone. Because every Vet has their own story of experiences of war and sees it a whole lot different in his or her own way. Their stories need to be told so people can understand the consequences of war.

THE WAR IS NOT OVER FOR ME

I thought the war was over with me. I thought when I left Vietnam and the Army my experiences of the war would stop. My fears would stop, my anxiety would stop and my worries about my guys would stop. And I would stop feeling like a hunted animal out in the jungle. What I didn't know, then, was that these feelings would haunt me till the day I die. It's like time has stopped for me. I live it over and over again, like I'm still 19. It's been over 50 some years and I still feel the presence of war like it was yesterday. War's smells, sounds and images pop back into my head at odd times. Even similar smells, sounds, or images trigger memories of my war experiences. I dream about those things and when I do, it feels so real again. Only folks who've been there can really understand it!

A lot of people look at me because of the way I look at them. I have that look like I am out in deep space, like I am staring right through them. That's because I'm thinking back to when I was in the war in Vietnam. It bothers me when I notice when they stare at me. They have that look like they are scared of me and ready to be on the defensive side. That's why I would get in a lot of fights because of that. If it wasn't for my wife being the kind of person she is, I would have gone nuts or I would be in prison, but I have been in county jail a few times. She has never left my side. She's been very understanding and feels for what I went through. Now that I look back on what I put her through, I sure put her through a lot of SHIT! I can't believe she put up with me. She's a very loving and caring woman to me. She learned to understand how I felt inside. She knew when to leave me alone and let me have my space when I needed it. She had to be a very strong woman to be with me. Because of all this PTSD I have in me.

A lot of times I just don't know how I handle it. I still wake up scared and sweating, and it feels so real to me in my dreams. I feel I'm still in a firefight, fighting for my life. In those firefights I still feel the terror and my sweat, and my hands shaking. And when I wake up from those dreams all my terror, my sweating, and my shaking don't go away, they're still there because I wake up soaked in sweat, and my heart's still pounding, and my hands are still shaking. The evidence of the dream stays with me even after I wake up. I must force my eyes open so I can see what my surroundings look like, and see that I'm actually in a "safe zone," I'm not back in the jungle. And it takes a while before I can calm myself back down and into reality. I've been feeling like that most of my life. Sometimes it gets to me. I don't know how many times I've thought, "I want to end things," but I don't. It's because I think of how much I've got to lose like my family, and my friends, and the ones that died keeping me alive.

I'm suffering for all of them. I think that's what keeps me going in life. I owe it to them to stay alive in this world, on Mother Earth. The pain and suffering will only end, I guess when I go to my Creator into Heaven and the Spirit World. I've already been in Hell – and I've made it this far. All I can do is wait it out for God, the Creator, to take me to my Ancestors into Heaven, and be free from this pain and suffering.

  Now you know how one Native American Grunt kid feels and lived. How he lived through the horror of war and how he dealt with life in the best way he knew how from the age of 19. It's like I am still 19 in my mind. I've got this to say: When you send young men and women off into harm's way, into war, you'd better hope it's worth it. Life is the highest price to pay, and nothing on Mother Earth can pay for it or bring a life back that was taken away. Life is the most important thing on Mother Earth and you only have one life. Once it's gone it's gone! Even though life is not fair you have to learn to deal with it and make the best of it. In the best way you know how. Nobody can do it for you. Because everybody has a different way of looking at life. Life is not fair! Life has so many different paths. You just hope you do the right things to keep you going. You hope you take the right path. That's all you can do is hope for the best in whatever you do. I found out if you learn by others and by their mistakes you will have a good life. Because you don't have to make those mistakes if you learn from others.

  "Once a Grunt always a Grunt."

  "Only when you experience war and shed blood in battle will you become a true Grunt and a true Warrior in our Native ways."

  "May the Creator bless us all that have walked the true path in the battle of war to become a true Warrior."

  That is how I survived my emotional experiences in the Vietnam War one step at a time.

**ALPHA COMPANY, 1ST BATTALION, 27TH INFANTRY,
25TH DIVISION, WOLFHOUND UNIT, WILL ALWAYS BE MY UNIT
ONCE A WOLFHOUND ALWAYS A WOLFHOUND
NO FEAR ON EARTH IS OUR MOTTO**

GLOSSARY

AIT .... Advanced Infantry Training

AK-47 .... Russian automatic assault rifle

11B (11Bravo).. Infantry or Grunt

Bunker.. Protective embankment or dugout

Bush ....Out in the jungle

Chopper...Helicopter

Chinook Helicopter ....Large transport helicopter powered
by two rotors and shaped like a breadbox with a rotor at each end

Claymore mine....................... Directional antipersonnel mine, command-detonated

CP.. Command Post

C-ration .... Combat meal

CQ .... Charge of Quarters

CO .... Command Officer, same as Captain

Company .... Approximately 160 men; made up four Platoons

Dust-Off .... Medical Evacuation helicopter that picks up the wounded and dead

FNG.. Fucking New Guy

Grunt .... Infantryman

Gunship............. Helicopter with machine guns and rockets; supports Infantry units

Ho Chi Minh slippers...Sandals made from tires-
....soles made from the tread, with straps from inner tubes

Hootch.. House or hut; dwelling

Hot LZ.................................... Hot Landing Zone (active battlefield or combat site)

HQ... Headquarters

In-country...The War Zone (in Vietnam)

LAW .... Light anti-tank weapon

LP..Listening Post

LT ....Lieutenant

MOS.. Military Occupational Specialty

NVA...North Vietnamese Army

Patrol................... Unit or person employed for reconnaissance, security, or combat

Platoon ....Approximately 40 men; four Squads make a Platoon

Point or Point Man .... First man leading the patrol of men

Post...A command; where the soldier is posted

RPG............... Rocket-propelled grenade (Ruchnoy Protivotankoviy Granatomyot)

RTO ....Radio Transmitter Operator

Stand-Down .... To take a break inside a base camp

Squad...Approximately 10 men; smallest team (unit)

Squelch........................... The sound of a radio button on the handset being pressed

Sweep .... Same as patrol

Unit .... Organization of personnel and materiel

VC ....Viet Cong (South Vietnamese Communists)

Sept 27, 1968

Dear Mom & dad

Well another day has pass again. Well we went on a night ambush and then a sweep at the same time

Well we took off about 1:00 PM to are ambush sight and it took us three hour to get there

The reason it took so long. We had to cross two river and the water was over are head.

Then we had to move out at 3 AM in the morning.

Then we came back to the bungle about two oclock in the afternoon. So it was a long day & night for us.

Well tomorrow we be going on another sweep again.

Well right now I am
under the bugle pulling
gard

Oh mon next time
don't saint me so
many stamp like you
did. Because the one
you send me got all
wet

Boy dam I had went
I got the hell out of
here. Boy sometime I
feel so bad and then
sometime I feel Ok.

Boy went started
thinking of home an
know I could be
there ifs it wasn't
for this army.

But then the army
show me alote of
thing, what I shouldn't
do and what I can do.
Well I just got off of
gard.

Well how is bill
and dad doing litty.
Oh did they go

hunting after all, and
then did they get
any deer.

Has dad and Bill
been going fishing
lately or they just
been saying, home

Ok how does Rose
and Linda look.

Hay have you seen
Lina, you know Ema
sister. Have you hear
from Jim lately or her
mom

Has Bill found his
job ok I mean did
he get his job yet.

Are you still looking
for a house or you
going to stay at the
one you at now.

Ok if dad can't find
me a hot Rod see
if he can get a
good deal on a 66 n 67
Super Sport Chev. Ok.

With a 4 speed
and 327 engine Ok
That if he can't find

me a hat Rob ok
so I guess I better
end for now and go
too sleep ok. So
until next time.

Love
   always
      from
         your
            Baby
               Son
         Joseph F Maa
            Who
               always
                  miss
                     you
                        all.
                  Love

September 27, 1968 [Joe to his mother]

Dear Mom & dad

Well another day has pass again. Well we went on a night ambush and then a sweep at the same time. Well we took off about 7:00PM to are ambush sight and it took us three hour to get there. The reson it took so long. We had to cross two river and the water was over are head. Then we had to move out at 3:00AM in the morning. Then we came back to the bridge about two oclock in the afternoon. So it was along day & night for us. Well tomorrow we be going on another sweep again. Well right now I'm under the bridge pulling gard. Ok mom next time don't sent me so many stamp like you did. Because the one you send me got all wet. Boy I'm glad went I get the hell out of here. Boy sometimes I feel so bad and then sometime I feel Ok. Boy went started thinking of home an know I could be there if it wasn't for this Army. But then the Army show me a lot of thing, what I shouldn't do and what I can do. Well I just got off of gard. Well how is Sel and dad doing latly. Ok did they go hunting after all, and then did they get any deer. Has dad and Sel been going fishing latly or they just been saying home. Ok how dose Rose and Linda look. Hay have you seen Lina, you know Erni's sister. Have you hear from Liz latly or her mom. Has Sel found his job ok I mean did he get his job yet. Are you still looking for a house or you going to stay at the one you at now. Ok if dad can't find me a hot Rod, see if he can get a good deal on a 66 or 67 Super Sport Chav. Ok. With a 4 speed and 327 engine Ok That if he can't find me a hot Rod ok so I guess I better end for now and go too sleep Ok. So until next time.

Love always from your Baby son Joseph F. Maes Who always miss you all. Love

November 21, 1968

Dear Mon & Dad

Well to started alon
Ok and everything is
just fine now.
Well guess what? I
think it the best time
to tell you now.
I got wounded on
the 19 of November. I
only got hit on the
leg and arm, them Ok
and everything alright
See I was the
only one to leave
the hospital the over
guys had to say, be-
cause they got it
worse then I did
Shit the Doc.
pack me and I
walk right out the
next and got on

2

a jeep to 25 Divi "ho".

So don't worry mom and dad dear Ch. Well now al got a jungle Heart now and that all al nud is just one not two three.

Oh al got ~~three~~ 7 letter today. Five from you and one from Lina and one from Bill Vernon.

Ch mom thanks for the thanksgiving cards too.

Oh you never told me ~~you~~ got a new color T.V. be glad get and ~~oka~~ watch T.V. again.

Well about Joe. if he want to get marrige well it up to him. He should

3

know what he doing
he fool around with
alote guid aready. so,
if think this is right
one let him go get
marriage tell him I
wish him the best
of luck ok.

Boy That Dennis
is realy to much
"ha" one of these days
one of them girls
is going hock him
"ha"

Hay did dad get
a Boat + trailer for
fishing "ha" Went did
he get it "ha". Boy saying
"ha" get to you "ha".

Well the only thing
Bill said to me is he
been going fishing and
hunting and working and
that he be taking
them picture. To
you. Goo —

Now for Lina she
Ok I think she is
a realy nice girl
Boy just think she
got six A and one B
in thir year quarter
boy dose she have
a head "ha" "haa" I
go again that "hat bit"

She told me about
the track team and
that they won the
CCC and about the
foot ball game they
had.

Oh she send me
one of her school
picture of her funly
she don't look to
bad at all.

Well that about it
man & dad clan Ok
and clin doing fine
so don't worry so
much Ok.

5

So until next time

Love
   always
      from
         your
            Baby
               son

Joseph F Mac

P/S God did it for
a good reason and
al know why too.
God is still with
me 100%.

Love
   always
      your
         son

Joseph F Mac

November 21, 1968 [Joe to his mother]

Dear Mom & Dad

Well to started I'm Ok and everything is just fine now. Well, guess what? I think it the best time to tell you now. I got wounded on the 17 of November. I only got hit on the leg and arm. I'm Ok and everything alright. See I was the only one to leave the hospital the other guys had to stay, because they got it worse then I did. Shit the Doc. pach me and I walk right out the next and got on a jeep to 25 Divi "ha" So don't worry mom and [tell] dad I'm OK. Well now I got a purple Heart now and that all I need is just one not two three. Ok I got 7 letter today. Five from you and one from Lina and one from Bill Vernon. Ok mom thanks for the thanksgiving cards too. Ok you never told me you got a new color T.V. be glad get and watch T.V. again. Well about Jr. if he want to get marriage well it up to him. He should what he doing he fool around with alot girl already so if think this is right one let him go get marriage tell him I wish him the best of luck Ok. Boy that Dennis is really to much "ha" one of these days one of them girls is going hook him "ha" Hay did dad get a Boat & Trailer for fishing "ha" Went did he get it "ha". Boy saying "ha" get to you "ha" Well the only thing Bill said to me is he been going fishing and hunting and working and that he is taking them pictures to Mr. George – Now for Lina she Ok I think she is a really, nice girl. Boy, just think she got six A and one B in this year quarter boy dose she have a head "ha" Hear I go again that "ha" bit." She told me about the track team and that they won the CCC and about the football games they had. Ok she send me one of her school picture of her finly she don't look to bad at all. Well that about it mom & dad I'm Ok and I'm doing fine so don't worry so much Ok. So until next time

Love always from your Baby son Joseph F Maes P/S God did it for a good reason and I know why too. God is still with me 100%.

Love always your son Joseph F Maes

April 15, 1969
Tuesday

Dearest Baby Son:

Well son only a few lines to let you know we are OK & every thing is OK. And hoping & praying that things are going alright with you also.

Well today the only thing that happened was that Fremont School had a Riot, they say it was a Bad one, Kids got hurt, and some were Taken into custody. you know put into Peterson Hall, so now the parents are Patroling the school, I guess all the police in Stockton were there. now they say that Fremont is the worst school of Stockton. O wow! Then today it was your

2

dads birthday, but he didn't
even have one beer, he had
even forgotten, its these
countiny the days to the 27th
that has us all tense.
He is now 49 years old.
He says his birthday will
be the day he sees you
getting off that plane, well
Sel is at work again, I'
m about to start getting
ready to go to work, I waited
for the mail man, but he
didn't stop today. I also
answered Nicky his letter.
I think now he is sorry
to have extended himself over
there, also he told me his
brother got drafted and that
he is at Ft. Lewis, and sure
hopes that they don't send him

3

Vietnam, like they did him.
And I guess Dennis is back
at Camp Pendelton again as
he has not come over, Then
Liz called said she was not
coming over till may be this
week end, she says her folks
are planing to move to Red Wood
City where she is now, as
her mother is not working
any more because they closed
down the Morpach Cannery
where she used to work.
Other than that, the girl
who works at Macis always
asks for you, & the one at
Martins Jewelry where we
got Selgas wrist watch, she
says she always says a
prayer for you at church.
And Jessie from Carters is
always asking about you.
Well son, its almost time
for me to start getting ready

4

so until tomorrow again,
oh, they want Sel to be a
patrol man, they sent him
a notice to go take a test.
O wow! He don't know if he
should or not.

well son lots of love from
your dad + brother + as always
all my love, blessings +
prayers to you.

God Bless You + Protect You.
Love you so very much
your mom
Josephine maes.

12 days more,
O Boy!

April 15, 1969 Tuesday [Joe's mother to him]

Dearest Baby Son

Well son only a few lines to let you know we are ok & every thing is OK and hoping & praying that things are going alright with you also. Well today the only thing that happened was that Fremont School had a Riot, they say it was a Bad one, Kids got hurt, and some were taken into Custody you know put into Peterson Hall, so now the parents are Patroling the school, I guess all the Police in Stockton were there. Now they say that Fremont is the worst school of Stockton. O Wow! Then today it was your dad's birthday, but he didn't even have one beer, he had even forgotten, it's these counting the days to the 27th that has us all tense. He is now 49 years old. He says his birthday will be the day he sees you getting off that plane. Well Sel is at work again, I'm about to start getting ready to go to work, I waited for the mail man, but he didn't stop today. I also answered Nicky his letter. I think now he is sorry to have extended himself over there, also he told me his brother got drafted and that he is at Ft. Lewis, and sure hopes that they don't send him Vietnam, like they did him. And I guess Dennis is back at Camp Pendelton again as he has not come over, then Liz called said she was not coming over till may be this weekend, she says her folks are planning to move to Redwood City where she is now, as her mother is not working any more because they closed down the Morpack Cannery where she used to work. Other than that, the girl who works at Mais always asks for you, & the one at Martins Jewelry where we got Selzo's wrist watch, she says she always says a prayer for you at church. And Jessie from Carters is always asking about you. Well son, it's almost time for me to start getting ready so until tomorrow again, ok, They want Sel to be a patrol man, they sent him a notice to go take a test. O Wow! He don't know if he should or not. Well son lots of love from your dad & brother & as always all my love, blessings & prayers to you.

God Bless You & Protect You. Love you so very much
Your Mom Josephine Maes. 12 days more, O Boy!

LAST LETTER

DEAR LETTER

GO UPON YOUR WAY
O'ER MOUNTAINS, PLAINS OR SEA
GOD BLESS ALL WHO SPEED
YOUR FLIGHT, TO YOUR FAR DESTINEY
ANID BLESS ALL THOSE BENEATH THE
ROOF, WHERE I WOULD BID YOU REST
BLESS MOST OF ALL THE ONE TO WHOM
DEAR LETTER, YOU'RE ADDRESSED.
"(SGT. JOSEPH MAES)"

(LAST LeTTek)

April 20, 1969
Sunday

Dearest Baby Son

Well here it is the last letter to go to Vietnam from your mom, it is the 365th letter I have written, not one day did I miss, I sure am glad that I went to school & learned to write, and also that you have been so good in writing home, as that is what has helped me to get thru all this. Well son today I changed the furniture all around, different from any other way I have had it before. I washed clothes, & cleaned up the house, It turned out to be a warm day today, Sil put some speakers on his car, he too is now just counting the

2

days. 1 week more he says.
I guess it seems shorter in
time to say 1 week instead
of 7 days. I bet to you and
us this will be the longest
week of the year. But Thank
God that's all there is
left now. The only one who
came over was Butch, with
a story that he might
have to get married, He says
"Wow! that "partying" sure
is lot of trouble," he says
It got me into trouble," you
know how he talks. He
always comes to see Sal, always
asks for you. Other than that
nothing much of any thing.
So son, after this letter, no
more will I write, I only hope
you get this letter. So Son

3

until I hold you in my
arms, Thanking God for
giving me the strength all
this year to see all this through
and also for Him to have
been at your side at all times
I'll close for now.
Love from your dad & brother
& as always all my love,
prayers & blessings to you.

God Bless you & Protect you
all the way home.
Love you so very much
Your mom.
           Josephine Marie

Bless all the Boys you
are leaving Behind also.

April 20, 1969 Sunday [Joe's mother to him]

Dearest Baby Son

Well here it is the last letter to go to Vietnam from your mom, it is the 365th letter I have written, not one day did I miss I sure am glad that I went to school & learned to write, and also that you have been so good in writing home, as that is what has helped me to get thru all this. Well son today I changed the furniture all around, different from any other way I have had it before. I washed clothes & cleaned up the house, it turned out to be a warm day today, Sel put some speakers in his car, he too is now just counting the days. 1 week more he says. I guess it seems shorter in time to say 1 week instead of 7 days. I bet to you and us this will be the longest week of the year. But Thank God that's all there is left now. The only one who came over was Butchi, with a story that he might <u>have</u> to get married. He says "wow! that "party-ing" sure is lot of trouble," he says it got me into trouble," you know how he talks. He always comes to see Sel, always asks for you. Other than that nothing much of any thing. So son, after this letter, no more will I write, I only hope you get this letter. So son until I hold you in my arms, Thanking God for giving me the strength all this year to see all this thru and also for Him to have been at your side at all times. I'll close for now.

Love from your dad & brother and as always all my love, prayers, and blessings to you. God bless you & protect you all the way home. Love you so very much your mom Josephine Maes Bless all the boys you are leaving behind also.

JOE'S MOTHER'S CALENDAR

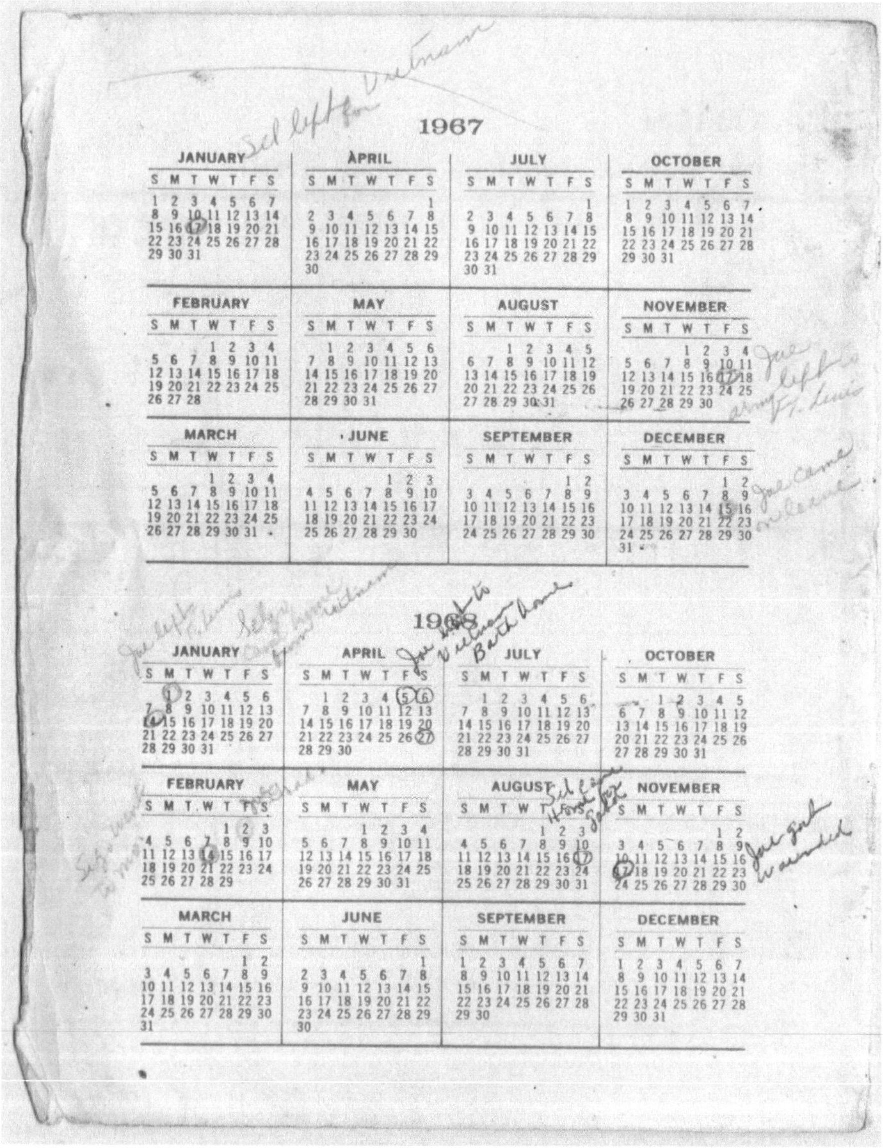

PRAYER TO THE GREAT CREATOR
AND TO THE SPIRITS OF MY ANCESTORS
IN THE TIME OF NEED

Oh Great Creator and the Spirit of my Ancestors, hear my voice in the wind, as the War goes on in this forgotten land of Vietnam.

Hear me! I need your strength and wisdom and guidance though this crisis I'm in.

Help me walk through the path of death and make my eyes ever behold what I have seen in battle.

Make me and my hands respect the things you have made and my ears sharp to hear your voice above the sounds of battle.

Make me wise so that I may understand the things of war which you have taught me and my people to be strong in our Native ways in battle.

Help me remain calm in the face of the enemy and all that comes toward me in battle.

Oh mighty Spirit, guide me through battle. Let me learn the lessons you have hidden in every leaf and rock in battle.

Help me seek pure thoughts and actions with the intention of helping each other in battle.

Help me find compassion and feeling without grief that overwhelms me in the site of battle.

I seek strength, not to be greater than my brother, but to fight my greatest enemy – myself. I will be ready to come to you with clean hands and straight eyes and a pure heart.

So when life fades, as the fading sunset and my spirit blows in the winds. May I come to you without shame?

Because I have spent my time in the hell of battle in the forgotten land of Vietnam.

Sgt. Joseph F. Maes. It was an honor to be asked to carry the Eagle Staff in the Grand Entry at a Pow Wow, and wearing my gourd blanket. It is a great honor to be able to call myself a Gourd Dancer. I am a True Vietnam Warrior.

This is our group, the Central Valley Vietnam Veterans of California. This was taken in the center of the Vietnam Wall in Washington, D.C. We went to honor all our fallen brothers and sisters whose names are etched on The Wall. Back row left to right: Steve Simons, Walt Raby, Augie Zapata, Brett Williams, Joe Martinez, David Romero (Taco), Dal Volbracht. Middle row left to right: Jeff Weatherill, Bob Willis, Joseph F. Maes, Celestino Dimas (Rick), Andy Rallojay, Terry Andree. Front row left to right: Selzo Maes, Jr, Allen Godine.

MY HEART IS BLACKENED

To my Native American Brothers and Sisters on this black granite wall with all your names. I stand here before you all! As a true Warrior that has been in battle as you all have been. My heart is blackened by the way things are.

We are still not recognized by the people of this monument as true Warriors of our land. I don't understand why Native Americans are not recognized by these people. They recognize others from other lands. All I know is my Ancestors are true founders of this land.

This government made so many promises to us. They only kept one promise: they took our land. They say there is freedom and justice for all. We had "freedom and justice" and that is why we have been almost exterminated.

If you tie a horse to a stake, do you expect he will grow fat? If you pen an Indian up on a small spot of earth and compel him to stay there, he will not be contented, nor will he grow and prosper.

These are words from some of our Great Chiefs. All that has been said and written is true in my People's words. Each man is good in the sight of the Great Spirit and more so to the one that's been in battle and saw what men can do to each other in battle.

Also to let my native Brothers and Sisters know on this black wall that they have not been forgotten by their Native Brothers and Sisters and by their Native people. Here I am before this wall to give them our blessing from the four directions and to the Great Spirit of the Spirit World.

CRY OF THE WOLFHOUNDS
A Company, 1ˢᵗ Battalion of 27ᵗʰ Infantry, 25ᵗʰ Division

Far across the wide Pacific, Vietnam is the spot.
Where we spend our days and nights in the land that God forgot.

Down with the snakes and lizards down when a man is blue.
Right in the middle of nowhere ten thousand miles from you.

We sweep by day and we freeze by night.
It is more than a man can stand.

We are not supposed to be convicts – we are defenders of our land.
We are soldiers of the First Wolfhounds, drawing our monthly pay.

Protecting guys with millions, while we draw two-sixty a day.
At home we have been forgotten – and no one gives a damn.

Because we are Soldiers in the army and we belong to Uncle Sam.
But when we pass though the Pearly Gates you will hear Saint Peter yell.

Fallout you Wolfhounds from Vietnam – you have spent your time in hell.

NEVER ENVY A VETERAN

Never be afraid to thank a veteran
When he goes off to war
He has no choice but to put himself in harm's way
He puts his life on the line
His life takes on the value of each American
An honor that cannot be seen in his medals and ribbons
So do not envy a veteran when he wears his medals and ribbons
Grieve with them, all those veterans
Who are not able to wear their well-earned medals and ribbons
Recognize the value of freedom
It is the ultimate price that many veterans have paid for what is deemed as free
Veterans have risked it all to keep our freedom
Show thanks to our veterans with a handshake or
Just say thank you and welcome them home
Show them the appreciation which they deserve . . .
They paid the price and some paid the ultimate price.

FREEDOM IS NOT FREE!

THE FUCKING NEW GUYS (FNGs) IN WAR

We the FNGs were taught to fight as one in the land of Vietnam
Through the jungle and the Monsoon rains
We FNGs were taught to kill and to take useless hills
To accept the war and then to bury the pain in vain

We the FNGs were taught to forget our losses
Not allowed to grieve for the Few and the Proud

We the FNGs sat in silence in disbelief
Crying in pain but never out loud not to give our positions away

WE the Proud FNGs were taught to live with senseless goals
We learned those hard lessons while in the land of hell

We lived from moment to moment, to overcome the torments
Never thinking we would return from this hell

Still we said our goodbyes and flew the friendly skies to the good OLD USA
War torn, dazed and alone and empty feeling as we land in the good OLD USA

We the FNGs learned well, to survive, to fight and to die
But we were never taught how to survive and to come home in one piece, so we cry

We taught ourselves to deal with our emotions
But if we can't deal with our mental emotions
You end up committing suicide in this great land of lies

But as time goes by we are dying a slow death within ourselves
We know it! But all we can do is take it one day at a time by ourselves

Our war will never end for us, till the day we DIE

SHE WAS THERE

I was there and got wounded there
The door opened up and there she was
With that look of hope in her eyes, for us.

I was there and got wounded there,
There she was, with that smile of safety.
She made me feel warm and safe.

I was there and got wounded there,
There she was with a soft voice that
Sounded like your Mom, sister, wife, or loved one.

I was there and got wounded there,
She was a nurse that we called Angel of Mercy,
Yes, she was there.

I was there and got wounded there,
She was there I could smell the sweetness
Of home in the air, because she was there
Our nurse our Angel of Mercy.

THE UNTOLD STORY OF A BOX OF C-RATIONS

In Vietnam a box of C-rations was
To fill our stomach to stop that deep hunger pain
And we wondered why

Like everything else in that treacherous country
The Viet Cong and NVA soldiers
Made booby traps out of them to inflict pain on us
And we wondered why

It was used as a calling card or friendship
To the Vietnamese people to help ease
The pain of hatred toward us
And we wondered why

When we looked at these empty cans
And we wondered what happened to our innocence
And that lost feeling that we left behind
We still carry all the internal pain
Which we feel.
We learned not to ask why
We learned to do or die
And we still wonder.

Q&A WITH AUTHOR JOSEPH F. MAES AND HIS FAMILY

When did you start writing the memoir? Why did you decide to do it?

Joe: I started writing about 15 years ago, in 2006, after I retired. I wanted my kids to understand why it was so hard for me to be close to them, and to understand me better. My story started small, just like two pages. Then it got longer – I didn't know I had so much in me. About four years later, I met a woman named Diana Marroquin. She was a veteran from the National Guard. I showed her my photo album, one that I made for the Wolfhound reunions. She said I should tell the whole story. She really helped bring it out of me. -

Susan (Jessica), Joe's wife: He wrote more after going to the Wolfhound reunions. We went to the very first one, in San Diego. After we got there, Joe said he couldn't do it. I went behind his back to William "Easy" Smith and told him we couldn't stay, we'd have to leave the next day. He said okay, but let's have dinner. I hoped we could get Joe to stay. At dinner the guys talked Joe into staying, without *telling* him to stay. So then we stayed the whole weekend. But Joe didn't meet anybody from the 1st Battalion, 27th Infantry, 25th Division. To this day he hasn't met up with any of them. We've been to five or six reunions now. The 25th reunion for the group will be in August 2021.

In writing your experiences, did you feel any relief by moving these images from your brain onto the page?

It was very emotional to do it. It opened up a lot of old memories, but by the end it was helpful. But not helpful at all at the beginning. It gave me too many flashbacks. Once I started opening up more and more, I felt more comfortable talking with Diana about what I was writing. My wife would stay in the other room. She'd give us privacy. I had nothing against telling her, but it's hard to talk to your spouse. It's easier to talk to a stranger. I didn't want to get my wife upset or traumatize her. A friend can walk away and you don't have to see them anymore. Diana is in Texas now.

What kind of mental health help have you requested and received?

The VA wasn't prepared for us, for the types of issues that we had. They had support for older guys. But it wasn't for young kids, kids traumatized in their youth. It's like we died within ourselves already, and they weren't prepared to deal with that. They were telling us to forget about the war, and there's no way in hell you're going to forget about it. That's why a lot of guys left the program. In a way it was like getting traumatized all over again. The VA is still figuring out how to help guys. Back then the VA would hire private contractors, and they didn't get it at all. The only thing that helped was to meet other veterans and make our own groups. We formed the Central Valley Vietnam Veterans. The best help is what we gave each other.

Did your father ever talk to you about his own military service?
No. He wouldn't talk about it.

Were your brother's experiences in Vietnam similar to yours?
He didn't talk about it. He wasn't in the Infantry, he was an Engineer, so he was in a support unit. Not in combat every day. Every vet's war is different, even if he's standing right next to you. But it only takes one incident to traumatize you, even for the guys in the back.

You talk about the strength that your identity as a Native American gave you in Vietnam – are there other elements of your Southern Ute culture that you'd like readers to know about?
I'm still kind of scared of showing my feelings out there in the world, and I don't like to talk about my culture too much. Because people will use what they hear in a way that it's not meant to be used. People talk about what they hear, but don't understand the real meaning of things for us. A lot of elements of Native American culture have been misunderstood and misused.

When did you visit The Wall? Why did you decide to do it?
Joe: I went on November 10th, 1991, for the dedication of The Wall. I went with 15 guys from the Central Valley Vietnam Veterans group. We went to say our goodbyes. There was a structure there, you could touch The Wall, and it meant something.

Susan (Jessica): While the boys were in DC, we women, the wives, wanted to represent them back in Stockton. We marched during a parade. It was a really different feeling. Your husband is alive but you're still honoring him by representing him and all the men who went to The Wall.

Over the years, which people in your life were the most supportive to you as a veteran?
Mainly my Mom and Dad. And my brother Selzo. Then when I got married, I got support from my wife and my kids, too – my daughter Zatanee and my son Joseph Jr. After we started the Central Valley Vietnam Veterans group, we supported each other. Especially Celestino "Rick" Dimas, Steve Simons, Walt Raby, Andy Rallojay, and Bob Willis. Diana Marroquin was a part of my life and really got me to open up.

Many Vietnam veterans have traveled back to Vietnam as a kind of therapeutic experience. Would you ever consider going back to Vietnam?
I would have liked to have gone back, way back then. Now, I don't know. Things have changed so much, things are not the same. Technology and everything has changed their country. I would be interested to go, but I can't now, with my health conditions. My friend Rick went. He said it's not the same and that you can't go everywhere you might want to anymore. He took his wife and explained a lot of things to her. She said that it's a beautiful country, if not for the war back then.

Do you like to hear people say "Thank you for your service"?

I'm not speaking for all vets, just myself. For me to hear that is like a slap in the face. I needed that thank you when I first came home. That would have helped me a lot with my PTSD. Let's put it this way, it's not too little, too late. It's nice to hear, but I can't take it sincerely. With older people, I feel like I'm helping them get over their neglect of us.

With young kids, it's nice to hear it. But I feel like they're getting brain-washed. There's no glory in war. If people tell young kids to say this, they should say it because they mean it, not just because someone went to war. Say it because someone served his country, not because of war. It's an honor to serve your country, but not an honor to go to war. Because if you look at it now, what did we accomplish with that war? Nothing. They're still communists, and the dominoes never fell. It was a bunch of BS.

Joe's daughter Zatanee: What was it like growing up in a household with a Vietnam veteran?

If I am being candid and completely frank, I don't know how to answer this question. It is like asking any child how it was growing up with their parents, to me he was just dad. There was nothing that I noticed to be different than any of my other friends and their fathers. There were some things that were obvious, don't horseplay or sneak up and scare people. But all my friends grew up with those rules.

Growing up I knew that there were certain times of the year that were harder for my dad. It was when I was older that he told me why those times were harder for him. In high school my dad had asked for his records of his time in Vietnam, and I asked if I could read them. He was willing to let me read over the documents, and I would ask questions about abbreviations. I remember growing up and going to various events or Vietnam Veteran memorials. My dad and his friends, who were also veterans, would get together with their families throughout the year and the kids would all hang out. This was like a second extended family. His group of friends would get together for the different holidays, go camping during the summer, and would be in the various parades throughout the year.

I remember there were times when it was harder for him at night and those were the times that we would go to Sacramento to the memorial. But the fondest memory I have growing up with my dad is when he would sing to me and my brother. Sometimes it was during the truck ride on the way home, other times it was when he was at home and he had his guitar. When I saw my dad singing or playing the guitar, he seemed to have a weight lifted off his shoulders.

Joe's son Joe Jr.: What were some of the challenges of growing up in a household with a Vietnam veteran?

I think this question itself shows the differences between those raised in a veteran household and those not. The "challenges" in my life were opportunities to learn what I could do and be free to fail knowing I would be OK.

Children will never listen to their parents growing up regardless of whether those parents are veterans or not. Rather they will observe the actions of their parents and internalize the results of those actions. Both of my parents worked tirelessly to provide for us and give us the best life they possibly could. This meant they weren't always there at track events and I was able to learn to not rely on external validation for motivation to continue doing things, I should be doing them because I enjoy them not because my parents liked to see me succeed. They weren't home after school to cook dinner and we learned how to cook for ourselves. I once burnt boiled eggs. After that I never had to rely on McDonald's or top ramen to feed myself in the army or college, because I knew how to cook a real meal from scratch that cost less than a "value" meal.

Watching not only my father and mother but the group of veterans and significant others that they associated with I knew mistakes would be made, but given the right community, there would always be someone there to support you regardless of the outcome. Now that I myself am out of the military and fortunate enough to have attended several different colleges, graduated from an accredited engineering program, and found a job that straddles the line between those who chose a trade over a degree, I see both the differences and similarities in my upbringing and those of the people around me. I was allowed to try many things growing up, from Taekwondo and cross country to rebuilding my first car. If there was something I wasn't able to do there was always someone to ask, or at the very least guidance on how to find a book that could help me understand how to continue.

Growing up in this veteran's household you worked hard and you earned what you got. I'm well into my 30's at this point and looking back at what many of my peers today would call challenges, I see those challenges have given me not only the knowledge of how far I can push myself but the confidence to push myself farther. I would like to thank both my parents because even though they were not always present they were always there when it mattered.

Joe's wife, Susan Jessica: What are the challenges and difficulties you faced being married to a Vietnam veteran?

We have been together for 50 years. I was 18 when I met Joseph in 1971, our first date was in the country in Turlock Ca., he kept saying "in-country", at that time I didn't understand the phase "in-country." We dated for almost ten years before we got married in 1980, I really didn't know about Vietnam. I would hear him speak to other Vietnam veterans, but didn't understand Agent Orange, long trips to Livermore for VA appointments, mood swings, always living on the edge of life always in a survival mode.

Living with a Vietnam vet I guess would be normal for me, yes, we've had ups and downs in our marriage it hasn't been all peaches and cream, you need a bit of sour cream to know you have a good marriage, because of his service time in Nam. You don't come home the same as when you left. I have half of a man, he didn't come home whole. He had a hard time with our children, don't get me wrong he loves them, but when they were babies and growing up it was very hard for him, he was afraid for me to get pregnant I didn't know that Agent Orange could affect babies, again early in our years together that darn Agent Orange, and war messed him up.

I do know other wives had similar thoughts. We would go fishing, hunting and camping, he would serenade me with his guitar. When we got married, sometimes he would take off and get his head to together so as not to get angry at home, I understood when he left. He also had me up on a pedestal in a white dress under a glass dome, he was very protective of me, I was naive of the street life. So, my life with Joe seemed to be a normal life because I don't know any other life. There are veterans that have had more than one wife, but once you get married it's till death do us part.

It was a difficult time for me and Joe when he found out some of his illnesses are due to Agent Orange, to have 45 radiation treatments for prostate cancer, ischemic heart, a stent put in his heart, lymph nodes removed, and having PTSD: Post Traumatic Stress Disorder. He even had a ruptured gall bladder with peritonitis and gangrene. I thought he was going to die. He used to think he was invincible, macho man, this is when he changed 180 degrees, I would say he was my hard cookie, he is now my soft cookie.

I took care of the kids as best as I knew how (kids don't come with manuals neither does a veteran), you are the spouse and learn to walk the line. Living with a Vietnam veteran is different to each one of us, who is married to one. There are challenges, they are walking time bombs, you just have to learn to love and stand by their side. There are no medals for wives who stand by their husband, we are veterans in our own way. If you think about it, I guess there are challenges and difficulties.

We must have patience with our veteran, always give your veteran your tender hugs, be sensitive to their needs and most of all devote your love and life to him. A veteran is always fighting his or her war, their war will never end for them till the day they die.

The VA's definition of PTSD is Post Traumatic Stress Disorder. My definition as a wife:

Patience
Tenderness
Sensitivity
Devotion

READER DISCUSSION QUESTIONS

1. What scenes from the book are most memorable? Why?

2. Does this book change any opinions you may have had about people who served in Vietnam?

3. Does this book give you a different or better understanding of the Vietnam War?

4. Does the narrative of a man who was drafted make you think differently about the use of the draft for Vietnam service?

5. How is Joe's identity as a Native American Southern Ute important to the narrative?

6. How is Joe's story different from other war stories you've read or seen? How is it similar?

7. Do you think returning veterans from the Gulf War, Iraq, and Afghanistan could identify with this story? Why or why not?

8. Do you have family members who served during wartime? Have any shared their experiences with you?

9. Do you think that reading this book would be helpful to other veterans, from Vietnam or other military conflicts?

10. What things do you feel inspired to learn more about after reading Joe's book? Stories from other veterans? The history of Vietnam? Southern Ute Native Americans?

ACKNOWLEDGMENTS

I want to thank all the people who helped me over the years as a veteran and specifically with this book, including the Central Valley Vietnam Veterans, Linda Vasquez, Linda Marquez, Richard Campos, and Stan Rapada.

I especially want to thank Diana Marroquin – without her this book probably wouldn't even exist. With us it was one veteran talking to another veteran, and she really drew the story out of me.

I also want to thank the Pieces to Peace Veterans Writing Project, run by Paula Sheil through the Tuleburg Press, with funding from the California Arts Council. Also, thanks to Amy Smith, who edited this book and ran the Pieces to Peace writers group, and to my fellow veteran group members, especially John Britto, Richard Soto, and Xochitl Paderas. Also, thanks to Joan Simpson.

Most of all, I want to thank my wife, Jessica, for everything she did for me over the years, including working on this book. I turned her into a veteran with all my trauma. I would have been locked up without her. She gave me the freedom to get away when I needed to, so I didn't take out all my troubles at home. She brought out the best side of me.